lasting hope

DEVOTIONS FOR LENT 2019

 AUGSBURG FORTRESS

Minneapolis

LASTING HOPE
Devotions for Lent 2019

pISBN 978-1-5064-4776-6
eISBN 978-1-5064-4777-3

Writers: Mary Hinkle Shore (March 6–16), Ron Valadez (March 17–23), Nathan Hilkert (March 24–30), Christina Garrett Klein (March 31–April 6), Bekki Lohrmann (April 7–13), Kevin L. Strickland (April 14–20)
Editor: Laurie J. Hanson
Cover image: Tamie Steffen-Hornstein, www.tamiehornstein.com
Cover design: Laurie Ingram
Interior design: Eileen Engebretson
Typesetting: Erin Keeffer

Manufactured in the U.S.A.

19 18   1 2 3 4 5 6 7 8 9 10

Welcome

The book of Psalms gives us a realistic look at the journey of faith for individuals and a community. From crying for help to singing songs of praise and thanksgiving—and everything in between—the psalms show faith with all its ups and downs, twists and turns.

More importantly, the book of Psalms points us to God. During times of celebration as well as suffering, loss, and lament, the psalm writers turn to God and remember God's promises—promises kept and promises still unfolding. God's faithfulness to these promises creates a durable, lasting hope in the psalmists and in the Israelite community.

Lasting Hope explores psalms assigned to Ash Wednesday, Sundays in Lent, and Holy Week in this liturgical year (year C of the Revised Common Lectionary).

- Psalm 51 (March 6 through 9)
- Psalm 91 (March 10 through 16)
- Psalm 27 (March 17 through 23)
- Psalm 63 (March 24 through 30)
- Psalm 32 (March 31 through April 6)
- Psalm 126 (April 7 through 13)
- Psalms 31, 116, 22, and 98 (April 14 through 20)

May Jesus, God's promised one, be with you on this Lenten journey and fill you with lasting hope.

Psalm 51:1-2

Have mercy on me, O God,
according to your steadfast love;
in your great compassion
blot out my offenses.
Wash me through and through
from my wickedness,
and cleanse me from my sin.

To ponder

God does not wish to regard our sins and punish us as we daily deserve but to deal graciously with us, to forgive according to God's own promise, and thus to grant us a joyful and cheerful conscience so that we may stand before God in prayer. . . .But such a confident and joyful heart can never come except when one knows that one's sins are forgiven.—Martin Luther, *The Large Catechism*

We begin with grace

Psalm 51 is traditionally known as King David's response after the prophet Nathan revealed to him the harm he had done to Bathsheba and her husband, Uriah. Like David, we often do not recognize an action as sin until someone shows us another perspective on it. Then we realize we were not just "blowing off steam" harmlessly: a friend was frightened by our outburst. We did not simply borrow that money: we took it without permission and have no idea how we will pay it back. That constant comparison of ourselves to a colleague who seems to have it all has turned into something toxic for both of us. Behavior we might once have glossed over is dangerous and powerful. It has the potential to shred loving connections with God and our neighbor.

When we realize such things, Psalm 51 gives us words to speak about them. In the first verse, we speak of God's grace three ways: as mercy, steadfast love, and great compassion. When we know God to be gracious, we have the courage to go forward. We can tell the truth and ask forgiveness.

Prayer

Most merciful God, help us to trust in your compassion and steadfast love. Free us from sin and raise us to new life. Amen.

March 7

Psalm 51:10

Create in me a clean heart, O God,
and renew a right spirit within me.

To ponder

"Heart" and "spirit." Here we're saying we want our inner core, our inside selves, to change anew. We know our sin is deep. And thus, we pray that the healing will be deep. Nothing like a little change, a New Year's resolution, a quick resolve in the morning breakfast to make this a better day. Nothing like this will or can do the job we need. The healing needs to go much deeper.

That's why we say and pray: "Create, create, create." We mean just that: CREATE!—Timothy Weber, "Mercy and Our Many Selves"

A future with hope

We often focus on the past when we ask for forgiveness. We call to mind things done and left undone, and we express sorrow to God or to those we have wounded. This focus on what is past, with its fearless truth-telling, begins the healing we seek, but it is only part of the picture. The future depends on God's re-creation.

Just as it is in God's nature to show mercy, so it is in God's nature to create. In the Old Testament, the Hebrew word for "create" used in Psalm 51:10 always refers to the activity of God. The One who created humanity in that One's image continues to share the divine life with human beings. The Creator fashions us anew to give us a future different from one shaped by our sin. God forgives. God does not allow our sin to set the trajectory of our future and the future of those we have hurt. "Create in me a clean heart," we pray. We are asking the God who made us to make us new.

Prayer

O God, we long to be what you meant us to be all along. Create us anew, that we may bear your image faithfully and share your creative spirit with the world. Amen.

Psalm 51:11-12

Cast me not away from your presence,
and take not your Holy Spirit from me.
Restore to me the joy of your salvation
and sustain me with your bountiful Spirit.

To ponder

A willingness to forgive is clearly the mark of a humanity touched by God—free from anxiety about identity and safety, free to reach out into what is other, as God does in Jesus Christ. But it may be that a willingness to be forgiven is no less the mark of a humanity touched by God. It is a matter of being prepared to acknowledge that I cannot grow or flourish without restored relationship, even when this means admitting the ways I have tried to avoid it, admitting sin. When I am forgiven by the one I have injured, I accept both that I have damaged a relationship, and that change is possible.—Rowan Williams, *Being Disciples*

A friend of sinners

A long time ago, I was taking a class that required reading texts in a foreign language. A student in the class made a novice mistake in translation. The teacher must have been particularly impatient that day because he responded to the mistake by saying to the student, "I should put you out for that." The class was shocked. Was the teacher joking, or would he really throw a student out of the classroom because of an error?

Might God "put us out" because we are sinners? Pondering a life separate from all that we associate with God is frightening. Imagine life without beauty, truth, love, mercy, or justice! So we pray, "Cast me not away from your presence."

As real as our fear might be that our sin will be too much for God, scripture tells us that God wants a relationship of love and trust with us, not separation. Casting out is not God's way; coming near is. God's love for the world is most vivid in Jesus, who was called "a friend of tax collectors and sinners" (Luke 7:34). He restored the relationship God seeks with us and shared God's bountiful Spirit with his friends.

Prayer

Free us from fear, O God. Come near to us in mercy and restore our trust and joy. Amen.

Psalm 51:17

The sacrifice of God is a troubled spirit;
a troubled and broken heart, O God,
you will not despise.

To ponder

God does not want "broken" or "crushed" persons in the sense of "oppressed" or "dysfunctional." Rather, God desires humble, contrite persons who are willing to offer God their whole selves. If pride is the fundamental sin that leads to idolatry, then the transformed psalmist now evidences a humility that inevitably leads to praise.—J. Clinton McCann Jr., "Psalms," *New Interpreter's Bible*

Lost and found

Sometimes even modern people are tempted to cry out in frustration, "What do you want from me, God?" It may be that things are simply not going our way, or it may be that something we desperately wanted to succeed falls apart. A friend says, "Someone up there doesn't like you," and we wonder whether it's true. Does God need something from us—some magic words, or maybe a large check in the offering plate—in order to redeem us from our sins and offer us a new beginning?

God's mercy does not come to us in this sort of exchange. The psalmist rejects the idea that God is waiting around for sacrifices and burnt offerings from us. To worry about offering God the right outward signs of devotion is to worry about the wrong thing. "Someone up there" (that is to say, God) likes—indeed, loves—us and all that God has made. That One seeks us out when we become lost.

Contrition is the sign of devotion appropriate to those who have been lost and now are found. To be contrite is to see our lostness and regret the pain we have caused. Contrite hearts are honest. They are open to the One who loved us in the beginning and who loves us still.

Prayer

Forgive us, O God, when we are overcome by sin or guilt. Mend our hearts and fill them with your love, that we may offer love to others. Amen.

Psalm 91:1-2

You who dwell in the shelter of the Most High,
who abide in the shadow of the Almighty—
you will say to the LORD,
"My refuge and my stronghold,
my God in whom I put my trust."

To ponder

Beneath the cross of Jesus I long to take my stand;
the shadow of a mighty rock within a weary land,
a home within a wilderness, a rest upon the way,
from the burning of the noontide heat and burdens of the day.
—Elizabeth C. Clephane, "Beneath the Cross of Jesus"

Shelter

Before the 2018 ELCA Youth Gathering, a friend from Texas and I were talking about how hot it would be in Houston during the last week of June. "We'll just have to drink water and look for shade," I said. "There is no shade in Houston," my friend replied.

No matter where you live, you've probably had the experience of looking for shade when the sun is beating down, or maybe, as a thunderstorm threatens, the experience of hurrying to find a place of safety. We know the need for shelter and the fear that comes when we cannot find it.

Psalm 91 begins by naming the Most High as shelter and shadow at times when the world is anything but safe. The threat could be from weather, or it could be from other elements of our lives that are beyond our control. Pain and the effects of illness can be as unrelenting as the burning sun on a hot day. Sometimes we need shelter from people who would hurt us. Sometimes our own bad habits threaten to undo us and hurt others. As danger swirls around us, God is worthy of trust. Amid all that would threaten harm, God offers a refuge and stronghold.

Prayer

Give us shelter, O God, from all that threatens the life you intend for us. Amen.

Psalm 91:9-10

Because you have made the Lord your refuge,
and the Most High your habitation,
no evil will befall you,
nor shall affliction come near your dwelling.

To ponder

Open ourselves to the suffering of others without limit and we can destroy ourselves, taking on more pain than we can bear. There is, however, no such thing as more pain than God can bear, and part of what it means to trust God is to know that God can and will bear whatever cost in suffering faithfulness in love may require. To know such a God loves us enables us to take risks

of a kind we could not otherwise dare.—William C. Placher,
Narratives of a Vulnerable God

Home

A spiritual director comments to those with whom she works,
"Fear is the cheapest house on the block. I'd like to see you living
in better conditions." The psalmist imagines better conditions: the
Most High is your habitation. We "live and move and have our
being" in God (Acts 17:28).

The poetry of the next part of the psalm is over the top. How
could it be true that "no evil will befall" someone in this life?
The forces arrayed against the whole creation's flourishing are
powerful. From the pain of deception and distrust, to the reality
of Alzheimer's disease and cancer, we know affliction. Surely the
Israelite people did as well. The psalmist is not proclaiming that
God's people will live a pain-free life, but rather that nothing will
be able to separate God's people from God's love (see Romans
8:38-39).

God is our dwelling place. Jesus took up residence with us so
that we might know our true home to be in God.

Prayer

God, we are grateful for your presence with us and our belonging
in you. Through all the trials of life, be our home. Protect us from
all that threatens our security in you. Amen.

Psalm 91:11-12

For God will give the angels charge over you,
to guard you in all your ways.
Upon their hands they will bear you up,
lest you strike your foot against a stone.

To ponder

Jesus is hungry in the wilderness, wrestling with a vocation sure to
lead to suffering and death. The devil offers a way out, offers perks,
proposes a big splash in the big media market.... Will [Jesus]
choose power, serve Satan? He could.... Jesus hangs on, though.
How? Only because he remembers the word of God, spoken long
ago in the wilderness through Moses to Israel, and knows it is a
word spoken to him.—Richard B. Hays, "Clinging to the Word"

16

Safety

The devil suggests that Jesus witness to the truth of Psalm 91 by throwing himself down from the pinnacle of the temple (see Luke 4:9-13). Surely God will send angels to uphold Jesus, right? (Imagine the U.S. Navy Blue Angels swooping down in formation to catch the tiny speck of a human on one of their wings and land him safely on the ground—without so much as a stubbed toe!)

Jesus refuses to twist the promise in these verses into a test of God's faithfulness, and in his refusal he shows us its true meaning. In hundreds of different ways (several of which are in this psalm), God is saying, "I intend your good, not your harm. Now and eternally, the whole company of heaven is at work to sustain, guard, and guide you." Because Jesus knew this, he had no need to run the experiment the devil suggested.

This psalm is for us when we are tempted to believe that all we can count on is our own wits or charm, income or status, or the deals we can make. None of that is true, but we can count on God, who gives the angels charge of us.

Prayer

Into your hands we commend ourselves, O God, our bodies and souls and all that is ours. Give your holy angels charge over us, so that the wicked foe may have no power over us; through Jesus Christ, our Savior and Lord.—Psalm prayer for Psalm 91, *ELW Leaders Desk Edition*

March 13

Psalm 91:13

You will tread upon the lion cub and viper;
you will trample down the lion and the serpent.

To ponder

God's protective care is not "mine" (just as the gospel is never mine); it comes always as gift, assuring me that God provides all I need precisely so I may take no thought for the morrow and give myself to the neighbor.—Frederick J. Gaiser, "It shall not reach you"

Keep going

The psalms often picture danger and enemies as wild animals. Given the traditional connection between the psalms and the youthful shepherd and poet David, this comparison makes sense. Imagine being a youngster left in charge of a flock of sheep. Their protection is your responsibility. What worries you most? Perhaps you are concerned about ravines and wandering sheep, but even more than these, you know the dangers of an attack by predators. There is almost no defense against wild animals who can strike with the speed of a snake or the force of a lion.

If you are not a shepherd or a cattle rancher, your worries and fears may have little to do with the attacks of wild animals. Yet the psalm verse still speaks to the scope of God's care. As you live out your calling to be a child of God, dangers may threaten to paralyze you. Don't stop because of them. Keep going. God's protection frees us from fear that would otherwise stop us in our tracks. God's care frees us to care for the people and things entrusted to us.

Prayer

Creator God, you have called human beings to care for all that you have made. When dangers surround us, give us the courage and freedom we need to love as you love. Amen.

Psalm 91:14

I will deliver those who cling to me;
I will uphold them, because they know my name.

To ponder

A promise loses its very character apart from the one who promises. If I am out of work and on relief, and the owner of the local grocery store promises me a job in two weeks, whether or not I now adopt a stance of hope in the world depends on the character of the one who promises. Does he have a history of faithful actions . . . ? Are there testimonies to his faithfulness? If so, my life has already changed. It changes with the issuance of the promise.—Richard Lischer, "Preaching and the Rhetoric of Promise"

The God who promises

As Psalm 91 ends, we see clearly that it would have been wrong to conclude from previous verses that those who are loved by God will never encounter trouble. Difficulties in life do not mean that God's favor has been withdrawn. Difficulties mean only that God's favor is especially needed.

God responds to the needs of God's beloved ones with the promise to show care and love. In verses 14 and 15, God says, "I will deliver…. I will uphold…. I will answer." Earlier, the psalmist offered assurances about God's provision and protection. Now the Almighty speaks words of comfort personally.

If you knew for sure that God would answer, how would you call out? What is the situation in which you need God to be with you? From what do you need rescue? The promises in Psalm 91 invite us to ask these questions and to put our answers in the form of prayer. Those promises—and the faithful character of the One who made them—embolden us to pray.

Prayer

Lord have mercy. Christ have mercy. Lord have mercy. Protect those who are in any trouble. Keep us from all that would harm us. Amen.

March 15

Psalm 91:15
They will call me, and I will answer them;
I will be with them in trouble; I will rescue and honor them.

To ponder
So many people have asked me what to do for depressed friends
and relatives and my answer is actually quite simple: blunt their
isolation. Do it with cups of tea, or with long talks, or by sitting
in a room nearby and staying silent or in whatever way suits
the circumstances, but do that. And do it willingly.—Andrew
Solomon, *The Noonday Demon*

God with us

The real danger of suffering is its potential to isolate us. Illness separates us from our routine, and it may physically separate us from other people. Grief feels like a burden no one else can understand, so we stop trying to put it into words and suffer in silence. Shame convinces us that everyone else is judging or laughing at us, or just dismissing us as nothing. We are tempted to believe we are all alone.

It is not true. We are not alone. God says, "I will be with them in trouble." Elsewhere in this psalm God is acting to shield God's people from harm. Here God's power is different. God is not only a shield against harm but also a companion in the midst of it. To be present with someone in suffering is already to break its greatest power. God promises to break the isolation that trouble forces on its victims.

Throughout his life, and in his death, Jesus embodies God's power to be with those who suffer. Jesus does not turn away from those who are in trouble. On the cross, he goes before us into the most isolating things we will ever face, namely, suffering and death. In the resurrection, he goes before us to welcome us to new life. He is with us in all things.

Prayer

Thank you, God, for your presence with us in times of trouble. When we feel alone, make yourself known to us. Amen.

Psalm 91:16
With long life will I satisfy them,
and show them my salvation.

To ponder
The words "given for you" and "shed for you for the forgiveness of sin" show us that forgiveness of sin, life, and salvation are given to us in the sacrament [of the altar] through these words, because where there is forgiveness of sin, there is also life and salvation.—Martin Luther, "Small Catechism"

But wait! There's more!

Years ago, Gary Larson drew a cartoon with the caption "God at His Computer." On the monitor screen was a man on a sidewalk. Above the man an upright piano was dangling, apparently being moved into an upper-level apartment. Meanwhile, the finger of an old man with flowing white hair and a robe hovered over a "SMITE" key on the keyboard. The cartoon was comical, but also a little unnerving if you identified with the fellow on the sidewalk!

The last verse of Psalm 91 lets us know that God does not sit at a computer all day considering whether to press the SMITE key. The Almighty is refuge, stronghold, and companion in the midst of trouble. And there's more: God will "carry and will save" (Isaiah 46:4), giving us life and salvation.

Prayer

We trust your promises, O God. Thank you for the salvation you have given us in Christ. Guide us as we find our life in him. Amen.

March 17 / Lent 2

Psalm 27:1-2

The LORD is my light and my salvation;
whom then shall I fear?
The LORD is the stronghold of my life;
of whom shall I be afraid?
When evildoers close in against me to devour my flesh,
they, my foes and my enemies, will stumble and fall.

To ponder

The only thing we have to fear is . . . fear itself—nameless, unreasoning, unjustified terror.—Franklin D. Roosevelt, first inaugural address

Fear

Both the psalmist and FDR attempt to instill confidence and courage in their audiences, and quite possibly in their own hearts as well. After proclaiming God as light, salvation, and stronghold the psalmist asks, "of whom shall I be afraid?" Almost as if in conversation with the psalmist, FDR opens his first inaugural address with those famous words "fear itself" to a crowd in the grip of the Great Depression.

We may be inspired with renewed confidence when we hear Psalm 27 in worship. And then we return home to our everyday struggles that challenge that confidence, to news headlines that flirt with despair, all threatening us with that old foe—fear. The hard truth is that our lives present us with many reasons to fear. But this does not negate the words of the psalmist nor of FDR, because they knew full well the real fears we face, and this makes their words all the more poignant.

Dear reader, fellow journeyer, God knows your fears and does not hold them against you, but shines a light for your path all the brighter, braces you with a saving arm, and fortifies that stronghold—built for such a time as this.

Prayer

O God, you give life and light to our hope. When we need it most, remind us that you rule over that ancient foe—fear. Continue to instill in us the confidence needed to face each day with courage and strength. Amen.

March 18

Psalm 27:4
One thing I ask of the LORD; one thing I seek;
that I may dwell in the house of the LORD
all the days of my life;
to gaze upon the beauty of the LORD
and to seek God in the temple.

To ponder
I long, as does every human being, to be at home wherever I find myself.—Maya Angelou, in *The End of the World and Other Teachable Moments*

Home

Most of us think of a church sanctuary when we hear the phrase "house of the Lord." For millennia, people of various faiths have designated certain places—usually structures of some kind—as holy places, places where the divine is given space to come in close.

Church sanctuaries can evoke strong emotions and memories in us. I pray they are positive ones for you. As we are called to "gaze upon the beauty of the LORD" and seek God in the house of the Lord, know most assuredly, dear seeker, that God does indeed show up there, again and again, without fail.

When we leave our sanctuaries, however, do we leave alone? Or does God go with us? And if God goes with us, are we not always in God's "house"? We are called to return to church sanctuaries to be fed and sent, and yet it is also important to remember that wherever we find ourselves, God is with us. This blessing is ours to share, for we know that many in our society long for a place to call home, a place to feel welcome, a place to feel safe, a place to be loved.

Prayer

God of house and home, thank you for welcoming us wherever we are, and for never failing to show up. Give me a welcoming heart, so that I may provide a place to call home, a safe place to be loved, especially for those who need it the most. Amen.

March 19

Psalm 27:6
Even now my head is lifted up
above my enemies who surround me.
Therefore I will offer sacrifice in the sanctuary,
sacrifices of rejoicing;
I will sing and make music to the LORD.

To ponder
The caged bird sings with a fearful trill,
of things unknown, but longed for still,
and his tune is heard on the distant hill,
for the caged bird sings of freedom.
—Maya Angelou, "Caged Bird"

Sing

Music has always played a major role in my life. Some of my oldest memories involve music. My mother taught me to play guitar and to sing and introduced me to Motown. Music has seen me through the lowest lows of my life and celebrated the highest highs.

Despite all this, there have been times when I lost the will to sing. Like many of us, over the years I have suffered from a few bouts of depression caused by stressors associated with life events. For me losing the will to sing is like losing the will to breathe. That's when I know something is really wrong. So to hear our psalmist sing while surrounded by enemies is baffling to me. Maya Angelou's bird singing of freedom from behind bars is difficult to wrap my head around.

In the low times of my life, however, others have surrounded me, loved me, supported me, lifted me—and even sung for me, when a tune was too heavy for me to carry. Who has seen you through rough times in your life? Who has been there to sing for you when you could not? Who has lifted you up in your lowest of lows? Do they know the effect they had on you?

Prayer

God of freedom's song, thank you for singing us through the waves of our lives. Thank you for sending us people to sing for us when we cannot. Keep us ever in tune, ready to sing for others who cannot sing for themselves. Amen.

Psalm 27:7-8

Hear my voice, O LORD, when I call;
have mercy on me and answer me.
My heart speaks your message—"Seek my face."
Your face, O LORD, I will seek.

To ponder

"What giants?" asked Sancho Panza.

"The ones you can see over there," answered his master, "with the huge arms, some of which are very nearly two leagues long."

"Now look, your grace," said Sancho, "what you see over there aren't giants, but windmills, and what seems to be arms are just their sails, that go around in the wind and turn the millstone."

"Obviously," replied Don Quijote, "you don't know much about adventures."—Miguel de Cervantes Saavedra, *The History of That Ingenious Gentleman, Don Quijote de la Mancha*

Adventure

Seeking God's face can be a disturbing idea, especially when your heart is telling you to do so. (However, ignoring your heart may be where real danger lies.) God, who is full of surprises, is the original plot-twister, and dealing with the unknown can be a little unnerving, to say the least. You just never know what's going to happen next.

But what if we thought of faith as an adventure, and seeking God as the quest to end all quests? Adventures are exciting, thrilling. They can be scary at times, but that's part of what makes them adventures. And as Sancho Panza discovered, adventures don't have to make sense or be logical. Sometimes the greatest adventures are those that happen within the heart and mind.

Lent can be a trying time. It probes deep into our souls, taking stock of what lies within. Lent calls us to follow our hearts and seek God—only to find God alongside us the whole time. Be courageous, O blessed adventurers! Enjoy the journey.

Prayer

God of adventure, grant grace and protection to all who seek your face. Empower us when obstacles obstruct our ability to see you—especially when those obstacles are us. Amen.

March 21

Psalm 27:9-10

Hide not your face from me,
turn not away from your servant in anger.
Cast me not away—you have been my helper;
forsake me not, O God of my salvation.
Though my father and my mother forsake me,
the LORD will take me in.

To ponder

Every day we are all called to become a "caress of God" for those who perhaps have forgotten their first caresses, or perhaps who never have felt a caress in their life.—Pope Francis, address to members of St. Peter's Circle

Embrace

Being held in someone's protecting and loving arms is a memorable experience. Maybe you have experienced this with a parent or grandparent, sibling, or spouse—or with your grown child who is now taking care of you. Maybe you have experienced this with a stranger, a rescue worker or emergency responder. Protection and love can come from some of the most unlikely places and people at times.

Our psalm passage for today shows someone yearning for that protecting, loving presence, but not finding it anywhere. And so, the psalmist turns directly to God, with hope and confidence that God will not turn away in a time of need: "the LORD will take me in."

Have you ever experienced this strong need for loving protection? How did God respond to your need? Who did God send as an answer to your plea?

Prayer

Embracing God, thank you for always being willing to take us in and shelter us under your protecting wings. Be with those who have not experienced this. And make us willing to be an answer to someone's prayers for protection, shelter, and embrace. Amen.

Psalm 27:11-12

Teach me your way, O LORD;
lead me on a level path,
because of my oppressors.
Subject me not to the will of my foes,
for they rise up against me,
false witnesses breathing violence.

To ponder

At last with an effort [Frodo Baggins] spoke, and wondered to
hear his own words, as if some other will was using his small
voice. "I will take the Ring," he said, "though I do not know the
way." —J. R. R. Tolkien, *The Fellowship of the Ring*

Level

What kind of path is "level"? What does it look like? Is it straight, without any twists and turns? Is it flat, without any steep inclines? Is it unlittered, without any obstacles? Is it fast, without any traffic? What if it's none of these things? Could our paths be made level not by their physical characteristics, but by the companionship we find as we travel on them?

Our psalmist continues to find turmoil, continues to be plagued by enemies, even to the point of violence. It's important to note that God doesn't pluck the psalmist out of these circumstances, nor does the psalmist ask God to do this. Rather, God provides companionship and accountability—loving and teaching on the difficult paths.

Frodo Baggins had a difficult path ahead of him, filled with obstacles and enemies. But he received companionship and guidance along the way. So it is with us. God not only provides God's very own presence, but also provides people to travel with us, to protect us as well as guide us when we stray—providing a level path.

Prayer

Traveling God, we thank you for walking with us wherever life may lead and for providing companions along the way. May we be willing to walk with others, especially when their paths are treacherous, even when we do not know the way. Amen.

March 23

Psalm 27:13-14
This I believe—
that I will see the goodness of the LORD
in the land of the living!
Wait for the LORD and be strong.
Take heart and wait for the LORD!

To ponder
More and more I find I want to be living in a Big Here and a Long Now.—Brian Eno, in *The Clock of the Long Now*

Now

Waiting sounds more like an Advent discipline, but it is certainly a part of our Lenten experience too. This past week, we have been traveling with the writer of Psalm 27, and it has been a roller coaster of a ride! We don't know exactly what was happening, but whatever it was, it shook the psalmist to the core. So it is with great joy that we see the writer end on such a positive note, waiting for the Lord with hope and confidence.

But how long are we expected to wait? For much of Christian history, people were trained to put all their hope in the afterlife, believing all their troubles would be taken away when they died. However, our psalmist challenges that notion! Despite fear, loneliness, abandonment, and violence, the psalmist proclaims: "This I believe—that I will see the goodness of the LORD in the land of the living!" While waiting for God, the psalmist comes to the conclusion that God's goodness can come, not at a much later time, but at any moment.

We still have a long way to go until Easter, dear traveler. But while you wait, remember that God's goodness may be seen at any moment—even here—even now.

Prayer

God of our past, thank you for always walking with us, right up to this very moment. May we also recognize you as the God of our present, seeing your goodness now, amid all that life brings us. Amen.

Psalm 63:1

O God, you are my God; eagerly I seek you;
my soul thirsts for you, my flesh faints for you,
as in a dry and weary land where there is no water.

To ponder

The whole life of a good Christian is a holy desire. Now what you
long for, you do not yet see: but by longing, you are made capable,
so that when that has come which you may see, you shall be filled.
—St. Augustine, Homily 4 on 1 John

Thirsty for living water

We Christians have often been known for the things we renounce, the things to which we say no. Just type "Christians are" into an internet search engine and pause to ponder the results.

Our baptismal liturgy begins with a list of things we reject or renounce: the devil, worldly forces that rebel against God, and the ways of sin. But our baptismal life does not stop with no! It continues into a full-voiced confession of our three-personed God's love for the universe. The psalm verse for today reminds us that a faithful life is one so filled with desire for God that spiritual desire becomes indistinguishable from the physical ache of hunger and thirst.

This Lent we may fast from some unnecessary pursuits and say no to certain practices. But we say no only to more fully say yes to the truest, deepest longings for God—longings God promises to satisfy for us in Jesus Christ.

Prayer

Resplendent God, you offer us far more than we can ask for or imagine. Teach us to say yes to all you offer to us, and to desire you, the source of all goodness and joy. In the name of the one who bore the cross for the sake of the world, Jesus Christ our Lord. Amen.

March 25

Psalm 63:2
Therefore I have gazed upon you
in your holy place,
that I might behold
your power and your glory.

To ponder

[Christian worship is] the last judgment of vision, forcing it
either to persist in projecting idols, or to accept prayer. Prayer
means, in this context, allowing the Other to look at me.—Jean-
Luc Marion, "The Blind Man of Siloe"

Already connected

Our actions in worship are about the power and glory of a God who is made present in our midst. We lift our voices together in song. We kneel and bow and reach out our hands. These rituals enact the gospel, God's good news for our lives, and engage our senses so that touch and taste and smell all confirm the saving message we also hear.

Our basic human tendency is to see any religious action as an if/then proposition. If I bury this statue of St. Joseph in my yard, then God ensures that my house is sold—or other, more creative (and insidious) forms of exchange. But the gospel of Christ is a matter of because/therefore. Because God has given us such a rich gift in Christ, therefore we can fully give ourselves to God, and to a world in desperate need of redemptive love.

Lenten practices such as fasting, praying, and feeding the hungry are not ways for us to make contact with God. Rather, these practices are ways in which we come to a fuller awareness that God is already in contact with us—already connected to us in ways we can hardly begin to fathom. As we gaze upon God and what God has done, we find that God is already looking lovingly upon us.

Prayer

God of glory, you come to us in humility. Help us to receive you gladly, and in our adoration, to be transformed into your likeness, through Jesus Christ our Lord. Amen.

Psalm 63:3

For your steadfast love is better than life itself;
my lips shall give you praise.

To ponder

The whole story of creation, incarnation and our incorporation
into the fellowship of Christ's body tells us that God desires us,
as if we were God, as if we were that unconditional response to
God's giving that God's self makes in the life of the trinity. We are
created so that we may be caught up in this; so that we may grow
into the wholehearted love of God by learning that God loves us
as God loves God.—Rowan Williams, "The Body's Grace"

Beloved

It might surprise you to learn that monks in medieval Europe preached on the Song of Solomon, which is filled with love poems, more than any other book of the Bible. Bernard of Clairvaux, whose writings greatly influenced Martin Luther, adored this book. Here he saw a magnificent portrait of God's love and a description of God's burning passion to be with the beloved for the sheer joy of it.

One of the basic struggles of Christian spirituality is a tendency to reduce Jesus to simply a figure who supplies or helps us obtain something good. Consider the ways in which you see or hear Christ described as the inspiration for certain actions or changes, or as a model of moral purity of one sort or another.

Life with Jesus is something different altogether. We seek Christ—and Christ seeks us—because he himself is good. Because he himself satisfies every desire. Because he alone demonstrates for us and to us what it means to burn with steadfast, unceasing, self-giving love. Love in a relationship that transforms us. Love that brings us the deepest delight, and fulfillment that exceeds our most ardent desire.

Prayer

Lord of love, you seek us unceasingly. Help us to know ourselves as beloved, and to be transformed by your grace, through Jesus Christ. Amen.

Psalm 63:4
So will I bless you as long as I live
and lift up my hands in your name.

To ponder

There was a young couple strolling along half a block ahead
of me. The sun had come up brilliantly after a heavy rain, and
the trees were glistening and very wet. On some impulse, plain
exuberance, I suppose, the fellow jumped up and caught hold of
a branch, and a storm of luminous water came pouring down on
the two of them, and they laughed and took off running, the girl
sweeping water off her hair and her dress as if she were a little
bit disgusted, but she wasn't. It was a beautiful thing to see, like

something from a myth. I don't know why I thought of that now, except perhaps because it is easy to believe in such moments that water was made primarily for blessing, and only secondarily for growing vegetables or doing the wash. I wish I had paid more attention to it.—Marilynne Robinson, *Gilead*

Lifelong blessing

Ritual has power. When I train leaders in my congregation to serve as assisting ministers, I tell them that what we do with our bodies in worship is as important as the words we say with our mouths. We beckon worshipers toward holy ground.

On our own and with others, our praise and worship of God ought to be enacted bodily, by kneeling; by lifting up our hands; with candles, icons, incense. As we receive God's grace in tangible ways, so too we praise God in tangible ways.

All the gestures of Christian worship exist to communicate in an unmistakable way God's promised blessing. The action of blessing another person or thing does not, of course, make something holy or sacred. Blessing acknowledges and declares the reality of something or (someone's) sacredness. The psalmist's act of blessing God makes sense: God does not need our blessing, but we need to be reminded of God's worthiness and glory.

Prayer

You bless us with your presence, Lord Jesus. May all we say and do magnify you and your steadfast love for us. Amen.

March 28

Psalm 63:5

My spirit is content,
as with the richest of foods,
and my mouth praises you with joyful lips.

To ponder

We're so caught up in our everyday lives that events of the past
are no longer in orbit around our minds. There are just too many
things we have to think about every day, too many new things
we have to learn. But still, no matter how much time passes, no
matter what takes place in the interim, there are some things we
can never assign to oblivion, memories we can never rub away.—
Haruki Murakami, *Kafka on the Shore*

By heart

My young children already have an expansive number of songs committed to memory. This can be frustrating, as my wife and I have endured hours of listening to earworms from the latest children's movies. But it can also be deeply moving. My oldest daughter has joined me to sing all the verses of "Amazing Grace" on visits to church members who are homebound.

Memory is a gift we make too little of. We no longer memorize poems in school, or scripture verses in Sunday school. But I believe that our memories, delicate and amazing vessels that they are, are being crammed full of other material. Have you tried to count the number of songs whose verses you know inside and out? Or experienced the words of a corny commercial jingle from your childhood rising unbidden to your lips? When we know something that well, we often say we know it by heart. That's an apt turn of phrase, isn't it?

Our lips must make the words time and again before something is written on our hearts. What would happen if we said the same scripture passage repeatedly, savoring it day in and day out? Would our mouths then be full of praise?

Prayer

May words of praise and thanksgiving be ever on our lips, O Lord, that in all of life's adversity and change, we might be ready to name your unending mercies, through Jesus Christ our Lord. Amen.

Psalm 63:7

For you have been my helper,
and under the shadow of your wings
I will rejoice.

To ponder

To pray "Thy kingdom come" is liberating precisely because, while it calls us to participate in what God is doing in the world, it also reminds us that God alone, in his providence, is bringing about the consummation of all things. And until then, we can't expect—and shouldn't seek—complete purity.—James K. A. Smith, "Faithful Compromise"

Cultivate trust

Alan Kreider, in his book *The Patient Ferment of the Early Church* (Baker Academic, 2016), argues that patience was the most important virtue for the early church. The church grew so explosively in its first two centuries of existence not so much because Christians proved the superiority of their ideas in intellectual debates. Nor did growth happen by convincing their neighbors that their understanding of justice was best. They attracted others to join their communities by embodying the patience that they first experienced in God. Instead of seeking to force their desired outcomes on society, the early Christians focused on cultivating trust in the risen Lord who promised to one day reign over all creation.

A mentor of mine once told me that ministry is like digging trenches in the desert. It's seemingly absurd and fruitless because results might not be seen for months or years. But the water that will come one day will need to be channeled to the places where it's needed most. How might this Lenten season provide an opportunity for us to recover trust in our God who has promised to redeem all of creation? How might we learn to let go of our anxiety about results and set to work digging trenches in the hope of rains yet to come?

Prayer

As you so patiently draw us to yourself, help us to patiently wait for your reign, sovereign God. Teach us to trust in you above all things, through Jesus Christ our Lord. Amen.

Psalm 63:8
My whole being clings to you; your right hand holds me fast.

To ponder
I know that "technological progress" can be defended, but I observe that the defenses are invariably quantitative—catalogs of statistics on the ownership of automobiles and television sets, for example, or on the increase of life expectancy—and I see that these statistics are always kept carefully apart from the related statistics of soil loss, pollution, social disintegration, and so forth. That is to say, there is never an effort to determine the net result of this progress.—Wendell Berry, in "Feminism, the Body, and the Machine"

In God's grasp

In my childhood, "tech-savvy" equaled America Online® and dot-matrix printers. But I'm also young enough to remember becoming the first person I knew who had internet access in their college dorm room. I text with my friends and map directions to the restaurant I just found on the internet. But I also take essayist Wendell Berry's warnings against technology seriously. Digital technology is quite simply the cultural reality in which most of us (relatively) affluent Westerners live. Yet, for all the gains that have been made, being so immersed in this digital world results in losses as well.

I was attending midweek worship at college chapel one day. I felt my phone vibrate in my pocket, midway through the liturgy, but ignored it. As the service ended, I took out my phone and began to respond to the texts while walking toward the exit of the church. I hit the clear glass window adjacent to the door, rebounded back, and narrowly missed the person behind me.

I often wonder whether I am grasping the important events unfolding around me—my infant daughter's experience of the world, or a parishioner's voice, or God's presence nearby. What is it that you hold fast to? Who or what holds fast to you?

Prayer

Help us to relinquish all that hinders us, so that we might grasp you and your eternal promise, through Jesus Christ our Lord. Amen.

March 31 / Lent 4

Psalm 32:1-2

Happy are they whose transgressions are forgiven,
and whose sin is put away!
Happy are they to whom the LORD imputes no guilt,
and in whose spirit there is no guile!

To ponder

If a child has been taught from her earliest years that she is not
lovable or competent, not worth anything to anybody or to the
world at large, that child is never going to truly believe God loves
her. . . . A child whose self-concept says, "I am lovable and competent" will be able to assert with confidence, "And God loves me,
too."—Ivy Beckwith, *Postmodern Children's Ministry*

Child-like faith

Each day, Rachel wakes up singing or talking to her toys, asking them if they would like some water or if they are still napping. This toddler arises with delight in her eyes, without remembering that she hit her babysitter because she was not finished playing and did not want to go to bed yet. This child does not yet understand what forgiveness is, but she does know that Jesus loves her and that saying "I'm sorry" and giving a hug will help.

In love, God forgives us, removing the sin that we have kept inside and disconnecting it from us so that we are no longer separated from God. It can be challenging to hear words of forgiveness when we feel our sin is so great, yet God's forgiveness is for the faithful and our belief and acceptance of that forgiveness is the first step into a full and happy relationship with God. Through forgiveness, we are renewed in spirit.

Whatever happened the night before, Rachel greets the morning with joy, knowing that she is loved. Each morning is a fresh start for this child and for us too. It is a new adventure, filled with hope and happiness.

Prayer

God, enliven our spirits to start anew with you each and every day. Amen.

Psalm 32:3-4

While I held my tongue,
my bones withered away,
because of my groaning all day long.
For your hand was heavy upon me
day and night;
my moisture was dried up
as in the heat of summer.

To ponder

Hope is not a matter of waiting for things outside us to get better.
It is about getting better inside about what is going on inside. It is
about becoming open to the God of newness. It is allowing our-

selves to let go of the present, to believe in the future we cannot see but can trust to God.—Joan D. Chittister, *Scarred by Struggle, Transformed by Hope*

Emerging

The winter air has left our bodies dry. We feel cracked and broken. Some days it seems there is not enough skin lotion and lip balm to soothe us all.

In times when it seems all hope has dried up, it is hard to do anything but groan. In a world that is full of brokenness and chaos, it can be difficult to speak. It is in those times that we must continue to actively seek God in our midst. Just because we cannot see the seeds of restoration buried deep in the soil does not mean that God's promised growth will not emerge.

God makes green our desert places, and God's hand is still filled with blessings for us when we are cracked and broken. In our distress we can call on God, the only one who can save us, and find our voice to speak up and shout out against the injustice and oppression of the world. We can have faith that through the brokenness around us new life will emerge, and it will be glorious.

Prayer

God made visible, help us find the words to speak of your glory, and guide us to serve and love in ways that show your saving work to all the world. Amen.

Psalm 32:5
Then I acknowledged my sin to you,
and did not conceal my guilt.
I said, "I will confess
my transgressions to the LORD."
Then you forgave me the guilt of my sin.

To ponder
When peace like a river attendeth my way,
when sorrows like sea billows roll;
whatever my lot, thou hast taught me to say,
it is well, it is well with my soul.
—Horatio G. Spafford, "When Peace like a River"

Flood of forgiveness

Think of the last time you were by a river or a stream. Remember the sounds, the smells, and all of God's creation living within and around that flowing water. The peace of a river is not one of stillness or silence, but one of activity and life. The peace of the river is filled with habitats, ecosystems, and organisms that are beautifully and wonderfully made.

Maybe you stepped into that river or stream and felt the smoothness of rocks that have felt the rush of the water. Or maybe you picked up a stone lying outside the water's reach and saw its jagged edges.

Sometimes we may feel like those jagged rocks, not flooded by life-giving water but drowning in sin. Still water does not make our jagged edges smooth. Only the rush of the Holy Spirit can do that. Each time we confess our sin, the Holy Spirit moves over the water and in forgiveness makes us smooth. Whether this water is like a raging rapid or a gentle stream, like the hymn writer Horatio Spafford we too can find peace in God's forgiveness.

Prayer

God who has moved across the waters, with forgiveness you grant new life where there once was death. Hear our sins with a compassionate heart and, in your mercy and love, smooth out our jagged and sinful selves. Amen.

Psalm 32:6

Therefore all the faithful
will make their prayers to you
in time of trouble;
when the great waters overflow,
they shall not reach them.

To ponder

The arc of history is longer than human vision. It bends. We abolished slavery, we granted universal suffrage. We have done hard things before. And every time it took a terrible fight between people who could not imagine changing the rules, and those who said, "We already did. We have made the world new."—Barbara Kingsolver, "How to Be Hopeful," commencement address

Unyielding hope

We are no strangers to troublesome times and circumstances. Bad things happen to good people every day, and we are at a loss to explain why these things happen and to reconcile them with our faith and who we believe God to be. We may question whether our thoughts and prayers are enough to wipe away the tears and mend the brokenness.

Our hope and faith in God, however, allow us to reframe these troubles and meet the challenges of today. Just as it is essential to be moved to action, we must continue to pray, knowing that God hears our cries, God knows our troubles, and God is at work. Our hope is grounded in God's promise to be faithful and never abandon or forsake us. As we pray together, our hope exposes our faith in Jesus, who sets out to save and change our world, and thereby change our troubles and change us.

Prayer

God, our hope, your ears are always open to hear us in our time of need. When troubling waters overwhelm us, receive our fears and anxieties and renew our hope in your promise of faithfulness. Amen.

April 4

Psalm 32:7
You are my hiding-place;
you preserve me from trouble;
you surround me with shouts of deliverance.

To ponder
We may encounter many defeats, but we must not be
defeated. . . . It may, in fact, be necessary to encounter defeats so
we can know who the hell we are. What can we overcome? What
makes us stumble? And fall? And miraculously rise? And go
on?—Maya Angelou, *And Still I Rise*

Safe and sound

A bird nest provides a place for eggs to be somewhat protected from outdoor elements such as weather, predators, or curious humans. For the hatchlings that emerge, the nest offers time and space to receive nourishment, grow stronger, and watch and learn from the parents to find food, recognize danger, fly, and eventually leave to build their own nests and start the cycle again.

We too need hiding places where we are covered by wings of love and renewed to confidently return to the task at hand. Sometimes it is difficult for us to ask for the time and space of a hiding place, even when we desperately need it. But God comes to us as our refuge, as rest for our weary selves, nourishing and restoring us. God surrounds us with a cloud of witnesses who eagerly proclaim God's saving acts of forgiveness and love in our coming in and our going out. And then, just as young birds stay in their nest only for a while, we are sent out, with shouts of deliverance echoing around us.

Prayer

Giver of rest and respite, make us whole in the sacred spaces you provide for us. Amen.

Psalm 32:8-9

"I will instruct you and teach you
in the way that you should go;
I will guide you with my eye.
Do not be like horse or mule,
which have no understanding;
who must be fitted with bit and bridle,
or else they will not stay near you."

To ponder

[Kids] don't remember what you try to teach them. They remember what you are.—Jim Henson, *It's Not Easy Being Green*

Hold on

One summer my father decided it was time for my younger cousin to learn how to ride a bike. My father persistently coached him through the tears so he would get near and finally get on the bike. The instruction to ride a bike was made easier as my dad walked and held onto the handlebars while my cousin got into the rhythm of pedaling. As he got the hang of things, my father started walking faster, then jogging, and finally running until the bike was going faster than my father.

My cousin was thrilled by his speed and shouted, "I'm doing it! I'm doing it!" only to realize that my father's hand was no longer on the handlebars. Confused, he looked back to see his uncle in the distance, and then looked forward just in time to crash into the lamppost at the end of our sidewalk. The next lesson focused on how to use the brakes!

By grace, we have a God who will accompany us and teach us which way we should go. Although we may fall, we don't need to look back, because God always holds us close and will never let us go.

Prayer

Loving God, you promise to teach us. Help us when we fall, lead us with your understanding, and guide us back to you. Amen.

Psalm 32:10-11
Great are the tribulations of the wicked;
but mercy embraces those who trust in the LORD.
Be glad, you righteous, and rejoice in the LORD;
shout for joy, all who are true of heart.

To ponder
To know the way,
we go the way,
we do the way.
The way we do,
the things we do,
it's all there in front of you.
But if you try too hard to see it,

you'll only become confused.
I am me and you are you.
As you can see;
but when you do
the things that you can do,
you will find the way.
The way will follow you.
—Benjamin Hoff, *The Tao of Pooh*

Surprises around the corner

One of the joys of summer is that it is prime season for hot air balloons. Turn a corner while driving, and you might just find a beautiful hot air balloon greeting you from a distance—a large, bright, colorful surprise that glides along effortlessly. Even more grand is seeing some twenty balloons together, filling the sky.

This is what God's mercy feels like: to be lifted up, time and time again, surrounded by the vibrant colors of God's grace and forgiveness. It is never-ending, and yet God's mercy often comes as a great surprise. When we feel we have done nothing to earn or deserve it, mercy comes to surprise us, because that's just who God is. All that's left to do is give shouts of praise and thanks to God, rejoicing in the merciful and bold surprises in our lives.

Prayer

God of grace, thank you for the endless mercy that you share so generously with us. Lift us up and fill our lungs with shouts of praise to you. Amen.

April 7 / Lent 5

Psalm 126:1

When the LORD restored
the fortunes of Zion,
then were we like those who dream.

To ponder

When there is nothing left in us that can please or comfort
our own minds, when we seem to be useless and worthy of all
contempt, when we seem to have failed, when we seem to be
destroyed and devoured, it is then that the deep and secret self-
ishness that is too close to us for us to identify is stripped away
from our souls. . . . It is in this abandonment that we are made
strong.—Thomas Merton, *New Seeds of Contemplation*

Never too far gone

Have you ever found yourself in a place where you could not find your way, where everything felt disorienting, murky, and hopeless? That is where the psalmist was. God's people, who were brought up out of slavery in Egypt, found themselves living in captivity again years later. They had lost everything that made them who they were. Yet the psalmist had the capacity to dream of life restored, as if they were already living in a new reality, looking back on God's restoration.

Often it is our past experiences of grace, mercy, and moving out from under the weight of a situation that carry us when it seems all hope is gone. The Israelite people sat in ruins, but they had a story to fall back on: we are the people that God delivered from slavery into freedom. God has built us up from ruin before!

The Israelites' story is our story. The death and resurrection of Christ is our story. It might look like things are beyond repair, but we have a track record that gives us reason to dream.

Prayer

God, your restoration is on the way, coming to meet us where we are. Make us bold in our hope and give us eyes to see it on the horizon. Amen.

April 8

Psalm 126:2a
Then was our mouth filled with laughter,
and our tongue with shouts of joy.

To ponder
The third great prayer, Wow, is often offered with a gasp, a sharp
intake of breath, when we can't think of another way to capture
the sight of shocking beauty . . . of a sudden unbidden insight
or an unexpected flash of grace. . . . "Wow" is about having one's
mind blown by the mesmerizing or miraculous: the veins in a leaf,
birdsong, volcanoes.—Anne Lamott, *Help, Thanks, Wow*

The graces make it possible

Sometimes your mouth is full of marbles, or at least that's how it seems because nothing, and I mean nothing, comes out right. Sometimes you'd rather not say what's been on the tip of your tongue because boy, oh boy, it could cut like a knife. Some days or seasons are like that.

But when you stop and step back and take in the graces that have come to you (and there have been so many graces), it's like the sensation of a morsel of chocolate touching your tongue. The sensation is one of sweetness, and the sweetness softens you. It begins in your mouth as you crack a smile, which bursts into a laugh. It begins on your tongue with a word of praise or thanks, but it soon spreads to your heart, to your mind, to your limbs.

Step back. Notice and name the graces. Not the heavy lifting you have done; not the accomplishments of which you might feel proud. Notice the things you have received that you could not have orchestrated if you tried: the fact that you were born at all, the yellow morning light, that your lungs are taking in oxygen without your even knowing it all the time, the people who love you, and so much more.

Prayer

Loving Spirit, you give us reason to shout for joy, for laughter, for gratitude because what you have done for us in Jesus is grace beyond our wildest imaginations. Amen.

April 9

Psalm 126:2b
Then they said among the nations,
"The LORD has done great things for them."

To ponder
Christianity roots its healing ministry in the good soil of the church as a community of ordinary people who come together to do things with God's help that they could not do in their own strength.—Una Kroll, *In Touch with Healing*

So good that the neighbors are talking
It isn't just God's people who are raving about their liberation. God delivers the Israelites from their captors in such a way that it

gets attention from other nations. Everybody notices and everybody is talking about it because this event is so momentous that clearly only God could have brought it about.

You probably know what it's like to be stuck in something that you cannot free yourself from—debt, a diagnosis, depression, or bereavement in the wake of death. These experiences can be like quicksand. The harder you try to force your way out of them, the more entrenched you become. You cannot simply will your way out of these things. In many cases you cannot easily work your way out of them either.

This passage from Psalm 126 invites us to still our bodies, minds, and efforts. There is quicksand, and we are going to remain still and calm in the midst of it and recall the things God has done that have moved us up and out of such stuckness.

Imagine a nation that has lost its land, its leaders, and its central meaning-making spaces and methods. Its people are hauled off to be slaves in someone else's land for generations. It is that nation of people that the neighboring nations are talking about, saying, "The LORD has done great things for them."

Prayer

Uplifting Spirit, bring about a healing and a deliverance so rich that people will gossip about it over the fence, saying, "Can you believe what God can do?" Amen.

April 10

Psalm 126:3

The LORD has done great things for us, and we are glad indeed.

To ponder

Nelson Mandela emerged from prison not spewing words of hatred or revenge.... He had been harassed for a long time before his arrest, making impossible a normal family life. By the time of his release on Feb. 11, 1990, he had spent all of twenty-seven years in jail. No one could say that he knew nothing about suffering.... Everything had been done to break his spirit and to make him hate-filled. In all this the system mercifully failed dismally. He emerged a whole person.—Desmond Tutu, *No Future Without Forgiveness*

Inextinguishable spirit

If you travel to South Africa and visit Robben Island, you will see the prison that held people like Nelson Mandela, people who stood in public opposition to the apartheid system of racial segregation. You can receive a tour of the remote, sea-surrounded prison from an ex-prisoner who will tell you firsthand of the horrors inflicted upon him during an extensive stay on the island. You will have to reckon with the unfathomable ways that human beings exert power and force over the lives of other humans, all in an attempt to maintain a position of dominance.

The miraculous thing about Nelson Mandela's story is that while he was in prison, while a powerful and dominating force attempted to diminish and extinguish his spirit, something was being cultivated in him. His spirit would not break. He maintained a level of wholeness that would not be snuffed out.

God has done great things, indeed! God frees captives from their bondage. But what is more, God is present in the suffering, cultivating something whole, with a power even greater than the powers of domination and fear. For this we can be glad indeed!

Prayer

God of the cross, you meet us in the place of the crucified, and it is there that you begin to cultivate your resurrection. Continue to meet this world in its suffering places and make it whole and glad indeed. Amen.

Psalm 126:4

Restore our fortunes, O Lord, like the watercourses of the Negeb.

To ponder

Prayer is a witness that the soul wills as God wills, and it eases the consciences and fits man for grace. And so he teaches us to pray and to have firm trust that we shall have it; for he beholds us in love, and wants to make us partners in his good will and work.—Gloria Durka, *Praying with Julian of Norwich*

Prayerful images

What images do you use in your prayers? Have you ever even considered using images to pray? The psalms are rich with images that individuals and communities have used to communicate the depth of their desires to God. In Psalm 23 the psalmist sings, "The LORD makes me lie down in green pastures." In Psalm 42 the psalmist prays, "As a deer longs for the water-brooks, so my soul longs for you, O God." In Psalm 22 the psalmist writes, "Packs of dogs close me in, a band of evildoers circles round me." Thirsty deer, packs of wild dogs, and green pastures are images that have been used to describe experiences in this life.

In Psalm 126 the image is of the watercourses of the Negeb, which were bone-dry waterbeds that became torrents of rushing water after rains fell. It is an image of a stark transformation from one reality to another.

If the psalmists teach us nothing else, they teach us that we can bring the entire spectrum of our lived experience before God in prayer, whether there are days when we feel as dried up as a parched riverbed or as afraid as someone surrounded by a pack of wild dogs or as relieved as sheep given rest in the lushness of green pasture. What is an image that describes your situation before God today? Present it with confidence to the one who has power to restore the watercourses of the Negeb.

Prayer

Tireless Creator, if you in a matter of moments can turn a dusty riverbed into a torrent of rushing water, then surely you can transform this world that it might teem with your abundance and life. Amen.

Psalm 126:5

Those who sowed with tears will reap with songs of joy.

To ponder

There is grief work to be done in the present that the future may come. There is mourning to be done for those who do not know of the deathliness of their situation. There is mourning to be done with those who know pain and suffering and lack the power or freedom to bring it to speech. The saying is a harsh one, for it sets this grief work as the precondition of joy. It announces that those who have not cared enough to grieve will not know joy.

The mourning is a precondition in another way too. It is not a formal, external requirement but rather the only door and route to joy.—Walter Brueggemann, *The Prophetic Imagination*

Enter into the tears

Grief work is hard. Our culture or world has not equipped us to be good at feeling our pain and acknowledging our sorrow. Emotions are judged as scary or bad or weak, and we are usually coached in overt or subtle ways to silence them or to do something about them: eat something sweet, turn up the TV, or throw yourself into a bathroom renovation project! But the truth is that tears are for crying and feelings are for feeling, and sometimes when we let it be that simple, something begins to shift.

The psalmist likens our tears to seeds and our grief work to that of a sower, planting our tears like seeds that God will grow into songs of joy. So often we draw back from our pain and the pain of others. But what we find throughout the history of God's people, including the Israelite people who first sang this psalm, is that in God we can enter deeply into the tears, knowing them to be the advent of our resurrection, the first notes in our songs of joy.

Prayer

Redemptive God, take our tears and sow them into the ground of your being that our dry, parched mouths might sing songs of joy. Amen.

Psalm 126:6

Those who go out weeping,
carrying the seed,
will come again with joy,
shouldering their sheaves.

To ponder

I promise you this blessing has not abandoned you. I promise you
this blessing is on its way back to you. I promise you—when you
are least expecting it, when you have given up your last hope—
this blessing will rise green and whole and new.—Jan Richardson,
Circle of Grace

Your life is a seed

One of the worst places to be is in a place where you feel that there is no potential. You look out over the horizon of your life, and it's one closed door after another; all endings and no beginnings, all weeping and no joy. Loss will do this to you, death and sickness will do this to you, even a terrible job will do this to you.

The role of potential in our lives is critical. The present can have its challenges, but if there is potential, your heart can still leap, your soul can still sing, and you have reason to keep putting one foot in front of the other. To have potential means there is still more to grow into and new life, in some form, is yet to come.

A seed is potential. Its present form is not its final form. There is life yet to be known in a seed. As people of God, we are afforded the opportunity to experience our lives like seeds. The job might be in gridlock, the death might be final, the loss might be tantamount, but through the mysterious workings of our God, these finite, hard experiences will crack open to reveal an abundance of life yet to be known.

Prayer

Holy God, you worked new life out of the deadest of ends for the ancient Israelites who first sang this psalm, and so we trust that you will work out new life for us as well. Grow joy where there is weeping and new potential where there is none, through Jesus Christ our Savior. Amen.

April 14 / Sunday of the Passion

Psalm 31:9-10

Have mercy on me, O LORD,
for I am in trouble;
my eye is consumed with sorrow,
and also my throat and my belly.
For my life is wasted with grief,
and my years with sighing;
my strength fails me because of affliction,
and my bones are consumed.

To ponder

Jesus feels the pain of others. He died for this world and weeps
over headlines. But he will not linger there with the daily

news—where my attention often gets stuck. He's got bigger fish to fry. The repentance of people like me.—Frank Honeycutt, 95 *Prosthesis*

Parading with paradox

Palm/Passion Sunday is a day full of paradox and reversals. It provides us with the paradox of life and, at the same time, the knowledge that none of us can escape the passion of Christ and his death—or our own. The grief expressed by the psalmist is one of the most real and unavoidable human emotions.

The reversal here is that death does not have the last word, nor are we left without hope. As Rowan Williams, former archbishop of Canterbury, once said, "God is never at the end of God's resources when we are at the end of ours. We really die, and God really remakes us. Creation and resurrection are inseparable activities in God's response to the death of God's loved ones."

Today we begin on the parade route of Holy Week. It may not be the one we wanted or expected, but maybe living in the tension and paradox on the parade route of life is exactly where we meet Jesus. The parade of Christ's passion is one that announces, "Jesus forgives," now and in paradise. Even in our grief, God is there.

Prayer

God who journeys with us in joy and suffering, we give thanks for your never-ending presence in our lives. Amen.

Psalm 31:11-12

I am the scorn of my enemies, a disgrace to my neighbors,
a dismay to my acquaintances;
when they see me in the street they avoid me.
Like the dead I am forgotten, out of mind;
I am as useless as a broken pot.

To ponder

Come, O Christ, among the ashes,
come to wipe our tears away,
death destroy and sorrow banish;
now and always, come and stay.
   —Susan R. Briehl, "Once We Sang and Danced"

Beauty in brokenness

In a centuries-old Japanese practice, pottery is repaired by filling breaks with a mixture of gold and lacquer. The flaws and repairs are believed to add to the history of an object, giving it beauty and value.

This understanding of "brokenness" is countercultural to the way many of us live and think. But God, who calls us this week to walk toward a cross, reminds us that even the brokenness of Christ's body and death on the cross is not useless.

We who are broken pots may feel forgotten, judged as useless by the world, but God takes our broken-potted selves and reminds us that we are loved. Loved in life and in death. Loved in brokenness and in newness. Loved to let others, even our enemies, know that Christ comes among the ashes and wipes our tears away.

Prayer

God who binds up the brokenhearted, give strength to the weary and hope to the hopeless. Amen.

April 16

Psalm 31:13-14

For I have heard the whispering of the crowd;
fear is all around;
they put their heads together against me;
they plot to take my life.
But as for me, I have trusted in you, O LORD.
I have said, "You are my God."

To ponder

The goal in handling dragons is not to destroy them, not merely to disassociate, but to make them disciples. Even when that seems an unlikely prospect.—Marshall Shelley, *Well-Intentioned Dragons*

Listening amid the whispers

As a child, I played the game "Telephone," where you would whisper something into your neighbor's ear and then they would pass it down the line and the last person would say aloud what they heard. The original message rarely made it to the end of the line.

This childhood game demonstrates something about living in the world with others. Whispered rumors can grow like wildfires. They can move from the lull of a whisper to the loud noise of fear that keeps us from living into the person God has called us to be. The psalmist dealt with this. Even some of Jesus' closest friends whispered unkind things about him, even to the point of death.

What does it take to quell those whispers and still that fear inside each of us? To speak to those voices and to that fear and say, "I have trusted in you, O LORD; you are my God"? It takes the promise that amid our greatest fears or fiercest opponents, God hears us and speaks a louder voice of love—even from a cross, where many whispers turned to loud taunts.

Prayer

O God, you hear us when we call. Help us to silence the voices of this world that prevent us from hearing your voice. Amen.

April 17

Psalm 31:15-16

My times are in your hand;
rescue me from the hand of my enemies,
and from those who persecute me.
Let your face shine upon your servant;
save me in your steadfast love.

To ponder

Though all the world with devils fill
and threaten to devour us,
we tremble not, we trust God's will:
they cannot overpow'r us.
—Martin Luther, "A Mighty Fortress Is Our God"

Rescued by steadfast love

One summer while serving as a camp counselor, I was trying to impress another counselor. She challenged me to swim from the boat to the shore. I didn't think we were that far out, and I didn't want to be beaten by her. I didn't know at the time that she was a professional swimmer. I was not. I jumped into the water and began to swim as hard and fast as I could, until I got a cramp in my legs. I panicked and felt as if I was going under. I screamed. I cried. Then a life preserver was thrown my way, and I was pulled back into the boat.

Often the rescue we need from our enemies is rescue from our own egos. We are often our own worst enemies and persecutors. As the psalmist cries out, "Let your face shine upon your servant; save me in your steadfast love." We too cry out. We cry out for God's face to shine on us and be ever present. We cry out for God to save us with God's steadfast love.

This steadfast love is never-ending and never tires. It's the type of love that is made manifest each time we tell the God-defying forces of this world that they cannot overpower us. This steadfast love is a love that will stretch itself upon a cruel cross, in the face of its enemies, and will rescue the whole world.

Prayer

God of steadfast love, thank you for rescuing us from ourselves and from the enemies of this world that get in the way of our receiving and sharing this love. Amen.

Psalm 116:1-2, 12-13

I love the LORD, who has heard my voice,
and listened to my supplication,
for the LORD has given ear to me
whenever I called....
How shall I repay the LORD
for all the good things God has done for me?
I will lift the cup of salvation
and call on the name of the LORD.

To ponder

Now we join in celebration at our Savior's invitation,
dressed no more in spirit somber, clothed instead in joy and wonder;

for the Lord of all existence, putting off divine transcendence, stoops again in love to meet us, with his very life to feed us.
—Joel W. Lundeen, "Now We Join in Celebration"

Tables of love

It has always amazed me how food brings people together. No matter the culture, the race, the age, food brings people together. When we gather around the table, breaking bread and sharing story, there is beauty to be found in common ground and common good.

Tonight, on this Maundy Thursday, the church across the world gathers around a table. Tables of love will be served and cups of salvation lifted up. The Lord hears our voices and calls us to share this feast of love with the whole world.

This is the love of the cross: love experienced around a table while bread is broken and wine is poured, a love that is felt as tired and worn feet are washed with a servant's heart. This is extravagant, wasteful, prodigal love: a love that is given and not deserved, love that is free, love that is given to all because God says so.

Prayer

God who feeds and God who loves, we give you thanks for your abundant feast of love and your call for us to share that with the whole world. Amen.

April 19 / Good Friday

Psalm 22:1, 7-8

My God, my God, why have you forsaken me?
Why so far from saving me,
so far from the words of my groaning? . . .
All who see me laugh me to scorn;
they curl their lips; they shake their heads.
"Trust in the LORD; let the LORD deliver;
let God rescue him if God so delights in him."

To ponder

God's justice is his mercy given to everyone as a grace that flows
from the death and resurrection of Jesus Christ. Thus, the Cross
of Christ is God's judgment on all of us and on the whole world,

because through it he offers us the certitude of love and new life.—Pope Francis, *The Name of God Is Mercy*

Cross-shaped love

Like the psalmist, like Jesus, we too have felt forsaken by God. We too have cried out, "My God, my God, why have you forsaken me?" Good Friday—God's Friday—reminds us that even in times when we feel deserted, God has not left the building nor abandoned us. Because of this, we have made the cross—intended as an instrument of death and finality—into an image and reminder of hope.

We sing tonight, "Behold the life-giving cross, on which hung the Savior of the whole world. Oh, come, let us worship him." We sing what was sung by our ancestors in the faith and will be sung by those to come. We sing and behold the cross that indeed is a reminder that even in what seems to be great loss and forsakenness, God is not finished yet.

Each of us is grafted onto this tree of life. Each time we think about it, we too can proclaim to the world: "Behold the life-giving cross, on which hung the Savior of the whole world."

Prayer

Listening God, hear the cries of your children and remind us that you never fail to hear us. Amen.

Psalm 98:1a, 4, 8

Sing a new song to the LORD, who has done marvelous things. . . .
Shout with joy to the LORD, all you lands;
lift up your voice, rejoice, and sing. . . .
Let the rivers clap their hands, and let the hills ring out with joy
before the LORD, who comes to judge the earth.

To ponder

A new creation comes to life and grows
as Christ's new body takes on flesh and blood.
The universe restored and whole will sing:
Hallelujah!
—John B. Geyer, "We Know That Christ Is Raised"

Singing new songs

Today the church lives in the vigil of the resurrection. It is that liminal space between Good Friday and Easter. This is the night! This is the night when mere spoken words cannot convey the great paschal mystery that Christ has died, Christ is risen, Christ will come again. This is the night to share this good news. We sing a new song to the Lord who has done marvelous things. This is the night we shout with joy to the Lord. This is the night when the church's song joins that of the psalmist, who helps us proclaim what is almost unimaginable in the resurrection: rivers clapping their hands and hills ringing out with joy before the Lord, who comes to judge the earth.

The good news of the resurrection that is first spoken in this liminal space is done so on this most holy night of the year. This is the night when we are all reminded that the cross is not the final word of God's great love, because Christ's body takes on flesh and blood in you and in me. This is the night when the universe is restored and we will forever sing hallelujah! We know that Christ is raised and dies no more. We too will rise! Hallelujah!

Prayer

God of new life, call us forth from the tombs of our lives to sing a new song to and for you. Amen.

Notes

March 6: Martin Luther, *The Large Catechism of Dr. Martin Luther, 1529: The Annotated Luther Study Edition*, ed. Kirsi I. Stjerna (Minneapolis: Fortress Press, 2016), 383. March 7: Timothy Weber, "Mercy and Our Many Selves: A Meditation on Psalm 51." *Currents in Theology and Mission* 13, no. 1 (February 1986): 45. March 8: Rowan Williams, *Being Disciples: Essentials of the Christian Life* (Grand Rapids: Eerdmans, 2016), 41. March 9: J. Clinton McCann Jr., "Psalms," *New Interpreter's Bible*, vol. 4 (Abingdon, 1996), 887. March 10: Elizabeth C. Clephane, "Beneath the Cross of Jesus," ELW 338. March 11: William C. Placher, *Narratives of a Vulnerable God* (Westminster/John Knox, 1994), 20. March 12: Richard B. Hays, "Clinging to the Word," *Christian Century* 109, no. 5: 124. March 13: Frederick J. Gaiser, "It shall not reach you': Talisman or Vocation? Reading Psalm 91 in Time of War," *Word & World* 25, no. 2 (Spring 2005): 198. March 14: Richard Lischer, "Preaching and the Rhetoric of Promise," *Word & World* 8, no. 1 (1988): 73-74. March 15: Andrew Solomon, *The Noonday Demon: An Atlas of Depression* (Scribner, 2001), 437. March 16: "Small Catechism of Martin Luther," ELW, 1166. March 17: Franklin D. Roosevelt, inaugural address, March 4, 1933, Washington, D.C. March 18: Maya Angelou, quoted in Michael Naas, *The End of the World and Other Teachable Moments: Jacques Derrida's Final Seminar* (Fordham University Press, 2014), 83. March 19: Maya Angelou, "Caged Bird" from *Shaker, Why Don't You Sing?* (Random House, 983). March 20: Miguel de Cervantes Saavedra, trans. Burton Raffel, *The History of That Ingenious Gentleman, Don Quijote de la Mancha* (W. W. Norton & Co., 1996), 38. March 21: Pope Francis, address to members of St. Peter's Circle, October 31, 2013. March 22: J. R. R. Tolkien, *The Fellowship of the Ring: The Lord of the Rings Series, Book 1* (Houghton Mifflin Harcourt, 2004), 270. March 23: Brian Eno, in Stewart Brand, *The Clock of the Long Now: Time and Responsibility* (Basic Books, 2000), 28. March 24: Augustine, Homily 4 on 1 John. Available at https://www.ecatholic2000.com/fathers/untitled-680.shtml. March 25: Jean-Luc Marion, "The Blind Man of Siloe," *Image*, no. 29. March 26: Rowan Williams, "The Body's Grace," Michael Harding memorial address, 1989. March 27: Marilynne Robinson, *Gilead: A Novel*, reprint ed. (Picador, 2006). March 28: Haruki Murakami, *Kafka on the Shore* (Vintage, 2006). March 29: James K. A. Smith, "Faithful Compromise," *Comment*, Spring 2014, March 1, 2014. March 30: Wendell Berry, "Feminism, the Body, and the Machine," *Cross Currents*, 53, no. 1 (Spring 2003). March 31: Ivy Beckwith, *Postmodern Children's Ministry: Ministry to Children in the 21st Century* (Zondervan/Youth Specialties, 2004), 48. April 1: Joan D. Chittister, *Scarred by Struggle, Transformed by Hope* (Eerdmans, 2003), 110. April 2: Horatio G. Spafford, "When Peace like a River," ELW 785. April 3: Barbara Kingsolver, "How to Be Hopeful," commencement address at Duke University, Durham, North Carolina, May 11, 2008. April 4: Maya Angelou, *Maya Angelou: And Still I Rise*, directed by Bob Hercules and Rita Coburn Whack (American Masters Film, PBS, February 27, 2017). April 5: Jim Henson, *It's Not Easy Being Green: And Other Things to Consider* (Hyperion Audiobooks, 2005). April 6: Benjamin Hoff, *The Tao of Pooh* (Methuen, 1982), 158. April 7: Thomas Merton, *New Seeds of Contemplation*, reprint ed. (New Directions, 2007), 258. April 8: Anne Lamott, *Help, Thanks, Wow: The Three Essential Prayers* (Riverhead Books, 2012), 71. April 9: Una Kroll, *In Touch with Healing* (BBC Books, 1991), 35. April 10: Desmond Tutu, *No Future Without Forgiveness* (Doubleday, 1999), 39. April 11: Gloria Durka, *Praying with Julian of Norwich* (Saint Mary's Press, 1989), 32. April 12: Walter Brueggemann, *The Prophetic Imagination*, 2nd ed. (Fortress Press, 2001), 119. April 13: Jan Richardson, *Circle of Grace: A Book of Blessings for the Seasons* (Wanton Gospeller Press, 2015), 118. April 14: Frank Honeycutt, *95 Prostheses: Appendages and Musings for the Body of Christ in Transition* (Cascade, 2018), 112. April 15: Susan R. Briehl, "Once We Sang and Danced," ELW 701. Text © GIA Publications, Inc. April 16: Marshall Shelley, *Well-Intentioned Dragons: Ministering to Problem People in the Church* (Bethany House, 1994), 34. April 17: Martin Luther, "A Mighty Fortress Is Our God," ELW 505. Text © 2006 Augsburg Fortress. April 18: Joel W. Lundeen, "Now We Join in Celebration," ELW 462. Text © Joel W. Lundeen, admin. Augsburg Fortress. April 19: Pope Francis, trans. Oonagh Stransky, *The Name of God Is Mercy* (Random House, 2016), 143. April 20: John B. Geyer, "We Know That Christ Is Raised," ELW 449. Text © John B. Geyer.

Also by Ann Turner

The Lost Swimmer

OUT OF THE

ICE

ANN TURNER

SIMON &
SCHUSTER

London · New York · Sydney · Toronto · New Delhi

A CBS COMPANY

First published in Australia by Simon & Schuster Pty Limited, 2016
First published in Great Britain by Simon & Schuster UK Ltd, 2017
A CBS COMPANY

1 3 5 7 9 10 8 6 4 2

Simon & Schuster UK Ltd
1st Floor
222 Gray's Inn Road
London WC1X 8HB

www.simonandschuster.co.uk

Simon & Schuster Australia, Sydney
Simon & Schuster India, New Delhi

A CIP catalogue record for this book
is available from the British Library

Paperback ISBN: 978-1-4711-5545-1
eBook ISBN: 978-1-4711-5546-8

Printed and bound by CPI Group (UK) Ltd, Croydon, CR0 4YY

MIX
Paper from
responsible sources
FSC® C020471

Simon & Schuster UK Ltd are committed to sourcing paper
that is made from wood grown in sustainable forests and support the Forest
Stewardship Council, the leading international forest certification organisation.
Our books displaying the FSC logo are printed on FSC certified paper.

For Joy and the boy,
with love

'Every heart sings a song, incomplete,
until another heart whispers back.'

Unknown

1

Penguins the size of small children, plump black and white bodies, robust little wings, propelled out of the sea and flew high onto the pack ice, chattering wildly beneath an Antarctic sky so vast and pale and clear it looked like it might shatter at any moment. The air was freezing but there was no wind, so I hauled off my polar-fleece jacket and shivered in my T-shirt, relishing the freedom after being indoors at base. Through the long winter months when the sun was just a lonely glow beneath the horizon I'd taken a stint as Station Leader, making sure the machinery and skeleton staff of plumbers, engineers, carpenters, doctor and cook kept whirring along. It was exhilarating to be back in the field, drinking in the sparkling light.

The Adélie penguins waddled across a bare outcrop and through a gap in a temporary fence housing a small metal weighbridge, where each bird was automatically weighed. They crossed to the rookery on the stony hill behind, each calling for their partner in a piercing shrill, creating an impenetrable wall of noise. I watched in awe as mate recognised mate, rubbing soft white chests together, tipping back their smooth black heads and stretching beaks to the sun, crying notes of pure joy. Mutualling – a heartfelt greeting after months at sea. They had reached the end of their long, annual migration. Spring was finally here.

Migratory. We were all migratory. I felt a deep melancholy as I witnessed the mass display of affection. Adélie penguins mate for life, something I'd yet to achieve. I was thirty-nine and single again. I had no one to come home to; unless you counted my mother, which I did not. And unlike me, Adélies are house proud, building nests of stones. There was much pecking as birds tried to steal each other's pebbles, rushing in and plucking them up, dashing away, getting chased.

Kate McMillan, an ornithologist and close friend, had just arrived for the season. A lanky 185 centimetres tall, thirty-three years old, she was pale-skinned and freckled, with a shock of unruly red hair that shimmered in the sun. She was doing a fine imitation of Charlie Chaplin as she fell into rhythm with the waddling penguins, causing no disruption as she placed coloured rocks on the ground for them. Red, blue, orange, yellow.

I looked down at my tablet and watched the images being streamed by the huge fixed camera that we'd set up yesterday with the help of our base engineers. Built like a tank in hard grey steel, the camera was programmed to swivel randomly to record the breeding cycle. It zoomed in to an enormous close-up of a penguin eye, beady black encased in a white ring, as the bird snapped up Kate's red stone. Then it zoomed back out to the chaos of the rookery where fights were erupting over the new pebbles. The penguins were completely trusting of our presence. Their predators were in the sky and sea, so they held no fear of us. Like all wildlife in this pristine wilderness the Adélies hadn't seen the awful destruction humans were capable of inflicting. It was a land of innocence.

Suddenly I saw a huge close-up of my own face. Behind sunglasses, my expression was ambiguous. My dark hair was looped up messily, my olive skin pale from not having seen sun since April. The camera zoomed out – I was tall and though not overweight the digital images fattened me up. I must do more exercise now the warmer weather was here.

The camera swivelled back to the penguins, and I took notes. Today I was carrying out an Environmental Impact Assessment on how the camera might affect the Adélies. Trained as a marine biologist, I had made my name studying the relationship between penguins and their tiny crustacean food, krill, in the Southern Ocean before spending a decade with my true loves, cetaceans, researching families of whales and dolphins. A second doctorate in environmental science ensured I stayed competitive. Through it all, Antarctica was the one underpinning strength of my life, the place that pulled me back from the darkness, and I would do anything to be here.

I was down this time on an eighteen-month contract with the Australian Antarctic Division, the longest I'd had – normally it was a twelve-month gig, but I'd taken the Station Leader position in the middle – and it would be my final summer before I had to go back to Victoria. Having been in the ice for a year already, there were a few quirks setting in. Kate said I had the *look* – like I was gazing through to a far horizon. I knew it in other winterers but I hadn't realised I had it myself. Even when you're surrounded by a small group of people in Antarctica, you're still more on your own than anywhere else. The landscape is broad and wide and your vision runs to it. You live in your head, the present can flow to the past – you spend hours reflecting. The other day I'd gone outside missing my left boot, and it was only when Kate laughed that I was *toasty* I realised I was standing in my sock. Toast is what the Americans call ice fever – when you start to burn out and the mind plays tricks. Everyone gets a bit toasty over winter, but I was generally fine.

Although I'd almost forgotten what the other world looked like. I was on leave from my university in Melbourne, where I'd torched a few bridges and I knew it meant I'd be stuck at Associate Professor level for some time. I adored my team of fellow scientists but I'd had a blow-up with a group of the most senior professors in my department. I shuddered at the thought. I was in no hurry to get back, even though I was passionate about my Antarctic Studies program that was growing more popular every year. I loved this generation of students. They looked at you directly, judged you for who you were in that moment, so different to the baby-boomers, who were always nosy. *What do you do? Are you married? Do you have children?* The students didn't take jobs as a birthright, unlike the old worn academics, too scared or greedy to leave, huddled over their posts like fat spiders. Of which my mother was one. Cristina Ana Alvarado,

Professor of Spanish Linguistics and Culture, stalwart of her School; a proud migrant success story.

We were Spanish, and *sacrifices* had been made. In Extremadura in western Spain, cherries grow in abundance in Valle del Jerte. That's where my Granny Maria and Papa Luis were born and raised, a place so beautiful they never wanted to leave. But they were both ten years old at the outbreak of the Spanish Civil War, and were sent on a boat to England in 1936 in a desperate attempt to keep them safe. Their parents perished in the war, killed by Franco's brutal Nationalists. Maria and Luis, heartbroken, yearned to go home to the shreds of family that were left, but it was too dangerous. As young, exiled adults they married, and when my mother Cristina came along, they vowed to stay in London to make a better life for her, a decision that sat heavily. Cristina felt responsible, and always tried to outperform. But she shattered their dreams when she met my dad, Mike Green, a young medical intern from Adelaide, who swept her off to Australia.

Dad was from establishment stock, and going through a belated hippy phase. I arrived two weeks after their marriage on a wild stretch of South Australian beach, much to the shame of Granny Maria and Papa Luis.

My childhood in Adelaide was perfect. We lived in a small house on the waterfront at Grange, a windswept seaside suburb. I learned to swim by the old wooden jetty and each summer pods of dolphins would arrive, ducking and weaving through the pale green waves. I'd run with the local kids along the beach, keeping up with the sleek grey fins as they rose and dipped. And sometimes there'd be another fin, one that stayed on the surface, cutting through the waves in a thick black silhouette. A shark; a white pointer. At weekends a tiny plane would circle the sharks and crowds of swimmers would flee, screaming, onto the baking sand. And when the tide was low I'd lie in warm pools, telling stories of dolphins and whales in faraway oceans to my friends.

All that changed when Dad, who'd excelled as a researcher in biological medicine at Adelaide University, found a promotion in Melbourne and we had to leave. I was devastated. I was nine years old.

We moved into a big creaking house in a dark leafy street in suburban Kew, far away from the beach. A green desert. And then, one year later, Dad moved out.

Mum ached to go back to London but she had a job as a lecturer, teaching Spanish, and as with all Alvarados she stayed to make a better life for her daughter. She insisted that I take my first surname – in Spanish tradition that meant her maiden name. I would be Laura Alvarado. I longed to be Laura Green. I worshipped my father and loved that he – and therefore I – was Australian. While Mum grew increasingly vexatious, difficult and angry, I blamed her and wondered what awful things she'd done to make Dad go. I'd grill her; she'd never answer unless it was to argue. I saw Dad at weekends for a couple of years, and then he moved to Sydney and was, more often than not, too busy to come down, or have me up to visit.

That left Mum and me in the too-big house in a cold, foreign place.

A penguin started to peck curiously at my leg, pulling the trouser fabric, letting it go, pulling again.

'No rock here, my love.'

He looked up and then pecked again. Another penguin dropped a stone between the tripod legs of the camera. The pecking penguin waddled off and returned with a blue stone of Kate's and dropped it on the leg of the tripod, where it rolled off. I photographed them and made notes. Had we erected the camera on their annual nesting spot? They were tagged with tiny radio antennae that stuck out through the oily feathers on the back of their necks. I looked them up on my satellite-tracking app – Isabel and Charles. I would follow them; make sure the camera didn't disturb them.

Elsewhere, young penguins arriving for their first breeding season were trying to coerce their way into established partnerships, to no avail. They'd rush in when one penguin was away, only to be pecked out, like a game of musical chairs in which they never won the chair. I sympathised. The camera swivelled and took arbitrary shots.

My nose grew numb from cold and a familiar sensation rushed through me. A storm was brewing. Down here, anything could change at any second. I looked across to Kate and knew she'd felt it too. I threw on my jacket and signalled for home; Kate gave me the thumbs up. We put on our skis.

The wind was fierce as we tilted against it, slowly making our way cross-country through icefields stretching wide to three horizons. Gales had whipped the surface into sastrugi, small ridges like frozen waves, with little peaks and troughs shadowed blue beneath sky that was turning a dark, foreboding grey. We took care to keep to the flagged area our safety engineer had set out, away from deep ice crevasses that could be fatal.

In Antarctica, people normally moved around on motorised equipment but we preferred to ski and it was much less disruptive to the Adélie colony. Our tiny Apple hut, a round red dome of warmth and shelter – looking just like its namesake, a cheery red apple – was a welcome sight in the vast white. I tried to pull open the door, but the wind kept blowing it closed. Kate helped, and together we managed to force it ajar long enough to slip inside. Shutting it, there was a beautiful muffled quiet. A blizzard was forming, and the katabatic winds, roaring downhill from the inland ice, grew so strong that everything started to rock.

We ate a quick meal of hot soup and biscuits in companionable silence. Kate was often not much of a talker, which always amused me given how loud her beloved penguins were. Afterwards, we slipped into sleeping bags and lay on single stretchers crammed close for body heat. Kate was absorbed in the footage the camera was recording and was now reprogramming it so that she could control where it filmed. I looked across at her screen and saw the penguins hunkered down, becoming white with snow and ice until they were indistinguishable from the landscape.

I checked my satellite-tracking app and found Isabel and Charles huddled together between the tripod legs, snug on their new nest. I, too, had found my mate down here once: at twenty-seven, in the abandoned Norwegian whaling station of Grytviken on South Georgia Island, I'd married Cameron Stewart, a dark-eyed, dark-haired, intense marine biologist the same age as me. We were part way through a summer investigation of humpback whales, which at that time were in decline. The bloody, awful history of the whaling station should have made us sad, but we were young and deeply in love, and instead it brought out an unexpected fighting instinct. We wanted to do something to respect the whales, to mark and pay homage to their terrible destruction. There was a small museum, and the woman in charge was also a chaplain. Cameron and I were sombre and respectful as we took our vows in front of empty pews in the old timber church that had been built for the whalers.

That night we slept in a tent by the harbour and stuck our heads out to watch the glittering array of stars in the deep sky, listening to a recording we'd made of humpback whales singing. Three pods, each with their own song, which the males sang to find their mate. They were eerily musical, sharing notes and arrangements with human compositions, like ethereal, modern performances.

We spent the next two weeks on board the *Antarctic Explorer* with a group of American scientists, diving with the humpbacks in their crystal-clear underwater world, vivid colours refracting light. With the rhythm of oxygen from my scuba tank, my protective diving gear keeping me in a warm cocoon, I felt more alive than ever before. We followed the humpbacks' songs, which developed each day and grew more complex. A high note here, a bass note there, a new coupling of tones. Our bodies vibrated as the songs swept through us. We named the whales, photographing them, memorising the distinctive black and white markings on the underside of their tail flukes. Each pattern was unique, like a fingerprint; there were no two alike. My favourite humpback was Lev, a calf, about ten months old. He was a friendly clown and had already found himself in trouble, with a diagonal scar running across his flukes. He'd swim so close

I could touch the long white pleats stretching from his mouth to his belly.

My phone started to ring, and I couldn't hide my reaction when I saw who it was. Kate glanced over, registered the caller, and waited to see what I'd do.

'Is it okay with you?' I asked. She grinned, green eyes lighting up. 'Wouldn't miss it for the world.' I punched her on the arm and put the phone on speaker.

'Hi Mum.'

'Laura, haven't you received my messages?' Cristina Ana Alvarado's strong, resonant voice boomed out. I could imagine her sitting where she always did at her kitchen table, running long fingers through stylishly-cut brown hair. Mum was an older, more fashionable version of me. Same olive skin, same dark eyes. I'd always wanted to take after my dad; he had brown hair and black eyes too, but he still managed to look like a white-bread Anglo-Saxon.

'Sorry, I've been busy.'

Kate snorted, too loudly.

'Who are you there with, honey? Is that Kate?'

'Yes, we're in the field.'

'Hi Cristina,' called Kate. Mum asked Kate how she was, but before waiting for an answer began to speak earnestly. Once she started, it was challenging to get her to stop.

'I don't suppose you've seen the news?'

'No, Mum, I've been—'

'That's the problem down there. You forget about every-one else.'

Kate nodded exaggeratedly and whispered, 'That's the point.'

'It's awful,' said Mum. 'I've just got home from a protest march. Those poor refugees are desperate. They're drowning in the Mediterranean as they try to get to Italy. And more innocent children have washed up on the shore, just like that little boy.'

My tablet beeped – Mum had sent a photograph of two girls, no more than six years old, neatly dressed in bright red parkas and jeans, lying face-down in shallow water, tiny arms stuck out to their sides, as if they were trying to hold hands. Drowned.

'Australia needs to take more refugees, it's barbaric.'

I nodded, unable to speak. The wind roared, rocking our Apple hut violently, and the connection broke up. Mum was still talking as the call was lost. I sat back, staring at the photo. Kate leaned over, and reeled away in shock. 'Wish I hadn't seen that,' she mumbled, quickly refocusing on her penguins. 'Your mother's right, we should be taking more.'

'She's always right on those things,' I said. *It's just everything else she's wrong about.* Like sending this terrible photo, already lodged in my mind, opening a portal into my memories that were pouring in, unstoppable. When Cameron and I had returned from Antarctica, I'd discovered I was pregnant. My mother heard the news of the marriage and pregnancy at the same time. I thought she'd be livid but she was ecstatic. In one swoop my family life improved, and Mum mellowed. Cam and I set up in a rented house in Elwood by the sea. We both had postdocs at Melbourne University and our world was each other, our work and most centrally our ever-growing, cutely kicking, adorable soon-to-arrive baby boy. Mum started a second career purchasing baby clothes and all the trappings of prams and bassinets and toys imaginable.

As the days grew closer to my full term I stopped working. Mum and Cam helped set up a cosy room filled with mobiles of penguins dangling from the ceiling, and colourful posters of whales of every species on the walls. We bought new furniture, and arranged the clothes in drawers from zero to twelve months. We were like blissfully nesting Adélies.

When my waters broke, Cam, Mum and I went to hospital as planned. Everything was going perfectly until intense pain exploded in me, and blood flowed like rain. Our baby was coming, clawing his way out in monstrous bursts, but something was terribly wrong. Specialists raced in and took over from the midwife. The contractions were fast. Too fast. I was rushed to the operating theatre. Mum held one hand, Cam the other, as I was wheeled along, and then to my horror they had to leave. An oxygen mask was clamped on my face, I was given blood to replace the gush of red seeping out, and rapidly prepared for an emergency C-section. Doctors swarmed. An intravenous drip in my arm and a general anaesthetic were the last things I remembered. When I woke up, my life had changed.

As I opened my eyes, the recovery room was silent. I looked around, waiting to hear for the first time the beautiful cry heralding my baby's arrival, expecting him to be close in a crib. My mother was nowhere to be seen. Cam, dark eyes sunken and bruised from tears, broke the news. Placental abruption. Sudden, unexpected. Starving our boy of oxygen. The doctors were unable to save him.

Stillborn.

Cam held me tight.

I asked to see my baby. The midwife was crying as she carried him in, swaddled in a hospital blanket, and placed him gently on my chest. Nothing made sense. He was beautiful, perfectly formed, with a head of black hair like Cam. Even in this miniature state I could see that he would take after his father – straight nose, narrow, pointed chin like an imp. I held his tiny crinkled hand and kissed him. My baby was limp, with no heartbeat. That wasn't possible. He'd been bucking playfully inside me for months, with a strong, healthy, throbbing heart.

He was as white as snow. A white I'd never seen.

We called him Hamish. A Scottish name, like his father. The midwife offered to take photographs. Cam said no. Every instinct in me needed to bathe Hamish, dress him in his soft blue pyjamas and wrap him in his own new woollen blanket. I was slow and careful as I washed his dark hair, my body numb and aching simultaneously. I tried to keep him warm, but he was as cold as ice. Cam stood shivering beside me, crying softly. He reached out his hand to touch Hamish; pulled it back, unable to.

After the funeral, with the pale coffin so small it looked like it housed a doll, we packed away the ultrasound scans of our growing boy, but we left his room furnished, with the penguin mobiles and whale posters. We kept his clothes. So many clothes. Cam and I couldn't talk about it. Milk still came, useless. I was fragile for weeks from the caesarean. I couldn't concentrate or care about my research. Mum tried to be supportive, but she was furious with the universe. It brought all the losses the Alvarados had faced rushing in. I blamed myself, my mind churning. What had I done? I hadn't smoked, drunk alcohol, taken drugs; I didn't have high blood pressure, wasn't overweight. I'd had none of the risk factors. But I was certain it was my fault, and I knew my mother blamed me too. She said I was being irrational but I couldn't shake the feeling. I withdrew further and further.

Cameron and I tried for another child, but nothing happened. I wanted a baby desperately, to raise a little boy or girl so differently to the way I'd been brought up. I wouldn't dominate; I'd make sure not to drive the father away. But Cam and I just weren't the same after Hamish. Two miserable years later we separated.

I felt so displaced I moved back in with Mum, which was a terrible mistake. We'd argue and make up and argue in a revolving psychodrama. And always, the face of my beautiful baby Hamish hovered. As soon as I closed my eyes. As soon as I woke.

I caught my breath, a hot flush burning my cheeks. In Antarctica ghosts could visit.

The blizzard was shrieking. I listened to the familiar roar, feeling the force of wind and ice and snow raging across the continent. It comforted me, even though it brought mortality knocking. Life could be so easily extinguished in extreme cold, if you were caught in the wrong place. Life was fragile. With sadness, I closed the image of the two drowned refugee girls, sickened by the injustice that they'd had to flee their homeland, only to meet death rather than a future of hope, the shared migrant dream.

I lay back and kept listening to the wind, grateful to be warm and sheltered, and then I tapped open a journal: *Bio-Medicine*

International. Mum had always wanted me to study Spanish literature, but there was something in my head that relaxed when I observed minute details with clean precision and recorded facts and figures, and I was addicted to collaboration, the teamwork that gave me an endless stream of tiny, tight-knit families.

As Antarctica howled, I scrolled to the long article by my father, Professor Michael Green, on the influenza virus and how susceptible the world was to a massive pandemic, greater than anything we'd ever seen. I kept abreast of Dad's research, even though I hadn't seen him since I first graduated from university, following in his footsteps with my science degree. When Hamish died, Dad had sent flowers and money, and written expressing his condolences – but he couldn't come to the funeral because he was overseas. Since then we'd had email contact, and left occasional phone messages. For the past decade Dad had been either away or too busy when I tried to catch up with him in Sydney. It saddened me, but I knew it was Mum's fault. I looked so much like her, and she'd treated him so badly. That didn't stop me feeling angry with him on my own behalf, but I always found myself slipping back into admiration. Dad had become a pre-eminent scholar, the most respected microbiologist in his field in the Asia–Pacific region. At least I could enjoy reading his work. It couldn't hurt me.

Or so I thought.

2

The morning was clear and pristine, as if the storm had forged everything anew in this ancient land. My heart swelled at the sight of endless white ice, lurid green flags marking out the safe path, red ones off to the edge warning of danger, as my skis made a rhythmic whoosh. Apart from the echo of cracking icebergs out to sea – smaller bergs calving off their mother-bergs – and the sound of my lungs working hard, there was a profound silence.

I relished this time between camp and base. In between those two different worlds – one of quiet focus, the other of group camaraderie – was a space that no words could describe. It was a place I'd give my life for.

I took it slowly, but far too soon the great red shed that formed the heart of our base grew large on the horizon, with quad bikes scooting up and away as people arrived back and others left for field trips. The base was still ensnared by sea ice which, as summer arrived, would melt and allow ships to sail close to unload their cargo. The buildings scattered along the coast gave the feel of a rundown frontier land. I envied Kate, who had stayed back in the Apple hut and would be joined this morning by Gretchen, another ornithologist who'd be her partner in the Adélie research. I'd only check in physically from time to time but would monitor the rookery every day via satellite. It would take three months to finalise my report on the new camera but in the meantime I'd oversee the continued repatriation of waste around the base, working with a team of newly arrived engineers. Beneath the ice were layers of domestic rubbish buried deep, leeching harmful contaminants, which had to be excavated. But before that, we had to deal with the surface waste: barrels filled with oil and an assortment of chemicals, old batteries, pipes, cables, and other refuse that in the past had simply been junked in the garbage field. Everything discarded must now go back to Australia. It would be a long, slow process: the barrels were leaking, and couldn't be easily moved. Here in the clear, freezing air, human waste and the uncaring ways of decades ago stood out like beacons of neglect. I often wondered if people back home would be less polluting if what they were doing was so starkly noticeable. Here you couldn't miss it.

'There you are, you dag!' Georgia Spiros's voice rang through the gaping dining area as I sat down to hot porridge. In her mid-forties, Georgia was tall, athletic and graciously slim, with sparkling black eyes and a grin that could melt ice. A senior detective in the Victoria Police, this was her third time as Station Leader – she'd just arrived to take over from me for the summer. The Australian Antarctic Division employed leaders from all civilian professions, who took leave to work in this extreme land.

The dining room was simply a shell with tables and chairs and a few comfortable sofas up one end, but Georgia managed to fill it with her exuberance. She came at me with open arms. I stood and hugged her. 'You need to fatten up,' she said. 'I can feel your ribs.'

'Lies will get you nowhere.'

'Tell that to a jury.'

She hugged me again, a great bear hug. There was nothing halfway about Georgia. If you were in, you were in.

'Missed you,' she said. 'And thanks for your notes. I feel completely up to speed. We'll have our formal meeting Monday, just to make sure everything's covered.'

'Absolutely,' I agreed warmly. Meetings with Georgia were always good fun. 'How are your kids?' I asked, and she punched my arm. Hard. 'Mad Greek *dag*,' I said. 'What's all that about?'

'Can't think about them. I just hope Jeff does his bit. Between you and me, I nearly didn't come. Stacey's doing her final year of school next year, and I'd like to be there at the start. But she told me I had to be in Antarctica or I'd drive them crazy. Even Alex weighed in. Just as long as I call every day, he said. And David sends his regards,' she added casually. I froze.

David White was my second ex-husband. Yes, I have two of them: the one area where I've outdone my mother. In my early thirties I was desperately lonely when Antarctica called again.

Returning to the icy wilderness had given me the first twinge of happiness after the loss of Hamish. It was a summer assignment studying whales in the Southern Ocean, with emphasis on how global warming might be affecting all the different species.

Our Station Leader that season was David White. He was tanned, blond-haired, blue-eyed, with a footballer's body; the physical antithesis of dark-haired, brown-eyed Cameron – and the difference didn't stop there. David, like Georgia, was a police detective who'd held a lifetime fascination with Antarctica. He'd won the job because he was gregarious, solid and adult, like he'd never even been a child. He made us all feel secure.

I was out in the field much of the time but when I came back, David was keen to hear my stories, particularly when I dived with the humpbacks and saw Lev again – now a fully grown forty-tonne whale, still with his diagonal scar and the black and white fluke markings I remembered vividly. As I swam near, Lev had moved his giant body gently with his long pectoral fins, like wings, so as not to crush me. He was as friendly as ever.

When the season ended David and I went back to Victoria, and two months later we caught up. He was stationed in Torquay on the Surf Coast and had a house further along the shore at Aireys Inlet. From his family room, perched high on a cliff, I saw migrating humpbacks the first day, their sleek black bodies surging through the aqua sea, hurling themselves high out of the water, breaching, then rolling playfully onto their backs to reveal their white pleats. They were following us from Antarctica, migrating to warmer waters for the winter. I grabbed David's binoculars from the windowsill. I could barely believe it as one whale started to lobtail, beating the water with its tail, its giant flukes rising up like a black and white butterfly – with a diagonal scar running through. My skin prickled, I flushed with joy: it was Lev. As I noted with excitement the date, time and location of the sighting, I couldn't help thinking it was a sign. I spent the rest of the year commuting up to Melbourne for work, returning to the fresh sea air at Aireys that revitalised me, and David who made me feel better than I had for a very long time. One morning he carved a question in the sand. *Marry me?* We were so happy, how could I not?

It was David who had introduced Georgia to Antarctica. That was a year before everything went wrong between him and me.

'DVD night tonight,' said Georgia. 'I've chosen a ripper. Quite arty-farty. Reckon you'll like it. Now do the vacuuming.'

Saturday was chores day at base. I considered myself lucky only to be vacuuming. Bathroom duty was much worse.

The dining room lights were dimmed and Georgia, beer in hand, stood at the front to introduce the film to the audience of winter tradies and newly-arrived scientists, mechanics, electricians, engineers, and an extra cook for the summer season. And Fran, our doctor, who had spent the past months growing a crop of hydroponic tomatoes but now faced the prospect of many more people to care for. (We loved Fran for those tomatoes – it was the only fresh fruit we had all winter.) We'd grown from a group of nine to about four dozen. The base was buzzing.

'This is a classic, set in the place I love almost as much as here. Can you guess where?' Georgia swigged her beer and topped it up straightaway from a large bottle. 'Open your eyes to Venice. Take it away.' She motioned dramatically to a bearded engineer who stood at the back of the room working the projector.

A little girl in a red raincoat was playing by a pond. Donald Sutherland appeared, sitting in a comfortable cottage, looking at a slide of a church. I caught my breath. I'd seen it before, and every ounce of me wanted to run from the room. The little girl in the red raincoat, his daughter, was going to drown in the pond. I couldn't move. I shut my eyes when it happened.

In Antarctica, there are rules. It's important to stick with the group; at times, that can save your life. If I left now it would send a terrible signal, because Saturday film nights were bonding exercises. In such a vast and potentially hostile environment, social isolation can set in, and Station Leaders always tried to forge connections between expeditioners.

I forced myself to watch the eerie landscape of Venice, its dark alleys where Julie Christie and Donald Sutherland get lost, the child – or *was* it a child? – in the red raincoat scampering away into the night. The body of a murdered woman hauled, upside-down, from a dank canal, her clothes falling away to reveal bruised flesh.

I knew that *Don't Look Now* was a good film, a great film, but I grew increasingly hot and claustrophobic, aware of the stale air from so many more people at close range. I was relieved when the lights came up.

Georgia was quickly by my side, hand gripping my shoulder as the audience clapped appreciatively and I joined in.

'Good, eh?'

'Brilliant.'

'Been to Venice?'

'I have.'

'Love it?'

I nodded. I did like Venice. But in the daytime and on the Grand Canal, not the malevolent, disjointed, empty Venice we'd just seen.

'Jeff and I are taking the kids once Stacey graduates. We'll stay at my favourite pensione, Hotel Leone Alato, in a little alley near St Mark's Square.' Georgia's grin was so dazzling it warmed me up.

'Got a moment?' she said.

I followed her into the small room that doubled as the communications centre and Station Leader's office. Georgia plonked herself behind the desk; I sat opposite.

'Strictly speaking I should wait and tell you this Monday, not on your night off, but the final approval's just come in.' Georgia had been steadily drinking through the film so was even more forthcoming than usual, but I had no idea what she was talking about.

'There's a field assignment for you at Alliance Station.'

I stared at her mutely as she smiled broadly back. We both knew that Alliance, a British base on South Safety Island in the Southern Ocean, was strictly off-limits to all but a team of elite scientists and a small support staff of technicians.

'An Environmental Impact Assessment of Fredelighavn, the old Norwegian whaling station at Placid Bay,' she continued. 'There's a push by some in the International Antarctic Council to open it as a museum.'

22

'What!' I blurted. 'But no one's allowed in because of the seal and penguin colonies. Not even the staff at Alliance.'

'That's being disputed,' Georgia replied matter-of-factly.

'Why? No one should go there. I've seen a few pictures from the seventies before it was closed off. It looked like paradise.'

Georgia nodded. 'That's why some people want to open it. They allowed a team of engineers in last summer to do a safety check. There's no asbestos, so unlike places like the old whaling station at Leith on South Georgia, tourists could go in safely. The buildings are evidently in very good condition, and with global warming there's been ice melt. That, and with some help from the engineers, has meant most of the sheds and houses are accessible.'

'What happens to the wildlife?' I asked, concerned.

'That's what you'd assess. Along with the suitability of the site.'

'I hate tourists,' I bridled. 'Why do they need access to so much of Antarctica? Can't they just leave it alone?'

'There are many who'd agree,' Georgia replied. 'Including, from what I hear, the staff at Alliance. The scientists don't want a bar of it. But Chile and Argentina are really pushing.'

I smiled wryly at the thought of my Spanish compatriots who hated the British, who also laid claim to some of the very same parts of Antarctica as the Brits, including South Safety Island.

'The Chinese are thinking of building a base on the island but there's a lot of quiet diplomacy against that,' said Georgia. 'Some think if Fredelighavn's opened, the Chinese will choose somewhere else. It's all just more jockeying for position before the Protocol expires.'

The Antarctic Treaty was drawn up in 1959 during the Cold War and came into force in 1961, reserving everything south of latitude 60°S as a place for science, with no military activity allowed; all sovereign claims were frozen. In 1991 the Madrid Protocol went further and banned all mining, but this was coming up for renegotiation in 2048. Although countries could stake no new claims, squatting on land with base stations was a game they played. There were likely vast oilfields and other riches to exploit beneath the ice. Countries were getting prepared.

Personally, I would have excluded tourism in the Treaty too – but they probably hadn't even thought about it in 1959.

'I might be biased,' I said.

'Nonsense. You're too good a scientist.'

'I could look at the evidence, I suppose.' Fredelighavn was the stuff of legend. South Georgia Island had six disused whaling stations, but Fredelighavn was the only one on South Safety. All the stations had expanded over their years of operation into small industrial settlements, but Fredelighavn was rumoured to have the most remarkable architecture, which was now overrun by the most extraordinary range and abundance of wildlife. I felt a magnetic pull to the promise of a natural wonderland.

And Alliance itself was an unusual base. The name, like those of most British bases, came from a nearby geographical location, Alliance Point, at the southern end of Placid Bay. But it had turned into another alliance: the British worked closely there with Americans and Australians. There was speculation that scientists studied viruses at Alliance. I'd once read a fleeting reference in one of my father's articles that led me to the same conclusion; it was nothing specific, but I'd always been curious. It was another incentive to take up the offer.

'There was a full background check on you,' said Georgia. 'You know no one's allowed there lightly, and this is a very important study. You were deemed politically neutral. Only people like me are aware how much you hate tourism. Your penguin and whale studies are revered.'

I tried not to blush, pleased they'd seemingly ignored my trouble with the professors in Melbourne. I knew those men would have done everything they could to hurt my chances.

'What about the Antarctic Heritage Trust?'

'You'll be talking to them, of course. If anything comes to fruition, they'd be the ones implementing. But the Council wanted someone at arm's length. They also want you to go to Grytviken Museum to check it out.'

I drew in my breath.

'What?' she said.

'I've been to Grytviken. Got married in the church.'

Georgia's eyes opened wide. She didn't know *everything* about me.

'I'm sure it's changed – I haven't been for over a decade,' I said.

'Cruise ships stop there. It's a favourite place.'

'I know.' It wasn't the first location I'd want to go to. I blocked the memories as quickly as they came: the ghastly flensing platform where the whales were cut up, the sheds full of the whale-processing machinery. And where I'd been so drawn to Cameron Stewart that I'd vowed to spend the rest of my life with him.

'And Nantucket,' Georgia continued.

'I've never been there,' I said, pulling myself back to the present. Nantucket. An island north of New York, across the Atlantic Ocean from Norway; another home of whalers plying their murderous trade.

'They have a state-of-the-art whaling museum and—'

'Am I the right person for this job?' I interrupted before she really got going. 'I'm not that keen on whalers.'

'You're respected. You're an expert. And people believe you'll be fair. Fearless even.' Georgia gave me a pointed look.

I grimaced. Being fearless is what had landed me in the mess with the professors. And with David White. Yet clearly I was coming out of that all right in these quarters.

'What about my current duties?'

'We'll get someone down to replace you. They want the report by the end of March. There's a lot to do. The Australian Antarctic Division's given their permission and sends their apologies for the short notice. Everything ran late getting approval from all the participant countries. It's a delicate matter.'

I paused, torn between desire to see the fabled place and a deep repulsion at what went on there. And I also wanted desperately to support those who were backing me.

'So, I guess I'll go,' I said. 'Best to have some control of the situation if they're going to open it up as a museum. And if the AAD's put me forward, I certainly don't want to cause trouble.'

Georgia laughed heartily. 'You'd be mad not to go. I can't wait to hear what it's like. And even though you're stationed at Alliance, you'll be reporting to me, and the AAD, which in turn will report to the International Antarctic Council.'

'Who'll be my team?' I asked, excitement growing.

There was a moment of awkward silence.

'At this point it's just you and one other – a German safety engineer, Professor Rutger Koch from Berlin University. He's done work for the Antarctic Council before. One of their favourites. And that's it, I'm afraid. Cost cutting. You'll be going into the buildings as part of your report and even though they've been checked, Koch will make sure everything's still stable.' Georgia shifted in her chair. 'Staff at Alliance will give you transport and technical support. But Laura, if you do find you need someone else, just call me and I'll see what I can do. In terms of protocol, your findings are strictly confidential. So no gossiping down there. No saying anything to anyone except Rutger unless you clear it with me.'

Lying on my bunk, I opened my laptop and tapped in *Fredelighavn*, searching for images of the abandoned whaling station. But after many tries with different key words, I still couldn't find any images. All I could see was a short piece that outlined how the bay and the whaling station had initially both been called Fredelighavn – *Peaceful Harbour* – but the bay's name had been changed to Placid Bay in 1911. In 1961 South Safety Island had come under the Antarctic Treaty, and in 1973 Placid Bay, and Fredelighavn Whaling Station with it, had been set as an Exclusion Zone, recognised as an exceptional wildlife-breeding site. No one, including scientists, was allowed in. It was completely off-limits.

I racked my brain to think where I'd seen the few photographs of Fredelighavn I remembered. I tried some different journals, but nothing came up. Was I thinking of the right place? When Georgia first raised the name, I was sure I had seen it. In my head were black and white images of sheds, white clapboard buildings and a church, stretching around a glistening bay, with penguins and seals everywhere.

I looked up Alliance base. Unlike most other bases, there was no comprehensive website, just a lean description: *British station committed to carrying out scientific research, with emphasis on inviting colleagues from the USA and Australia to participate in certain programs on an annual basis*; and a paragraph proudly stating it had an airport with a blue ice runway – where the ice stayed thick and hard all year, allowing wheeled aircraft to land.

I tapped *Rutger Koch* into the search engine and found he'd been to Antarctica as many times as I had. In his late thirties, he was tanned, fair-haired, square-jawed, with intelligent grey eyes. Manly. A Germanic David White. Even from the photos I was attracted. I stopped myself immediately. I was just lonely, and he'd certainly be attached. Strong, good-looking men had proved bad for me, and I was going there purely for work. I dropped him a quick email introducing myself.

We winterers were a close mob; we'd become an endearingly eccentric family. I tried to hold back tears, not wanting to look like an idiot, as I said goodbye. By the time I returned at the end of the season to catch the plane back to Australia, most would have already flown out, replaced by fresh personnel.

I saved my biggest hug for Georgia. Georgia, who I wanted to ask about David White but couldn't bring myself to. I wondered if he'd had children yet.

'Look after yourself, mate,' said Georgia, punching my arm.

'You too,' I said, although I suspected she wouldn't have any problems.

The warm Hägglunds, like an orange truck with huge rubber tracks and two cabins – on this day, one for passengers and one for gear – took me to Wilkins Runway, a field of ice high above sea level, from where I was flown to the USA's McMurdo base. We landed on its sea-ice runway, where security was high. The peaceful continent wasn't allowed to arm itself, but the American guards seemed very military. I was kept at the airfield until my flight arrived. A small British-run Dash 7 took me, with its strong propellers, over the vast white continent, across the frozen Weddell Sea and Antarctic Peninsula, descending over a blue and white patchwork of broken sea ice to the expansive South Safety Island, sitting at a latitude of 62°15'S, outside the Antarctic circle but just within the area governed by the Antarctic Treaty.

The plane banked sharply around the north-east coast as it came in to land, quickly obstructing my view of the sparkling Placid Bay but flying over the abandoned buildings of Fredelighavn. There was a whitewashed church with a surprising golden orb on the top of its steeple, and the black and white mass of an Adélie rookery. Along the shore sprawled red-roofed sheds, with industrial smoke towers sprouting from them, and the huge, wooden-planked flensing platform. On the beach, gigantic whale skeletons were strewn about. Close to the mountains that rose on both sides were clusters of large round oil tanks. And among more sheds was a small settlement of red-roofed houses. It didn't look like the photographs I remembered at all. But then, they'd been taken at sea level, not from above.

My stomach moved uncomfortably as I took in this pristine slaughter yard, a feeling not helped by the rough landing on the long blue ice runway; it took minutes before the Dash 7 finally turned towards the airfield buildings.

I emerged from the plane to be met by a tall, prim man in his early sixties wearing a starched white shirt and bow tie beneath his bulky polar jacket.

'Welcome to Alliance, Doctor Alvarado,' he said formally, shaking my hand in a weak, clammy grip, his lips pulled tight like string. 'Professor Harold Connaught, Base Commander. I have a Hägglunds waiting.' He insisted on carrying my luggage – a large suitcase and a smaller carry-on bag – but even with this British chivalry, he left me with the distinct impression that he wasn't glad to see me.

3

The airfield at Alliance was bigger than I had imagined. High on a plateau, a Twin Otter plane with skis beneath its wheels sat on the ice. Nearby, a hangar housed another Dash 7 and a Twin Otter plane with large floats above its wheels. Several outbuildings hid their function and contents behind huge steel doors; and inside a shed were three Hägglunds, their enormous rubber tracks and sleek glass windows making them look like giant all-seeing bugs. Unlike the usual orange metal frame, these had been hand-painted with sunsets and icebergs and Antarctic wildlife images. Connaught watched my surprise with clinical interest.

'We had an artist-in-residence here,' he said.

'Oh.' I couldn't hide my amazement at this supposedly secretive station having such a thing. The shadow of a smile crossed Connaught's lips but he said nothing. We continued on in silence to another Hägglunds, painted in three-dimensional trompe l'oeil style to look like a helicopter, with its blades appearing to stick out into thin air.

'Novel,' I said.

'We thought so,' he replied glibly as he opened a door in the front cabin, standing away to allow me to haul myself up.

'Hi, I'm Travis Roberts,' said a young American behind the controls, wearing a fluorescent orange jacket and moleskin trousers, offering me his smooth boyish hand. He looked about nineteen but I presumed he was older. He was pink-cheeked, with blue eyes and glossy brown hair, and slightly overweight. His smile was trusting, his teeth perfect. He had the air of someone from a very good family, and from my limited knowledge I guessed he was speaking in a cultured New York accent.

As we shook hands his grip was confident and reassured, strong without crushing. He looked me squarely in the eyes. I took an immediate liking to him.

Whales often hunt in pods: humpbacks blow nets of bubbles to confuse fish, orcas surround their prey and close the circle ever tighter. I knew that if I was to have a good summer here I'd need to find a new family. Travis Roberts could be my little brother for the season. I flashed him a smile and his perfect white teeth grinned back as he roared the Hägglunds to life.

As we left the airfield, mountains rose large on the horizon. White and craggy, with icy blue folds of shadow tumbling like silk, they could have been out of a fairytale. Pointed tips ran down to a solid triangular base. All it needed was a herd of frosted deer in front to be a Christmas postcard. Or a group of penguins. But we were inland and there was no wildlife in sight.

'Great to be here,' I said and Connaught ignored me, turning to look out the window.

'And we're pleased to see you,' said Travis. 'You're the first female company this season, like the first robin of spring.'

'Surely not.' I was used to being in the minority but not the only one. 'Will there be others coming?'

'Not for a few weeks,' said Connaught without shifting his gaze from where it was now fixed in the middle distance between the mountains and us.

'You'll be sharing with me, a couple of other engineers and your German colleague when he arrives later tonight,' said Travis, 'in Block Number Three.'

'Hope you don't snore?' I asked.

He laughed loudly. 'Separate rooms. And we each get a bathroom.'

'Luxury,' I sighed and Travis slapped my thigh, his fingers pressing in slightly, lingering for a moment. He was such a puppy that it felt more playful than sleazy. Still, I must take care not to lead my little brother on if I wanted to avoid his wandering hands. I'd met plenty of boys like Travis in the science world and I'd learned the hard way that clarity of intent was crucial. I'd been accused of giving mixed messages. These days I tried to be more aware, and not send the wrong signal.

My eyes widened as Alliance Station came into view, like a floating mirage in the ice. I wasn't sure what I'd expected but

I hadn't imagined it would be so modern. The buildings were raised on stilts and beautifully designed – sheeted in steel that glowed a pearly blue, making them simultaneously stand out but also fit in with their icy surroundings. Their windows were large and reflected the starkly beautiful ice field and mountains, and behind this mirror image was a shimmering, a beckoning. It was the most inviting base I'd ever seen, a vision suffused with hope, at one with its environment, with no rundown buildings or leaking detritus from the past. As we moved closer it sat ever more lightly on the ice. It looked like it could simply be packed up and taken back to England and no one would ever know it had been there.

'I wish all bases were like this,' I said.

'It's the future,' said Travis. 'Everything's more up to the minute than the minute. It's taken the design from the Brits' Halley base – the raised buildings – but here it's at a whole new level. So to speak.' He roared with laughter and slapped my thigh again as he drove the Hägglunds past the main building, which was the size of a large office block. Up close I realised that although it was on stilts, there was an inner part that went right down to the ice. And on closer inspection, it looked like it went through the ice.

'Does that go underground?' I asked.

'Sure does.' Travis waved his hand. 'There's a series of chambers under the ice.'

'That's enough,' snapped Connaught and we both turned in surprise. 'Doctor Alvarado is here to carry out an EIA on Fredelighavn.'

Travis nodded, impressed.

'She won't be coming into the main building. The mess hall is over there.' Connaught pointed to a building with glass on all four sides. It was like a beautiful chalet on stilts. 'And the gymnasium is there.' A smaller building hung suspended down an immaculate road of ice. 'Any entertainment is in the mess hall. There's also a library and mini-supermarket there for your supplies. Gratis, you won't need to pay for anything. And of course there's a bar. Whether you pay for that depends on what you drink and when. We have quite a few theme nights where the liquor is on the house.'

I nodded, amazed at the facilities and curious about who was funding them. Perhaps the Americans were chipping in with the budget? Travis stopped the Hägglunds at the third in a row of sleek buildings, raised on elegant steel poles about four metres off the ground, with a wide metal staircase up to the first floor. 'Home sweet home,' he said. Connaught stayed in the back while Travis grabbed my bags and led me up.

Inside was spacious and light. Floor-to-ceiling windows captured the brilliant blue sky and a widescreen view of the mountains glinting in the distance. Down a polished timber corridor was a series of colourful doors. Travis opened the fourth door, which was bright green, and a spacious bedroom with ensuite bathroom lay in front of us.

'This is a five-star hotel,' I said as I took in the king-size bed, leather sofa and chairs, small desk and glorious mountain vista. 'How will I ever leave?'

Travis placed my luggage down. 'Careful what you wish for,' he joked. 'Now, if you'd like to give me your computer and phone and tablet if you have one – anything you want connected to the internet – I'll take them to Jerry, our go-to IT guy, and he'll check there are no bugs. Then we'll give you the Alliance code and you can use them. Don't think we're being intrusive, it's just a standard thing down here.'

'Standard protocol at my base too,' I said, turning them on and handing them over, including my digital camera, which was linked wirelessly to everything else. I was prepared for this, so there was nothing they could see that I didn't want them to. 'I was hoping to do some work this afternoon. Shall I come and collect them?'

'This won't take long. I'll bring them straight back.' Travis smiled and left.

Without my lifelines there was nothing much to do. I unpacked, carefully folding clothes into drawers and hanging items in the large wardrobe. My new room was quiet and hushed. I moved to the bed and lay down. It was supremely comfortable, not like the lumpy bunks at base, but I didn't feel like sleeping, I felt like working. I was growing impatient and just as I started to think of taking a shower to kill time, there was a knock on the door.

'Dinner's at eight,' said Travis as he presented me with my electronic babies and a printout of the access code. 'See you there.' He grinned, shutting the door with a loud click.

I plugged my phone into the docking station on the desk in the corner and put on Beethoven's piano sonatas. The soft tones of *Moonlight* lilted out, which fitted the mood perfectly. I was starting to feel at home. I fluffed the pillows, lay back on the bed, nestled the computer on my lap and looked up the esteemed Professor Harold Connaught. He was attached to a new, regional university in the Midlands in England. That was my first surprise. I'd assumed he'd be from Oxford or Cambridge. Reading further, I saw that he had indeed been at Cambridge, and also for a short time at Harvard. Why then, and how, had he ended up in the university equivalent of a desert? And yet, to head Alliance Station was a prestigious job. He was a puzzle. After I'd read everything I could on him, I punched in *History of Alliance Station*. Nothing came up. It took many tries tapping in every conceivable way of asking the question before I found what I wanted. Finally I saw, buried deep in British Antarctic Survey documents, that the base had been opened in 1975 – two years after the Fredelighavn whaling station had become an Exclusion Zone. There were no photos, but in any case it had been completely rebuilt since then into this modern masterpiece, which could be no more than a few years old. Intriguingly, whatever buildings had originally been here had been demolished and taken away. When? The pristine quality of Alliance was so unusual.

I kept looking for more details but couldn't find anything, so I moved on to Norwegian sites to try to find information about the history of Fredelighavn. The first hour was fruitless and left me with throbbing temples. I turned off Beethoven, frustrated. It was growing cold in the room, so I found the heating control unit, fired it up, and then went back to my search, feeling cosy and a little bit sleepy.

My eyes were drooping and my back hurting from not sitting properly at a desk when I came across something useful. The English translation was a bit strange, but through the wonky grammar I could ascertain that by the turn of the twentieth century, when the Northern Hemisphere whales had been hunted almost to extinction, the whalers turned to the Southern Ocean for its plentiful bounty. In 1908, a Danish geologist in a voyage under Norwegian Captain Hans Jensen surveyed South Safety Island, and the calm waters in an eastern bay did not go unnoticed; he called the bay Fredelighavn – *Peaceful Harbour* – and viewed the remains of sealers' huts, scattered along the beach, as a positive sign. In the same year, the British claimed South Safety Island as British territory.

In 1909, Captain Jensen returned with thirty men and started to build the Fredelighavn Whaling Station, set just back from the beach. Jensen applied to become a British citizen in 1911, the same year the British renamed the bay Placid Bay in a show of empire, but the whaling station retained its name of Fredelighavn due to the British having given the Norwegian financiers a fifty-year lease to run it.

Fredelighavn was accessible by boat from November until March, after which the sea ice came in and closed it until the following November – then the sea ice melted again and granted passage. The surrounding ocean was full of whales and the station thrived, killing more than a thousand whales each season.

I had to stop reading and take a walk around the room, looking out at the ice-mountains to try to calm down. I remembered Lev as he swam past, the attention he paid not to collide with me – he *cared*. And his singing, his guttural notes swirling through me. Whales' communication skills are more efficient than ours. They are intelligent, evolved mammals, who would have cried as they were slaughtered, like children. They would have known what was happening as they were tortured and killed, and their songs silenced. I needed alcohol. There was nothing.

I checked the time – still an hour before dinner. I forced myself to read on. The article was written with a ghastly excitement. It treated the whole history as a great endeavour carried out under extremely difficult conditions. Fredelighavn was further south than most other whaling stations, and was the most productive.

Whale oil was initially sought after for candles and lights. The whalers ate the whale meat, rendered the blubber for oil and let the carcasses wash back into the sea, where many skeletons were soon brought back onto the beach by the tide. In later years the whalers extracted oil from the meat and bones, too, and then ground the bones into meal for fertiliser and pet food, wasting nothing. The beautiful creatures – southern right whales (named because their carcasses produced the most oil, making them *right*), sperm whales and killer whales were hunted ruthlessly, and then in time the largest of the baleen whales – rorquals – blue whales, humpback whales, fin whales, Antarctic minke whales and sei whales were all harpooned from steam-powered catcher boats and hauled to the shore of Alliance Bay.

Over the first few years at Fredelighavn the settlement sprang up as men came for the summer kill. They built the church with pride and vigour. Every few weeks a boat arrived bringing supplies for the whalers, and shipped the oil away to be sold at high prices around the world.

In 1915 the demand for whale oil increased as the First World War raged. Captain Jensen left to fight in the trenches, and was replaced by Captain Lars Halvorsen, from Larvik, Norway, who brought three young sons and an unusually pretty wife, Ingerline, who set about making improvements. It was Ingerline who raised the money for the gleaming orb atop the church steeple and, in 1925, organised for a cinema to be built. She encouraged men to bring their families with them each summer. The settlement grew, and Fredelighavn prospered, killing whales in ever-increasing numbers, now more than three thousand each year; whales that came, as they had done for millennia, to breed peacefully in the clear waters. It was nothing short of mass murder.

I checked my watch again. It was finally time for dinner. But now I wasn't hungry.

I took a quick shower, needing to cleanse myself after reading the violent history. No amount of scrubbing could help.

I rugged up in my best trousers, cream woollen jumper and matching scarf, hauled on a golden-yellow windproof jacket that I hoped set off my dark hair and eyes – I wanted to make a good impression meeting my fellow scientists – and went into the mellow light. The sun wouldn't set for more than a couple of hours at this time of year, but the long evening twilight was deep, an exquisite shade of blue. My boots crunched on the clean ice as I tried to get the images of the bloodied whales out of my head.

The mess hall was another work of art, with its huge picture windows on all sides revealing the mountains and the glowing steel buildings of the base. Down lights cast soft pools of illumination onto the pale timber floor and leather chairs surrounded cutting-edge glass tables, around which sat about fifty men. It was much busier than I had expected. The room was buzzing but the sound ebbed for a moment as I walked in and people glanced my way. Then the noise quickly picked up again as the men resumed their conversations. I tried to establish the scientists from the tradespeople. Usually it was easy to tell but here they all looked similar, and everyone was well groomed. There was no long hair and sloppy clothes like I was used to, and I was relieved that I'd dressed for dinner. Professor Connaught seemed to have set the style and standard, although thankfully no one else was wearing a bow tie. I looked around for Rutger Koch and was disappointed when I couldn't see him.

Connaught sat at the far end of the room, close to the bar, with two men in their fifties, no doubt scientists. At a table near him was a group of men in their mid-forties. I picked them for scientists too.

'Here you are.' Travis, looking decidedly attractive in a blue shirt and blue jumper that matched his eyes, took me by the elbow and steered me over to sit with his friends, none who seemed older than twenty-five. So, I was to be at the children's table; had Connaught arranged it? As I sat down Connaught glanced up. When I took a proper look his way he turned to have a deep discussion with his neighbour.

Before I could ponder the man's petty unfriendliness, Travis launched into introductions. The youngsters momentarily stopped eating their chunks of gravy-dipped bread, having already finished most of their meal.

'This is Jack Dixon and Simon Huxtable.' They shook my hand with sweaty palms – Jack was short and chubby, with a mop of curly dark hair, brown eyes and a large nose. He wore a T-shirt with a moose on the front, which bore a strange resemblance to him. 'Jack's an electrical engineer like me,' said Travis. 'And because we're short-staffed, we both work on the Häggies too.' Travis stopped and looked at Jack with mock intensity. 'But we never call you Jack, do we?'

Jack made shy eye contact with me. 'You can call me Moose, I guess,' he said in a quiet American accent, blushing. Travis slapped him on the back approvingly.

Simon Huxtable was tall with neat, short-cropped black hair. Well-toned muscles bulged beneath a white shirt that was carefully rolled at the sleeves.

'Simon's our chief pilot,' continued Travis happily. 'He's who you need if there's a sudden whiteout. He'll bring the bird in every time. Flies with Stan over there, his co-pilot.' Stan gave a broad, toothy grin and a little wave from a nearby table.

'If I need to fly I'll certainly have you, then,' I said to Simon and he smiled warmly.

'We have four pilots. But Reg over there,' Travis pointed to a man in his late fifties with greying hair, a neat beard and a bulbous nose a strange blue-red in colour. 'We wouldn't fly with him.' They all grinned.

'I wouldn't either,' I said for solidarity, and Travis reached down and squeezed my thigh. I needed to talk through the little-brother rules with him sometime.

'Vino?' Travis poured a large glass of white wine. 'Hope you don't want red? We're out of it.'

'Too many theme nights,' said Simon in a polished Australian accent, laughing.

'White's perfect. Has Professor Koch arrived yet?' I asked.

'Not yet,' said Travis. I sipped the wine, which was rough to the point of undrinkable. 'So what do they research down here?' I said.

Travis answered casually. 'A few clinical experiments. High tech.'

'What in?'

He shrugged. 'Not my area.'

I nodded, trying to think of a way to join another table to learn more about the local research. Across the room was a group of men in their mid-to-late thirties. I stood. 'Better get some food before it's all gone.'

'We'll keep your spot warm,' called Travis as I walked over to the servery, where a very large and unfriendly-looking cook was dispensing a choice of two meaty roast dinners with frozen vegetables that had been boiled limp. I chose the beef awash in gravy and headed for my chosen table. The men looked up in alarm. They were dressed like triplets in dark blue polo-neck jumpers and matching trousers. They were thin, tall and clearly worked out in the gym. Up close, their clean-shaven skin was pale.

'Mind if I join you?' I said, sitting down without an invitation. Their conversation stopped abruptly. 'Laura Alvarado,' I said, offering my hand.

Each shook my hand tentatively. Adam and Matthew were English, and Bruce was Australian. I waited for their surnames but none were given.

'Scientists down for the summer like me?' I took a stab.

'Yep,' said Bruce.

'Where are you from?' I asked brightly. Their eyes were shifting to each other, clearly annoyed at the interruption.

'Sydney,' said Bruce.

'Sydney Uni?'

Bruce grunted assent. I weighed up whether to ask him if he knew my father but, as it turned out, he didn't want any conversation at all.

'Sorry, Laura,' he said politely. 'We were just discussing something we need to sort out by tonight. Would you mind?'

The others looked at me impassively, and I could feel Connaught's eyes upon me. I stood, dinner in hand. 'No problem.' I nodded goodbye, trying to keep my chin up as I walked across and sat down beside Connaught, who nearly choked.

'Good set-up you've got here,' I said, turning to his dinner partners. 'Laura Alvarado. Down here for the summer.' These at least had the decency to pretend to be interested. After my previous humiliation I was grateful, and I was determined to seem confident and undeterred, despite feeling the opposite.

The men introduced themselves, again by their first names only – Jacob and Ewan. Neither shook my hand.

'Anyone know the weather forecast?' I asked.

'It's meant to be fine,' said Jacob politely.

'Excellent.' I turned to Connaught. 'I was hoping to organise transport to Placid Bay.'

Jacob and Ewan sat forward attentively. 'That's where I'll be doing my EIA,' I said to them.

'Why?' asked Jacob.

I shrugged. 'It's just a preliminary report.'

'What's being planned?' Ewan looked at me curiously.

'Nothing yet.'

'She won't tell us anything, and we won't tell her anything,' said Connaught, yawning. 'But unfortunately, Laura, your fellow team member Professor Koch has a problem with his gallbladder. They had to turn his plane back to Argentina. He'll be operated on tonight in Ushuaia. He assured me he'll be here as soon as he can.'

'The poor thing,' I said, taken aback. 'What are Ushuaia's hospitals like?'

Connaught stared at me. 'As if I'd know that.'

Ewan and Jacob smothered laughs.

'You may still go to Fredelighavn,' continued Connaught. 'But as it's an Exclusion Zone, I'm not able to send anyone in with you. It's beyond my station to approve that. Speak to Travis – he'll organise a Hägglunds.' Connaught stood abruptly. 'Goodnight all.' He sauntered off.

'That's us too,' said Jacob, rising with Ewan, who tipped his head in a mute farewell. I tried to become invisible as I was left to eat my dinner alone. When I glanced across to Travis's table, Travis had left. I chewed on the tough beef and focused on the news about Rutger. Could I ask Georgia if I could go back until he arrived? I poured a large glass of white wine from the bottle that had been abandoned by my ex-tablemates. It was top quality. I downed it quickly and refilled my glass. Drinking copious amounts of alcohol in the Antarctic was a tradition, and one that I'd grown to enjoy.

By the time I'd finished, the room had emptied and I was feeling stronger. It was like the first day in any new job: things always seemed foreign. There was a saying that went around among expeditioners: people who fell off the earth because they couldn't fit in ended up together at the bottom of the world. We were probably all lovable misfits in one way or another. There was no normal in Antarctica. Although I knew that what I'd witnessed tonight had been genuinely nasty: the scientists were freezing me out. I certainly wouldn't be putting in a good word for any of them back home. But I couldn't say much at all because I didn't know their surnames. And that meant I couldn't look up their backgrounds either, which I was sure was intentional. It made me all the more curious to find out what it was they were researching in the main building.

Back in my room I Skyped Georgia, who, unlike anyone else I knew, looked great on screen and managed to talk directly to the camera, creating an intimacy like she was there with you. She'd already heard the news and came straight to the point.

'The problem is it's a big task, and there's no room for movement. The clock's ticking. I'll see who I can authorise to get down there with you until Professor Koch arrives. Don't worry, I've got your back,' she said.

The cop bible. They looked out for each other above all else. I blocked out thoughts of David White as quickly as they rose, and thanked her.

'Koch is evidently very fit, and it's keyhole surgery,' she said, 'so they're not expecting this to take long. But I'd like you to start straightaway. Go to Fredelighavn tomorrow, if that's okay?'

Scientists are used to teams. We would never usually go out into the field alone. I wished I could argue the point; say that we could catch up if we only missed a week or so.

'Okay,' I said instead.

'I'll send you the engineers' report on the buildings. They were given a clean bill of health for safety last summer: they're unusually well preserved. But with the winter storms things could have changed, so take care. You know what you're doing. And Laura – it's an honour Australia's been chosen, and you in particular. It's the right thing to do to go down.'

I wished I felt the same. I spent the next few hours reading the report on Fredelighavn's structures, which did seem extraordinarily intact. The report was very dry in its details and annoyingly did not include photographs. My stomach dipped. If the weather held, I would be seeing it for myself in the morning.

4

The air was still and freezing, the light a piercing blue as I crunched along the ice not knowing exactly where I was going. No one had bothered to tell me where I'd find Travis, and I hadn't seen him at breakfast, where I'd sat alone. My head was pounding – my body still adjusting from the days of no sunlight in winter to now having constant sunlight with only a couple of hours of night, and even that wasn't black night. I'd slept badly. And I wished Rutger Koch was here.

There was no activity in the streets. No quad bikes roaring towards and away from the buildings, people returning, people going out, like my own base.

I tried to take in everything about the main building as I passed: it was comparatively large, and the centre that dropped underground was sheeted with thick steel. It looked like a giant insect giving birth.

I turned down another street and saw Travis up ahead, wheeling a red skidoo – a snowmobile, similar to a quad bike but with skis instead of tractor wheels, like a motorised sled with a windscreen in front of its long, low seat – out of a shed I hadn't seen yesterday.

'Hey there, Laura,' he called genially as I walked up. If he was annoyed I hadn't returned to his table last night, he was hiding it.

'So a nice warm Häggie for the lady? Or would you prefer a skidoo? Or both. I can take you down in the Häggie and leave a skidoo there for your return. Or you can drive yourself but I wouldn't advise it until you've been there once. We went out yesterday and flagged the way for you.'

'I'd like you to show me.' I didn't add that it was also regulation to do it that way. Would he really have let me go off alone?

We then went through a lengthy process of approving my pre-approved field trip. Unlike the days when it was just entered into a logbook, this was all computerised. Supposedly more efficient but it took forever, particularly because Rutger wasn't with me, which the computer didn't like any more than I did. Finally, we were cleared to go.

Travis led me to where he had a Hägglunds prepared with a tow-tray that was carrying a strapped-in skidoo. So, he'd just been testing me after all.

Today's Hägglunds was painted with penguins and seals.

'Your artist-in-residence was busy,' I said.

For a moment Travis looked bemused. 'Oh, him. Yeah, he painted fast. Bit of a lowlife. Drank like a fish. Then scampered off home quick as you please. Family emergency. I don't think he was cut out for the cold. Or the lack of girls.' Travis grinned. 'That reminds me. Tonight's a theme night. Come as your favourite fantasy. I can organise a costume if you like. We have a store.'

'Sounds good,' I said, thinking it actually sounded grotesque. I was used to fancy dress nights, which were another Antarctic tradition, but usually they were on weekends and good, wholesome, light-hearted fun. Down here if they were anything like last night I couldn't look forward to it.

'Häggie awaits. Hop in.' Travis went around to the driver's side.

In the front cabin there were pin-ups of bare-breasted women. I caught my breath. In the Australian bases there was no way they'd have anything like that, and I doubted the British Antarctic Survey would allow it either. In fact, I was certain. Alliance seemed to operate outside the established rules. Travis caught my expression, and quickly ripped them down.

'Beautiful day for a motor,' he said as he fired up the engine and we crawled into the street. Travis drove slowly until we were off the base, then roared the Hägglunds to life.

'Don't you love it?' he cried as we raced along. 'Best place on earth!'

I felt a familiar surge of happiness as we flew across the ice. We were heading towards the coast, bright green flags mapping out the safe drive zone. Red flags stood sentry over the dangerous thin ice. 'Point out everything I need to know?' I asked.

'Will do,' Travis replied cheerfully. 'Would you like me to come in with you when we get there?'

'I'd love you to. But I can't . . . You know it's an Exclusion Zone.'

'Asked and answered.' He winked. 'But I'll give you my cell phone number. If you're worried, just call.'

'So my phone will work at Placid Bay?' I'd brought it in the hope it would. Around all Australian bases we had good reception these days, but the whaling station was a distance out from Alliance.

'Well, not right there, it's too far away. But as you're driving back you'll get into range.'

I was uneasy about being alone in a foreign place, particularly with the hostile reception I'd received. I had a shortwave radio with me, but I didn't know who I'd connect with at base if I needed to use it.

As we roared along Travis dutifully pointed out the terrain, and I carefully observed. He told me he'd fitted the skidoo with an on-board computer that warned of danger areas. I was relieved I'd have that in addition to the flags pointing the way, but it also paid to hear as much as possible about the problem spots. On the ice, a thorough safety code was vital.

After thirty minutes, Fredelighavn rose before us.

The buildings were much larger at ground level, towering wooden structures in all the colours of the rainbow. 'Wow,' I said, 'I hadn't expected that.'

'Different, hey? More colourful than you thought?'

'It just didn't look like that from the air.'

'That's because you were seeing the roofs and bits and pieces. Looks red from above, doesn't it?'

He was right. It had looked uniformly red. Not the purples and pinks and blues that were unfolding on the horizon. In Antarctica buildings were always painted strong colours to help them be seen in whiteout blizzard conditions, but these colours, while still bright, were elegant.

'It's beautiful,' I said before I caught my words. How could this slaughter yard ever be beautiful? How could it be more than a graveyard, a terrible monument to an abusive past?

And yet the buildings kept revealing themselves as we approached. It was a picturesque village.

'Whoo-eee,' whooped Travis, and turned to me. 'Knew you'd love it! Wait till you walk around inside.'

'Have you been in?' I asked, confused.

'They don't track us on weekends – time off, we do what we want. Best diving on the island. We could go some time?'

'Certainly,' I said, 'if I wanted to break every rule in the book, which I don't.'

'Suit yourself,' he shrugged, breaking eye contact.

It infuriated me Connaught had a culture of staff that thought nothing of ignoring protocol. I would be including *that* in my report.

'Do others go with you on your weekends away?' I asked casually.

'Yeah, of course.'

'Well, then, perhaps I will some time.' I smiled. Finding who had been in the Exclusion Zone would now be a priority, and best if I did it from the inside.

Travis slapped my thigh. 'Thought you'd come round.'

52

I flashed him another smile, then quickly grew serious. We were miles from base and I didn't want him to think I was encouraging intimacy.

'If you drop me off by the first house, that'll be fine.' We stopped by a bright purple house raised high, presumably on stilts that were buried in ice. It had a highly angled corrugated-iron roof tethered to the ground with thick steel straps. Icy snowdrifts swept up the steps to the porch, but the doorway was accessible.

I strapped on my backpack, inside which was food, a second jacket in case the weather turned, the shortwave radio, emergency flares and bottles of water. I flung a second bag over my shoulder, which held my phone, tablet, digital camera, a sophisticated GPS, a high-powered torch and a first-aid kit. Travis quickly manoeuvred the snowmobile onto the ice and hung a helmet with a full-face visor on its handlebar.

The buildings stretching around us reminded me of Burano, a colourful village on an island I'd visited when I went to Venice years ago. I'd been desperately trying to take my mind off the loss of Hamish and breaking up with Cameron, and the gorgeous buildings had surprised me, momentarily lifting my spirits. These houses of Fredelighavn were similar, luminous in rich plum, fragile pink, deep sienna, pale blue, indigo, orange, yellow, ochre. All were timber, with horizontal boards cladding the walls and corrugated-iron roofs rusted a uniform red. In some places I could see the wooden stilts raising the houses above the ice that was piled high around the streets; ice that blocked windows in places, the result of blizzards powering through over the years. But in recent times there had been warmer summer temperatures and ice-melt, and that, with the help of the engineers, had left the buildings remarkably visible. There were also mountain ranges to the north and south of the village, and across the island to the west, which had provided protection.

'Sure you'll be okay?' asked Travis, leaning towards me protectively.

I nodded, quashing my apprehension at going in alone.

'I'll be seeing you, then,' he said. 'I'll have that costume waiting for the party. Be back by eight, okay?'

'If I'm not, come searching.'

'Don't worry, I will.' Travis looked at me seriously. 'Have a great day.' He grinned and his face lit up. Good little brother, I thought, taking care of family.

I waved as the Hägglunds took off, its rubber treads flying across the ice. As the hum of the engine receded, I became aware of the deep silence surrounding me.

I took another look at the purple house with its extraordinarily steep roof. It had faded white wood in its two front colonial paned windows and around the porch that protected its front door. All its paint was peeling but had been preserved in the cold, dry air – enough to give an absolute impression of what it would have been like in its heyday. It was cute and Norwegian, a little piece of home. On the edge of the world.

I laughed and was alarmed at the echo of my voice. I listened for other sounds. In the distance, I could hear the distinct wall of noise of an Adélie penguin rookery. I breathed more easily, relieved to be near something familiar.

I put on my skis and set off in the direction of the sea. The village was deep and set back from the coast at this point.

I couldn't even see the water, but I could see the tall smoke stacks from the whale-processing cookeries on the shore. To my left, a distance away, huge oil tanks, about fifty in number – round, with pointed roofs of corrugated iron – rose up the slope of the mountains. I knew from my time at Grytviken that some would have held the whale-oil, and others fuel-oil. A network of underground pipes would connect the tanks to the cookeries, from where the processed whale-oil would be pumped up to the tanks, and then, when the ships came, pumped out to them for delivery to markets across the world.

In the reverse direction, the fuel-oil would be brought from Norway and pumped off the ships, to run the generators for electricity.

My skis swooshed on the ice. I looked back to the skidoo, sitting beside the purple house. It was my escape route back to base. I felt a moment's queasiness at leaving it.

No one else is here, I kept telling myself, trying to block out the knowledge that Travis had come when he wasn't meant to – and that he'd been with friends.

'That was on a weekend,' I mumbled aloud.

I focused on the task ahead and moved down a street with colourful houses on both sides, their tin roofs kept firmly in place by steel cables fixed to the ground; in a few places the ends of harpoons were visible – the wires must have been attached to the harpoon, and then the harpoon stuck through the ice, its barbed, pointy end digging in to the earth below. Silence evaporated: the houses were creaking and cracking in the cold. Some sounded like they were sighing, as if they were alive. I stopped, feeling like I was being watched. I looked around, but there was no one there. My breathing grew rapid, little clouds of heat puffing into the clear day.

I was beside a house painted pale lemon, with a hot pink porch and windows. I was eager to get to the penguins, but my survey included the houses. As a kid, I always ate my least favourite food first, saving delicacies like jamon for last. I hadn't changed. I took off my skis and trod up the slope of ice that covered the stairs. I put my hand on the doorknob that was carved in the shape of a whale and shuddered at the thought of what had gone on at Fredelighavn.

The door made a high-pitched brittle sound like snapping bones as it swung open. I paused on the hearth and peered inside. Everything looked as solid as the engineers had reported. There was a short passage and a set of stairs leading up to another floor. I flicked on my torch. The timber floorboards sank as I walked; they were dry and fragile but intact. A pretty pink lightshade hung above me and the passage walls were painted in lime green. I drew in the air, an odd mixture of stale wood and fabric, and salty freshness from the sea.

The first room off the passage was the lounge. With all its furniture. I stepped back in surprise. When they'd left, they'd taken virtually nothing. I hadn't been able to find the date the whaling station had closed, but looking at the design, it seemed that time had stopped here in the late 1950s or early 1960s. That would fit with other whaling stations like Grytviken, which had closed in 1963 when the slaughter had been so great that there were no whales left. But of course on South Safety, they would have had to end the slaughter by 1961, when the Antarctic Treaty came into force, because native wildlife became protected.

I ran a gloved hand around my chin and it made a noise like rubbing on paper – my skin was dehydrated from the cold. I walked around the small lounge room. There were bright fabrics on the two lounges, two armchairs and curtains, all in a loud pink blossom pattern that reminded me of a Marimekko design. The kind of thing people were buying now for its retro beauty.

This sort of homeliness was like nothing I'd seen down here, and I found the domesticity strangely alarming. I had to try hard to remember I was in Antarctica.

One of the coffee tables was made from a pale European wood. Larch perhaps? It was from an older period. An antique. On it was an ashtray; I almost expected a smoking pipe. Then I smelled something and turned. On another coffee table sat another ashtray – and this one was full of cigarette butts. I went over rapidly to see if they seemed recent. There were bright pink lipstick marks on at least half the butts, but it was impossible to tell how old they were; Antarctic air is so dry and freezing, it preserves. The butts could have been here for weeks, months, years or decades. I took photos, intrigued. My guess was the butts were original, from the fifties. At this time, I would touch nothing. After my report there would be another team sent in to forensically go through everything.

That was why I was so angry that Travis had been. Had he touched anything in Fredelighavn? Contaminated anything? I assumed the previous engineers wouldn't have disturbed the site last summer, because they were trained and briefed.

I took more photos of the room and then continued down the passage. On my right was a tiny bedroom containing a single bed covered in a thick blanket with a pink woollen crocheted rug on top. Lovingly handmade and not so lovingly left behind. A flea-bitten Steiff teddy bear lay propped on the pink pillowslip; one eye was missing, the other glassy eye stared out accusingly, as if it blamed me for its abandonment.

Colourful floral curtains seemed eerily new. There was no deterioration at all. On the walls were pictures of horses cut from magazines, and on a dressing table stood little carved wooden horses, cows and goats. A sweet rural scene, totally incongruous with where we were. Why couldn't the little girl at least have taken these tokens with her?

These artefacts would have to be carefully preserved and conserved and moved into a main museum building. Tourists couldn't be let loose in such an environment. A Steiff teddy would be stolen for sure. It was so cute even I wanted to pick it up. I photographed it instead.

I moved on. Slightly down from this room on the opposite side was another small bedroom. This one had carved wooden models of sailing ships, and a series of beautiful wooden fish painted brightly in blues and reds and yellows and greens. There were little white yachts sailing jauntily on the cotton curtains. The bedspread was again crocheted, but in a deep blue. The little boy loved the sea. What had he thought about the whales? And why had he left his carvings, which were clearly painstakingly made and with great pride?

It was like plague had come and wiped this family quickly off the earth, but I knew that couldn't be the case.

I walked further into the belly of the house and arrived in a neat Scandinavian kitchen full of carved, pale wooden cupboards. A gorgeous teak table was bathed in sunlight streaming through the window. I couldn't believe my eyes: there were blue and white coffee mugs still on the table, with a brown liquid in them, frozen solid. Why had these people left in such a hurry?

I went to the nearest cupboard and opened it. Cans of herrings, sardines, pork and tomatoes were neatly stacked. I opened another cupboard: paper bags of sugar and salt and rice stared out at me.

Ernest Shackleton had left his supplies at his famous hut in Antarctica, as had Scott. They were entirely preserved. I therefore shouldn't have been surprised and yet I was. They had been explorers and left their provisions for future need and also because they couldn't carry them. Here we were at a port, or a harbour at least, where boats came and went with their cargo.

Why was nothing packed up?

Had they intended to return?

I would have to co-opt historians to shed light before I finalised my report.

At the back of the house was a latrine-style toilet: a raised timber box with a hole in it, similar to those the explorers such as Mawson had used in their huts. The wooden lid was closed. I had no intention of opening it.

I retreated through the house to the front staircase and looked up. Shadows were falling through a fine lace curtain, flickering on a forest-green wall.

Was it safe to go up? I knew I should probably wait until Rutger arrived, but the engineers' report had given the houses a clean bill of health last summer, and I was curious. My feet creaked on the stairs, the wood worn into mellow grooves. Every year they'd acquired this rich patina thousands of whales had been slaughtered. Suddenly I wanted to run. For the first time in years I yearned to go back to Melbourne to my mother and hide in our big family home in Kew. It held some bad memories but nothing like this.

I reached the landing, my hand resting on the smooth wood of the railing, polished from wear to a fine, silky feel that was almost warm to the touch.

On the upstairs level was the master bedroom. Again, the decor was fashionable 1950s. There was a small double bed with a striking cover in a geometric print of yellow, pink and green. The woman of the house surely loved it.

And yet had left it behind.

There were exquisite carvings of marine life, predominantly whales, capturing the different species in profound detail. Had the man who made them also slaughtered them? I had no doubt.

Perplexed and sad, I retraced my steps and went out the front door into the clear, cold air. I was thankful to be back in the street, away from this abandoned home. I made notes on my tablet, realising I hadn't taken anywhere near enough photographs. I called it *The House of the Carvers*, in a nod to Pompeii. That's what it had felt like because it seemed to have been so quickly vacated, as if the family were fleeing a volcanic eruption.

I picked up my skis and walked past more colourful houses towards the chattering of the bay. But before I arrived, a huge building loomed large on my right; its giant red doors hung open, askew, their hinges broken – and inside, I could hear and smell penguins. I walked carefully into the gloom. Snow and ice lay around in a shed full of rusted machinery: ancient tractor-tyred vehicles, all dilapidated. Around them, hundreds of Adélies had carried stones to make their nests. I photographed the birds in the glowering green light that was seeping through grimy windows high up in the timber walls.

The penguins looked at me, growing increasingly disturbed. As I walked further in they started to waddle away. There was no doubt – they were frightened. I backed off, sharing their alarm.

Out in the street I could still hear the raucous squawks of terror from the penguins. An invader had been.

It was so completely out of character for the Adélies. What had Travis and his friends done down here? Or was it the engineers who had come last summer?

Shaken, I continued on towards the bay past other corrugated-iron sheds, their doors closed, and one brick building. I thought of going into the latter, curious that it was of a different construction, but I was distracted by the unmistakable oily, fishy smell of seals. I looked around and saw an open door into a large pink wooden building. I walked across and peered inside. It was very dark and there were no windows, so I flicked on my torch as I entered. Among drifts of snow that had turned to solid ice, the room was full of comfortable lounge chairs arranged in rows, and in between the chairs, and sometimes on the chairs, was a colony of Weddell seals. I was in a cinema. The cinema that Captain Halvorsen's wife Ingerline had built in the 1920s. Most of the seals were facing the screen at the far end, like they were watching a movie. At the back of the room was an old projector, with a reel of film still threaded into it. The huge seals lay around, their sleek grey bodies dappled with white and black splotches, whiskered faces now raised to inspect me. An enormous seal started to bark, and others joined in.

They came at me aggressively and I backed away at lightning speed, my body tingling in shock. Weddell seals were usually placid, calm and untroubled by humans.

One young seal cut me off.

'It's okay, I'm not going to hurt you.' But now the biggest seal in the room, a bull stretching almost four metres long, weighing about 500 kilos, was lunging at me. I ran. He followed me into the street and I kept running. Looking back, I saw he'd stopped outside the cinema and was propped on his front flippers, tipping his head to the sun and roaring. I didn't slow my pace until I reached the harbour. Doubling over with stitch, I looked back. The bull seal was nowhere in sight, but I still felt like I was being watched.

Placid Bay stretched in front of me, sparkling in the sunlight. I turned again to look at the settlement. This was the view I remembered, but now it was in colour. The buildings were pink and green and orange, red and blue and yellow. A rainbow village. Fredelighavn didn't feel like it had stood empty for decades – it didn't seem like a ghost town. There was a strange sense of occupancy. Perhaps because of the wildlife? I turned back to the sea. To my right was a vast Adélie penguin rookery, streaked red from krill the penguins ate, stretching up a steep slope to Alliance Point. To my left, a distance away along the bay, gentoo penguins were nesting. Gigantic southern elephant seals sunned themselves on the beach.

I'd walked into a version of Paradise: a loud, noisy, hooting and honking world of happiness. Except in this scene, wrecks of old whaling catcher ships hulked in and out of the water near four wooden jetties stretching along the shore; the catcher ships, like everything else, had just been left. And strewn along the beach were huge whale bones, skeletons of the beautiful, gentle creatures that had been slaughtered, their bleached ribs rising up to the sky, casting shadows. Bile rose in a tart gush, washing my mouth with acid.

The ships were at strange angles to each other but most were fully intact. It was probably cheaper to scuttle them here than sail them back to Norway. There was no longer a use for them, because the prey had been killed to the edge of extinction. As I took photographs, a bull elephant seal, five metres long and slug-like, weighing around 3000 kilos, rose and roared through its long nose. I backed away, wary, but two seals, cows, lifted their heads and roared back. A mating ritual. The other seals remained sleeping, supremely relaxed. I left the love triangle to its courting, and walked towards the Adélies up at Alliance Point. They were just like the ones I knew from Australian Antarctic Territory, and I hoped that here, where they would have naturally nested for hundreds, even thousands of years, they wouldn't be frightened of a human like the ones I'd just seen in the machinery shed.

The rookery was a thriving, thronging mass of black and white. The noise was deafening. I put down my skis and walked up and among the Adélies, imitating Charlie Chaplin, swinging from side to side like them.

Without warning the penguins came at me in a group, squawking and pecking. I put my hands down to fend them off and brought them back up bloodied – sharp beaks had gone right through my gloves. I couldn't believe it. I tried to stay calm and continued to walk through the rookery, wanting to show them I was no threat, but the birds came at me again, swarming and thrusting their beaks.

I had no time to photograph their strange behaviour, no choice but to grab my skis and flee. I ran along the shore, stopping when I reached the huge expanse of the wooden-slatted flensing platform, turned silver with age. Catching my breath, I pulled out my first-aid kit. My arms were bleeding as well as my hands. There were a couple of deeper punctures on both legs where the beaks had gone through my trousers, deep into my flesh. Trembling, I dabbed on liquid disinfectant, then antibiotic cream. I was stunned. It was so unusual to be attacked aggressively by wildlife in Antarctica. When putting radio antennae on penguins you could get a few scratches and bites, but nothing like this – nothing with this force and anger. I took out my tablet and made myself focus enough to make notes, recording the time and details of what had just happened.

I ate an energy bar, but I didn't have any appetite. In front of me was the slipway into the sea, where the whales would have been brought after having been harpooned from the catcher boats and hauled to the harbour.

From the slipway, the whales were winched up to the flensing platform to meet the flensers, men with long knives who peeled the blubber away in strips. Then more men with knives, lemmers, cut the meat from the bones. I saw winches that would have been used to turn the whales as they were sliced up; a winch that would have hoisted the bones up to the bone cookery loft afterwards; and other winches that would have taken the blubber and meat to their processing plants, one on each side of the flensing platform.

I felt deep shame at what had been done to the whales. Reluctantly, I went to inspect the nearest shed, a long, red, corrugated-iron building with tall towers to let out the steam. I turned on my torch and slashed light through the gaping doors into the darkness. Giant metal vats, about ten times my height – pressure cookers – were lined up in two rows of eight, stretching about thirty metres into the deep gloom. Ladders were propped at several points, leading to a timber platform above. I walked through the cookers, coming out into an area that made my pulse quicken. Long saws lay along a vast table like something out of a nightmare, their jagged teeth rusty but deadly. Other circular saws stood in front of conveyor belts that rose to the upper platform. It was here the men would have cut the whale meat into smaller pieces, before sending it up to boil in the cookers. Nauseous, I walked out a door at the end, back onto the flensing platform. I breathed deeply and stared out to sea, where icebergs crowded further out, covered with Adélie penguins. One bird peered over the edge, decided it was safe and plunged down into the water. The rest of the Adélies followed in a single movement.

After making a few quick notes, I walked to the opposite side of the flensing platform to another long tin shed. The door screeched as I opened it. I flashed my torch around and saw more tall cookers, again in parallel lines. I counted two rows of five. Conveyor belts ran from the floor through three storeys of platforms above. This was the blubber cookery, simpler than the meat cookery. The blubber would have been taken up on the belts and dropped into the top of the vats to burn off and distil the oil.

Far away at the end of the shed, long knives and massive jagged-toothed saws orange with rust hung along the wall, with coils of thick rope, like a murderer's lair.

Goosebumps pricked my arms and I shone the torch behind me and to both sides, again feeling like I was being watched.

I couldn't see anyone or anything. Perhaps there were ghosts here, given the atrocities that had taken place. But I believed in ghosts of memory, not the supernatural. My baby Hamish floated before me, a trace of pale face, a blur of dark hair. A stab of sadness rushed through me like a physical blow. I waited, allowing a moment to think of him – and then I braced myself and continued through the shed.

At the back, beside the knives, was a room with a dirty glass wall looking out into the building – some sort of manager's office. As I headed for it I heard a rustling behind me. I swung around, and caught out of the corner of my eye a figure moving in the gloom. Large, thickset; the size of a man. I flicked off my torch and stood stock-still, holding my breath, heart pounding. I had no weapon to defend myself, and became acutely aware of the knives and saws nearby. Had he just helped himself to one? Was he coming for me?

Who was he? Absolutely no one but me should be down here; he must be one of the men from Alliance. The hair on the back of my neck stood on end as I headed in the darkness towards the rusty weapons, trying to make no sound, keeping my skis out in front so I could swing them into his ribs if he attacked.

The back of my throat burned in the icy air. Slowly, quietly, I inched towards the knives. The distance seemed to have increased, or perhaps I was walking in the wrong direction. But instinctively I felt I was in the right spot.

Suddenly a cold, rusty saw was under my fingers. I'd reached the wall. Steadily I moved to my left. I felt along quietly and the wooden handle of a knife slipped under my hand. I reached around it and pulled. Its blade was stuck tight on the wall, rusted on – it wouldn't come. But it made a noise, a muffled one that seemed horribly loud. I listened. Had I given away where I was? From outside, I could hear penguins calling to each other. At any moment I expected a hand to grab me, or worse.

I waited and waited for what seemed like an eternity. I couldn't hear any other movement. Perhaps it was just my mind playing tricks after all. I inched along the wall until my fingers found the next knife – a smaller one. I lifted it gently, and after a moment's resistance it came away with a shriek. I grabbed it tightly and moved away as fast as I could. Whoever was here would surely have heard that. I needed to get out, back to the snowmobile. Or did he know where that was too? Would he beat me there if he didn't trap me first?

I was gripping the knife and the torch, and my skis were under my arm. With my backpack and bag, it was too much to carry. Slowly I bent and put the skis quietly on the ground. I stayed crouched, listening intently. All I could hear was my own thumping pulse.

Then a movement caught my eye, darker black in the black. It was definitely a man, and close, only three metres from me. I desperately tried to think what to do. I felt safer hunched on the ground; standing, there was more of me to see. My calves and thighs were strong. I could spring up like a coil. I stayed where I was. Still; like a hunter.

Minutes ticked by slowly. My limbs began to ice up. Soon I'd have to move or I'd be so frozen I couldn't react properly. And then I heard a rusty screech and saw a figure silhouetted in the open doorway, up the other end past the cookers. He was medium height and muscular.

And he was running outside.

I let out my breath in a long exhale, then tried to breathe normally but it was impossible, I was too tense. I stood and stretched, shaking my arms to warm up as I decided whether to pick up my skis or head off without them. The man was out there somewhere, and that made me cramp with nerves. At least he was running. I'd disturbed him. Was he as scared of me as I was of him?

I decided to leave my skis. Preparing to go, I had a sudden impulse to check that I was alone in the shed. I flicked on my torch and shone it around. As it cut through the darkness I re-assured myself there was no one else. But then I caught sight of a strip of material, red, cotton, poking from beside the nearest cooker. I froze. Was it attached to a person? It looked limp, more like discarded clothing. I played the light straight on it, and nothing moved. I wanted to go over and pick it up but I was too scared. What if I walked straight into a trap? I turned and ran instead, out of the building, up a street away from the harbour, a different street to the one I'd been in before, my arms pumping and legs moving with a will of their own, my head swivelling to see I wasn't being followed.

I had no idea where I was. I ran up one street with sheds, then another with houses. Finally, like a miracle, the snowmobile came into view. I grabbed the helmet from the handlebars, and flung it on. As I took off I slid the rusty knife under a strap on the seat in front of me, within easy reach.

As soon as I was a distance from Fredelighavn, I plucked out my phone from my bag. No black dots on the screen – out of range. After several more minutes I checked again – the signal was there, but weak. I tried to call Georgia but it wouldn't connect. I phoned Travis instead and was thankful when he picked up instantly.

'There was someone here,' I blurted. 'A man.'

'Laura, is that you?' Travis sounded alarmed.

'Travis, did you hear? There was someone here. *At Fredelighavn.* Someone who didn't want to be seen.'

Travis was silent. I could hear him breathing.

'Just ... Travis, I want you to know in case something happens to me. And if it does, you must tell my boss what I've just told you. Georgia Spiros.'

'Laura, calm down. Start again. Are you okay?'

'I'm fine. But there was someone in the blubber cookery. I thought they were stalking me but now I'm not sure. They shouldn't have been there and they certainly didn't want to be seen. So who were they and what were they doing?'

Alliance came into view, like a modernist painting in the ice. Travis was waiting in the doorway of the shed. I slipped the knife into my bag as I approached.

'Laura, you had me worried.'

I stood up from the snowmobile, my body so cold it felt like it would snap in half.

'What happened down there?' he asked, frowning.

Now I was back, I just wanted to call Georgia.

'Let's talk about it tonight? Right now I need to get warm.'

'Come on,' Travis said reassuringly. 'I'll walk you to your room.'

5

I woke struggling, lashing out with my arms. When I opened my eyes I was horrified I wasn't alone. A man dressed in black jeans, a black V-neck jumper and a Venetian cat mask was standing over me, backing away. And beneath the sheets I was naked.

'Hey, eh, it's okay,' he stuttered. I screamed.

'Eh, don't do that!'

His gloved hands ripped at the mask and pulled it off. It was Travis.

'What the hell were you doing?' I demanded.

'It's okay.'

'Stop saying that.'

Travis was breathing hard.

'What are you doing in my room?'

'I knocked for ages. When I couldn't raise you . . . I'm sorry. I just thought after what you'd been through today . . . I panicked. And you never did finish telling me what happened down there. Your door was unlocked, so I came in. I was trying to wake you, I was really worried.'

I stared at him. It was an absolute unspoken law in Antarctica never to enter anyone's room uninvited. At base everyone lived close by, so the little privacy there was came in one's room. It was sacrosanct space, even if the door wasn't locked. My mind ticked over. I'd come in, thrown myself in a hot shower and then dropped into bed, about to phone Georgia. I must have fallen asleep. I'd assumed the door locked automatically as it felt so much like a hotel, which I now realised was foolish of me. At my own base I'd never need to lock up, but at Alliance I wouldn't ever have had the door open knowingly.

'Please go, Travis,' I said, feeling completely vulnerable.

He took a few steps towards the door and then stopped. 'It's almost eleven o'clock. Are you still coming to the theme night?'

I checked my watch, alarmed. I'd slept for hours. The last thing I wanted was to go to a party, but I'd promised Travis and I hated breaking my word to anyone. And my instincts told me his concern was genuine – even if my rational thoughts were far more wary. 'Okay. Why don't you go back to your room and I'll come and get you?'

Travis nodded, relieved. 'Take as much time as you need.' He indicated a fancy-dress outfit on a chair – a bright red leotard that looked homemade, and a holster with jewelled guns. 'It was the best I could find, sorry. It's a superhero.

And I brought you some food before it had all gone.' There was a bowl covered by a plate, and a spoon and fork, sitting on my desk. Travis closed the door, and I sprang up with the sheet around me and pulled a latch across. There was no other lock, the door being operated by an electronic card. It was so unusual that it didn't lock automatically when you were inside. A creepy detail designed by Connaught?

As I lifted the plate, the delicious aroma of spaghetti Bolognese met me. I gulped the pasta down gratefully, and then I threw on my outfit – bulking up the leotard with my own thick black woollen tights and a warm shirt beneath it. I attached the cowboy holster, shuddering at the thought of the rusty knife in my bag and what had happened today. I put on my boots, a cap, scarf and coat.

Before I left I phoned Georgia, but she didn't pick up. I sent an email, telling her about the man and the odd behaviour of the penguins and seals; asking her to call me.

The air was freezing and a deep blue light hung over the glistening ice. It was almost midnight by the time Travis and I arrived at the party, which was still in full swing. At the door Travis's friend Moose – his moose T-shirt now coupled with a pair of moose horns on his head – offered a choice of masks. He had the glazed expression of someone who'd drunk too much alcohol. Travis already had his Venetian cat mask; I took a simple piece of black cardboard that hid my eyes.

'I hadn't realised it was a masked ball,' I said as Travis crooked his arm through mine and drew me close.

'Aren't we all in masks down here all the time, anyway?' he whispered.

'Why do you say that?' I tried to keep my voice steady.

'Just joking. Let's get a drink.'

I ordered us two strong whiskies and found they weren't on the house after all.

'Only white wine, sorry,' said a sweet skinny boy behind the bar, his arms so thin and strong you could see the sinews. His sandy hair was cut stylishly around a narrow face, and he wore a black velvet mask through which his green eyes peered. He introduced himself as Guy. 'Any spirits are full cost.'

'Guy, start a tab for me,' I said.

'Way to go, Laura.' Travis's teeth shone white beneath his sequined cat's head. He slapped me on the back. Hard. He was over-excited. The only man here with a date. I could feel eyes upon us. The band seemed to be made up of scientists and they were playing very daggy cover tunes. To my horror the lead singer was Connaught. He had a deep, hypnotic voice and wore a beaked mask and a body-hugging leotard.

'This is more like Venetian Carnevale,' I said.

Travis shrugged. 'We have limited outfits. We do Venetian Carnevale quite often. I suppose it's always a bit of a variation. But you look different.' He stroked my arm and I pulled away, aware of how much younger he was.

'You know I think of you like a little brother,' I said and he looked alarmed. 'I just want to be friends, Travis. Is that okay?'

His lips tensed. I could see he was hurt, even behind the mask. But he pretended otherwise.

'Of course. That's what we are. So what happened today? You gave me a scare, Laura. And then I guess I gave you one.' He smiled sheepishly. 'But what *did* happen?'

I thought for a minute. I was tired and he *had* entered my room uninvited. 'Another time,' I said. 'And thanks for the food. It was very thoughtful. Shall we dance?'

Travis moved well on the dance floor, which was just the dining room with the tables and chairs pushed against the walls. He kept pressing closer and I kept moving him away. My eyes were on the scientists who were grooving around me, generally looking like idiots as they swayed and stomped along. All were wearing masks. Most seemed like they'd been drinking.

'So why's your fantasy a cat?' I asked as I moved quickly to avoid Travis touching me again.

'We always had cats growing up. I love them. I love penguins and whales too. But a cat's sexier, don't you think?'

I had to admit that in his well-fitting black jeans and tight V-neck jumper revealing a strong, toned chest, I noticed his muscles and was less aware of his puppy fat. And the more I looked, the less I saw any overweight bulges. Maybe I'd been mistaken and thought he was pudgy because of the way he'd been dressing? We all wore a lot of layers down here.

Right now, Travis's physique seemed very desirable. Romances were common in Antarctica and could just be short-term. What went on in the ice, could stay in the ice, no strings attached. But the last thing I wanted was a holiday romance with my little brother. Therapy bills would cost a fortune in years to come if that happened.

I quickly looked around the room, wondering if the man who had been in the blubber cookery was here, dancing, watching. Knowing who I was and enjoying the fact that I didn't know him. Or did I? Had we met? Was he one of the horrible scientists from the first night? I tried to find them in the crowd. With the masks and outfits, I couldn't tell if they were here. The image of the red material by the vat flashed before me. It could have been a T-shirt; the more I thought about it, the more convinced I became. Had the man been trying to retrieve it? Something that gave away he'd been there? I closed my eyes and tried to picture the silhouette and the size of the man as he fled. He was medium height and thickset. Fit. There were at least two dozen men in the room who matched that description.

I was unsettled as I shimmied about. I should be meeting new people, forging contacts . . . There was a man beside me who I hadn't seen before. He was thin and extremely tall with huge glasses, dressed in a giant squid outfit with a mask beneath the glasses shading most of his face. He had long blond hair. He was a dork but he danced with good rhythm. If only it wasn't Connaught singing I might be able to relax a little.

'Hi there,' I said, 'I'm Laura.' If they went by first names only, I would too.

'Jasper,' he replied in a richly toned English accent. 'Very pleased to meet you, Laura.' He squeezed my hand.

'So what brings you here?' I asked.

'Research.'

'What kind?'

He danced around me. I could feel Travis close, dancing behind the pair of us. I didn't look back.

Jasper was weighing up his answer. 'A few clinical experiments, down here amongst the ice and all that. Can't say more, unfortunately. I know that's unusual. I was at Halley before. Much more open. Connaught keeps us on a tight rein.'

As I nodded, frustrated, he leaned forward and breathed into my ear. 'No real reason not to tell you more, of course. Just orders. I think Connaught likes the drama. Look at him, writhing like a worm.'

I laughed; Jasper was refreshing. 'Can I have a few guesses what you're doing?'

'Why not?'

'Are there viruses involved?'

Jasper stepped back. 'Why would you ask that?'

'Something I read a few years ago. Alliance is a fascinating place.'

'Well, you know. Yes, in a word. We have excellent lab facilities,' he breathed in, 'and yes we are doing some cultures to test various viruses. Now that's all I'm telling you, Laura. Has that earned me a drink?'

'Whisky? Or white wine?' I asked, hoping he'd tell me more if alcohol loosened his lips.

He roared with laughter. 'Anything but the white.'

I flashed Travis a smile and touched him lightly on the elbow. I couldn't afford to put him offside. 'Another drink?'

'You bet. I'll come and help.'

Travis walked close beside me but didn't speak. Jasper joined us as I ordered three large single malts, dreading to think what my tab would be by the end of the night. The skinny barman, Guy, was generous with his pour, the amber liquid flowing freely into the tumblers. 'I won't forget that,' I said, and he winked.

Travis, Jasper and I chatted as we downed our whiskies swiftly, and then we started dancing as a trio.

Was I dreaming or was I awake? My head felt like I'd been ten rounds in a boxing ring – and lost. I groaned, disoriented, and tried to work out where I was. My limbs seemed to be stuck under a steam roller. My mind was blank, my vision out of focus. I thought I should panic. I fell back to sleep.

'Laura, wake up. What the hell happened to you?'

I opened my eyes a crack and the light blinded me. I covered my face with my hands.

'Laura, can you get up?'

'What?'

'I'm going to lift you.'

Slowly I realised I was talking to Kate. She hauled me to my feet and propelled me across the room. My room. I could see the snow-covered mountains through the window. The sun was shining in a vivid blue sky.

'How long have you been here?' she asked.

'What do you mean?'

'You were slumped in the corner. Here, get into bed.' She flung back the sheets and lowered me in. I sprawled out, trying to gather my thoughts. I felt my body to check that all my clothes were intact; relief flooded through when they were. The combination of stockings and leotard would have made it difficult to do anything that wasn't immediately obvious. My memory was blurred.

'What time is it, Kate? When did you get here?'

'It's six o'clock in the evening, and I arrived at midday. I only barged into your room a few minutes ago when I thought it was absolutely absurd you weren't up. I heard there was a party last night.'

I nodded, trying to recall what had happened. My mind remained stubbornly blank.

'There's a guy called Travis. Cute. Young,' said Kate. 'He's really worried about you but he wouldn't come into your room. He was the one who pushed me – your door wasn't locked. And Georgia's been on my back too. You were meant to call her.'

'Someone's exploded a firecracker in my brain.'

Kate laughed, her red hair falling forward in a shining veil as she leaned over me, tucking the bedclothes snugly about.

'It's called a hangover. I've heard the Brits are even bigger boozers than we are.'

'But I swear I didn't drink that much. I know my limits.' I tried again to remember last night. Nothing. 'I think my drink was spiked,' I said, alarmed.

'Yeah, sure, Laura. Try convincing Georgia.'

I stared ahead, squinting in an attempt to remember. All I could recall was dancing with Travis and the tall scientist. Was his name Jasper? And then it was just a huge blank. I'd lost hours.

'Seriously. I'm certain I didn't drink enough to feel like this.' I had no idea how I'd got back to my room.

'You probably just imbibed more than you thought. No big deal, just don't make a habit of it. But you'll have to flag away today. We won't be able to go to Fredelighavn until tomorrow.'

'No, trust me, Kate. Someone spiked my drink.' I tried to think if Jasper or Travis could have done it. I remembered gulping down whisky. The skinny barman Guy was a possibility. I had a vague recollection he'd winked at me.

And that was everything I knew.

'Do you have any idea who?' Kate's freckled face had tightened. 'That's absolutely awful if it's true. You'll have to report it.'

'To Connaught?' I snorted. 'If he'd seen someone do that he would have egged them on. That's if he didn't do it himself.'

'But why would he?'

'To humiliate me. Hoping I'd humiliate myself in any case. Or to frighten me. Make sure I don't step out of line.'

'It'd be very risky. He'd lose his job if he got caught. I can't imagine it. He met me at the airport. A very slippery snake. But I do agree he's not fond of you.'

'I don't think he wants me doing my EIA.'

'Mmm. It seemed a bit more personal. Did you have a run-in?'

'What did he say?'

'When I mentioned you he made a couple of snide remarks.'

'Like what?' I sat up, my stomach feeling sick now as well as my head.

'Acted like you were a troublemaker.'

I let out a strangled laugh. 'I've barely spoken to him.'

'Said you were nosy and ask too many questions.'

So, he was telling stories about me. I'd had that before. With the professors. 'That's a lie. And anyway, no one gives answers.'

'I stuck up for you.' Kate sat beside me on the bed. 'I told him I've known you for years. He glared at me and shut up, like I'd poked him in the eye.' Kate grinned, the skin around her pale eyes creasing with laughter. 'He'll be telling stories about me now too. And I'm glad. He's a fully minted cretin.'

'From a very insignificant university. He'd been in the Ivy League and now isn't, but he gets this post. I can't work it out.'

'How about the other scientists?'

'Well, if you can get some surnames out of them we can look them up. Connaught's got them all on a first-name-only basis with me.'

Kate frowned. 'That's unusual.'

'Highly irregular. The whole place is.' I filled her in on what happened at Fredelighavn. Unlike last night, I could remember that with crystal clarity and gave her a blow-by-blow description.

Kate pulled back the covers and hopped in beside me. 'Now I'm creeped out,' she said. 'You have to tell Georgia.'

I checked the time: we'd talked so much it was almost eight o'clock. I hurried to the computer and Skyped Georgia.

By the time I'd told her everything, for once Georgia's face wasn't warm. It was a sea of anger.

'I'd like to come down myself,' she said. 'But unfortunately that's not possible with everything going on here. There's thirty scientists arriving tomorrow and I need to supervise safety drills and the inevitable rooming crisis and whatever.' She tapped her desk and stopped, deep in thought.

'My strong feeling is we don't say anything to Connaught at this point. Put it in writing, Laura, and send it to me. I'll draft a report, which I'm going to sit on until we know more. It's very serious that anyone was down there at Fredelighavn, and if Connaught's responsible, I'm going to advise he lose his job. So we have to do this methodically and by the book. And watch your back. Kate needs to as well.'

'Hi Georgia, I'm right here!' called Kate, from the bed.

'Oh. Now this is what I mean – *by the book*. Laura, you should have told me Kate was listening. Think every bureaucratic thought and do it.'

'That sounds like fun,' mumbled Kate.

'What was that?' said Georgia sharply.

'We definitely will,' I said. 'Sorry. I'll write everything up tonight.'

'I hope you're wrong about the drink spiking. If it happens again, I'll be over in a flash. In a police capacity.'

'But do you have any jurisdiction at a British base?' I asked.

'I have contacts.' Georgia was very serious. 'Have you heard anything from Professor Koch?'

'No, have you?'

'He has to have a second operation. They removed the gall-bladder but found gallstones in his bile duct. He'll be there for another week. I thought he might have contacted you.'

I grabbed my phone and checked my email. There was a message from Rutger explaining just that. 'Sorry, Georgia, yes, he has told me.'

She glared at me. 'If your drink was spiked I'm not blaming you, but do keep abreast of things from now on, okay?'

I apologised again.

'Look after each other,' she said. 'And get back to me sharp on your return from the whaling station tomorrow.' She snapped off the connection.

'Wow, I've never seen her so angry,' said Kate.

'Me neither.' If Georgia was that furious, it made me frightened. I knew she wasn't really angry with me but with the situation. 'I'm never drinking again,' I said.

'Famous last words. Make a bet?'

I groaned. 'I guess we'd better get to dinner.'

'How about I bring something back to the room?'

'That would be the best thing that's happened in my life.'

'People say that about me all the time,' said Kate, hopping off the bed. 'And I'll let Travis know you're okay.' She paused. 'You don't think he did it, do you?'

'No. I certainly hope not.'

'He didn't seem the type, but then I guess you never know. I take it you don't want wine?'

I threw a pillow at her and she darted out the door.

Kate's red hair was sprawled over the pillow beside me: we'd both felt more comfortable not sleeping alone. It was 6am and the sun was blazing, high in the sky.

'Did you know you snore?' Kate said grumpily. 'I've barely slept.'

I didn't know I snored, that was new. It hit me with a thud the things you can be ignorant about when you're single.

'Don't believe you,' I said. 'Anyway, you never mentioned it before in the hut.'

'I'd meant to.' Kate grinned.

I whacked her arm. 'Want the first shower or will you go to your own room?'

'I guess I'll go to my room. But can I stay here again tonight? Alliance is scaring me. I'm used to penguins.'

I didn't want to remind her the penguins we were about to meet could be nasty too. 'Promise I won't snore,' I said.

'Lucky I have a forgiving nature.'

Half an hour later we were clomping through snow that had fallen in drifts overnight. When we entered the breakfast room conversation stopped. Everyone stared at Kate, who, with her tall, statuesque figure and flaming hair, was used to attention. She smiled at everyone and yelled to the room. 'I'm Kate. Look forward to meeting you all.' Occasionally she was just as loud as her penguins.

A few tables of men stood to invite her to join them. I wondered what I always did wrong: it couldn't have been more different to my introduction. Kate made a beeline for Travis and his friends – Moose and Simon-the-good-pilot – who all tried to pull up a chair for her.

'So how are you?' Travis asked me stiffly when the others went up for second helpings.

'Has anyone heard what happened?'

'Everyone. You know how rumours fly.'

'What are they saying?' My heart beat faster. I hated being the centre of gossip.

'You were blind drunk.'

'Travis, how much *did* I drink?'

I watched him closely. He looked concerned but not guilty.

'I don't know. You were dancing with me and that Jasper guy, and then you sat down. I went to get more drinks and when I turned around I couldn't see you.'

'Where was Jasper?'

'With me.'

'So where did I go?'

'No idea.' Travis shook his head from side to side.

'Don't you think that's odd – that I just disappeared?'

'Of course I do. I thought you must've gone off with someone else, but it seemed very quick. I was worried. I asked around, and everyone teased me. I was the idiot who'd been stood up. Then I drank myself stupid.'

I could picture it all too easily. The herd mentality, the boysie ribbing of the guy who'd lost his girl.

'And the boy at the bar. Guy. Where was he?'

'Behind the bar.' Travis peered hard at me. 'You don't think Guy did anything? He's the sweetest kid. And he's gay.'

I sighed. I had no suspects left. Except if Travis was lying. His open, boyish face was staring at me with deep concern. If he wasn't telling the truth, then he was completely psychotic and able to hide anything. It wasn't a good alternative.

'*Someone* must have seen where I went.'

'No one I could find. And you didn't just go back to your room?'

'I don't think so. I don't know. But if people saw me drunk, they must've seen me after you did. Because I wasn't drunk when I was with you, was I?'

'I'll ask around again,' said Travis. 'So you can't remember anything?'

'No,' I replied grimly.

'But you really are,' he searched awkwardly for words, 'okay?'

I nodded. 'Don't worry. Yeah.'

He stared at me.

'I'd know if they'd done anything, Travis. But someone did spike my drink. I couldn't have got that drunk any other way.'

Travis leaned forward, surprised. 'Have you ever had your drink spiked before?'

'No, but I've read about it.'

He suddenly looked ten years older, and, like Georgia, furious. 'Leave it with me.' He stood abruptly. 'I'm going to get to the bottom of this.' He strode off.

'What was that about?' Kate sat down with another bowl of porridge.

'I'm hoping Travis can find who the perpetrator was. That's if it really wasn't him, which I'm pretty sure . . .' I scoped the room. 'I need to speak to Jasper and the kid at the bar. See if they saw anything.'

Men stared as I walked past to where Jasper was sitting with other scientists. Without his squid costume, he was still easy to spot as he towered over everyone. His long blond hair was tied neatly in a pony tail, and his large glasses framed a face that was thin and kind. I called him away. He swore he hadn't seen me after I'd sat down and he'd gone with Travis to the bar. His story fitted Travis's like a glove. So either they were both telling the truth – or both lying.

I did a quick search for the skinny barman, Guy, but he wasn't in the room. The whole time I tried to shake the feeling of being a victim. My anger raged. I'd been abused and it was awful not knowing who'd done it. I reassured myself that Kate would be with me from now on, and that it could have been much worse. Was it a warning? As difficult as it was, I resolved to not let it frighten me. But if they'd done it to me, had they done it to other women at Alliance before me?

At the supply store, Kate and I packed emergency gear and then went to the shed where Moose had a Hägglunds ready. He looked at me nervously, clearly having heard the gossip.

'Moose, did you see who I left the party with the other night?'

'I only dimly remember you coming in.' He shrugged awkwardly. 'I was a bit sozzled. Sorry.' Moose didn't make eye contact as he finished the obligatory paperwork. I hoped it was only because he was shy.

We headed off.

I still had the rusty knife in my bag.

6

I concentrated hard as I drove through the crystal landscape, the ice sparkling, tinged with fluorescent blue. Neither of us spoke, but I could feel Kate's excitement. She was about to meet new penguins, and for her that was about as good as it gets.

Fredelighavn came into view and the colours were intense and deceptive. The air was so clear it was distorting things, making the houses appear different shades.

I pulled up by the purple house, which now looked pink. Snow had fallen overnight here too, erasing my tracks – and any footprints I'd hoped to find from the man when he ran from the shed.

Kate hopped out as soon as we stopped moving, already rugged up. She grabbed her bag and put on skis. I strapped on my backpack, hung my bag across my body and within minutes we moved past the House of the Carvers that was creaking and snapping in the cold. Kate was up ahead, bound for the Adélie colony. I had other plans.

'Wait up!' I called, my voice booming, echoing fiercely. Kate stopped abruptly.

'Sh. You'll wake the dead,' she said.

'We need to make a detour. I have to get my skis from the blubber cookery first.' Her face dropped but she didn't argue. I led the way to the door, where Kate took off her skis and we both switched on our torches. As we shone them inside the building Kate winced as the rusty saws and knives were illuminated in the beam of light.

'Instruments of torture,' she muttered. I hadn't told her I was carrying one.

I walked tentatively towards them, knowing that my skis must be near the saws. I could make out the outline of a missing knife and was glad that it was mine. In the dark it was hard to locate the skis, and for one moment I thought they'd gone. But then I found them, several metres from where I'd expected. I stood over them and looked around, calculating. The knives and saws were quite a distance away across the room. I was sure I hadn't been in this spot. I left the skis and marched over to the huge rusted pressure cooker where I'd seen the red material.

'Is this where they boiled the blubber?' asked Kate and I jumped.

'Hey, calm down, I'm right beside you,' she said.

But my attention was elsewhere: the red material – the T-shirt or whatever it was – had disappeared. I walked around the vat, my throat tightening: it was definitely not there.

'It's gone,' I said. 'The material I saw. That man must have come back and taken it.' I took photos with a flash, cursing myself for not doing this the other day.

'Are you sure you're in the right spot?' said Kate, shining her torch along the pressure cookers. 'There are quite a few of these.'

I headed along them, walking around their huge circumferences, checking everywhere. No red material.

'Someone's been here,' I said firmly. 'Georgia's going to have to talk to Connaught. Send a strong message that this place is off-limits.'

Kate stared at me, wide-eyed. 'Can we go to the penguins?'

I retrieved my skis, taking more photos, and kept shining my torch around the blubber cookery. It was a haunted place, misery sitting like fog even when the day was clear. For a moment I saw the whales thrashing around in the sea, screaming in pain, crying like children, and imagined the sour smell of their blubber as it boiled in the vats that loomed above me. Their cries merged with the cry of Hamish – the cry I'd never heard, and tears sprang, hot and wet. I brushed them away as I forced myself to bring my feelings under control.

By the time I went outside, Kate had already put on her skis and was stomping up and down impatiently, trying to keep warm. The temperature was dropping by the minute. Even our breath was icing up.

I quickly strapped on my skis and we headed off. The harbour opened up before us, a dazzling blue. It looked more like Saint Tropez than Antarctica – if you ignored the scuttled ships sticking out like monster's teeth, rusting eyesores in the pure water.

And to our right, further up the bay towards Alliance Point, was an extraordinary sight: thousands of Adélie penguins were dancing on the ice, little black and white bodies swaying from side to side as they hopped from foot to foot, their tiny wings thrust out, their beaks towards the sun. They were shrieking a deafening song of happiness. The wall of noise intensified as we approached. Kate was grinning from ear to ear.

'Careful,' I called but she'd forgotten all about me. She crouched down and undid her skis, then stood and drank in the sight of the dancing birds. When she walked towards them her tall, slender body started to sway as she fell into their rhythm.

I stayed behind and watched, curious to see how the penguins reacted today. I pulled out my camera and started to film, recording Kate's path through the Adélies. The noise cracked my ears; I wished I'd brought earplugs.

I zoomed in on Kate as she moved freely among the Adélies, her agile steps so light she appeared to float. She was as one with them and they seemed to treat her as their own. No birds attacked.

After half an hour Kate came back, ecstatic. 'They're beautiful,' she announced breathlessly. 'Completely unused to humans.'

I frowned, unsure what to say. Perhaps I had a bad effect on the penguins, just like I had on most men at Alliance. But then the scientist in me kicked in.

'Let's go through the rookery,' I said.

We headed up to the rocky slope where thousands more Adélies had gathered. I let Kate get ahead, again recording her movements. All went well – the penguins chattered around her, gathering stones, sitting on their nests. She fell into pace with the little be-suited birds and walked confidently among them. I was intrigued – maybe it really was just me they didn't like – and I decided to wait ten minutes before I walked through. In that time all was normal with Kate and the rookery.

I switched off my camera, not wanting to do anything that might scare the penguins. The stench was overwhelming as I headed in. Penguins were hunched on their nests. They looked up and didn't seem at all concerned by my presence. I kept going, wary from the recent attack. The birds went about their business, ignoring me as I headed for Kate. She turned happily and started to walk towards me. A few birds stopped and stared, and the rookery grew unnaturally quiet. And then the penguins rushed at us, pecking and squawking, chasing us away. Careful not to tread on nests, we retreated as fast as we could as the Adélies came forward fiercely, pecking at my gloved hands, attacking Kate's legs.

We grabbed our skis, getting swarmed, and ran. As we reached the beach, the penguins crowded around us, attacking from all sides.

On the icy sand I slipped and twisted an ankle. Ignoring the pain, I raced towards the village. Kate was close behind. We ran up a street and the penguins stopped following, staying on the beach, where they marched up and down like sentries, crying loudly to each other, severely agitated.

'What the hell was that?' said Kate, wheezing, pulling off her ripped gloves. 'I'm bleeding. They went right through.' She lifted up her trouser leg, which was torn from the beaks, but Kate had been prepared with thick wads of clothing, and the penguins hadn't been able to get through the padded material.

I inspected my hands and limbs, which were okay. I'd been prepared today too, and worn my thickest gloves and clothes. I put weight on my ankle, and it was fine. 'Here, I've got disinfectant.'

I treated the wounds on Kate's hands; a few were deep. I wrapped a bandage around.

'Someone's *made* the Adélies that way,' said Kate, furious.

'The weird thing is they weren't perturbed on the ice. They were completely normal and uninhibited there,' I pointed out.

'People have been in that rookery and done something awful. There's no other explanation. And probably more than once. Those birds were defending their nests. Did you get any of that on film?'

'No,' I shook my head. 'I didn't want to disturb them. I'm sorry.'

'I don't want to go back and cause them more anguish. But tomorrow we'll have to. It should be recorded.' Kate's eyes were dark with anger. 'Whoever's done this will pay.'

'Travis and his mates came here to dive.' I paused. 'So perhaps we should too – see how that affects the Adélies.'

Kate exhaled with a puff of her cheeks. The sweat on her face was starting to freeze into solid lumps of droplets. She picked them off. 'Do we have scuba gear?'

'We'll borrow Travis's,' I said. 'I'll get Georgia to approve the dive but we won't tell Connaught. I don't want that bastard knowing anything. That is, until he gets his marching orders. With what's gone on here, he can't be allowed to stay.' I stopped. I'd had the same feeling when I'd discovered what the senior professors in my department had been doing. Fixing results of an experiment to match the data they needed to get a larger, more lucrative research grant. I'd stumbled across the doctored inputs accidentally when I'd stayed late one night finishing work on one of my own lab experiments. I'd gone home furious, and discussed everything with David, who'd been adamant that I not be a whistle-blower. In his line of work, detectives stuck together, and when you found out someone was doing the wrong thing you talked to them, or subtly dropped in a reference so they stopped of their own accord. To his mind, you never reported your colleagues.

I'd thought it over for a few days, nervous the professors might destroy evidence. What they were doing went against every ethical procedure. I couldn't let it rest.

When I reported them all hell broke loose, but the Academy closed ranks. They were top scientists. They were investigated over a matter of months, found guilty of misconduct and rapped on the knuckles. Then everything went back to normal. Except I was ostracised, and David left me, calling me obsessed and stubborn, and someone he couldn't spend his life with. It certainly wasn't the first thing we'd disagreed on, just the worst – and the last.

'Laura?' Kate was tapping me on the arm. 'Come back to me. I know you're thinking about what happened to you with those professors. But we can't be frightened. Anyway, Georgia will know what to do.'

'We'll assemble the evidence,' I said. 'We'll be meticulous. By the time we've finished, Connaught will have nowhere to turn.' I wished I felt as confident as I sounded. Deep down I knew that whatever we discovered could be ignored if people wanted to keep it hidden. But ultimately I was reporting to the Antarctic Council, and there'd certainly be some countries keen to hear the news. That is if the Australians were willing to unleash a political storm.

'Shall we see the movie buffs now?' asked Kate.

I wasn't in a hurry to revisit the cinema.

'We can just poke our heads in,' she said. 'It's important to see if the seals go crazy like the Adélies. And we need to see the other Adélies in the shed too. Can we do that first?'

I led the way to the building full of old equipment, where the penguins were hunkered down on their nests. Kate stood in the doorway and took everything in.

'I'd rather not disturb them,' she said finally. She took photos without a flash, the penguins looking green in the light through the filthy windows.

'So, let's see what's playing,' said Kate. I reluctantly took her to the cinema, but when we shone our torches inside, we found the seals had gone.

'They must be at sea,' I said.

Kate stepped inside, sending a shaft of light over the empty seats, the stage and screen at the front, the projector at the back – the projector that looked different.

'That's odd.' I walked up to it. 'I swear this roll of film is fatter.'

'Spool. It's a spool of film, isn't it? Although, come to think of it, it's a reel,' said Kate.

'It's changed, whatever you want to call it. This one's bigger. There's more of it.'

Kate joined me, hooking a length of film out of the projector. 'Back in the way past, my dad was a projectionist for a film club,' she said. 'He used to thread these babies up.' She shone her torch through the celluloid and frowned.

'What is it?' I asked.

Kate flicked her torch nervously around the cinema and then unspooled more film, studying the frames, looping celluloid onto the ground.

'Careful,' I warned.

'This film's not from the fifties, it's more recent. I've seen it. It's Australian. A kind of horror film, or kind of not, with a child. Children. I reckon it was made in the late eighties because I was a kid when Dad showed it. It made an impact. Whoever's doing this is shoving it in your face. They're playing games, Laura.'

'Maybe they thought we wouldn't notice because of the seals.'

'And where *are* the seals? Out to sea, or have they been driven away?'

I took a look at the film, but it didn't mean anything to me, and then we walked around the empty cinema. The icy drifts lying about were too frozen for anyone to leave footprints.

'It still smells like seal,' said Kate, wrinkling her nose.

But my attention had been taken by something under a seat: a piece of popcorn. I photographed it. 'Look at this. Do you think it's fresh?'

Kate frowned. 'One way to find out.' She bent down and picked it up. And popped it in her mouth.

'Eh, you're destroying evidence!'

She swallowed. 'That's fresh, just as I thought. It's not only seals coming to these movies.' She made a face. 'Yuck, it's got a bit of a rancid seal aftertaste.'

I aimed a filthy look at her. 'You shouldn't have eaten that.'

'It was a scientific experiment.' She ignored my death stare. 'So who's having movie nights? And why old films?' Kate moved around inspecting the room.

'Can we find the title of the film?'

'Sure.' Kate went over to the projector. 'Want a viewing?'

'How?'

'Let's see if it works.' She followed a lead that ended in an old rectangular battery pack the size of a large shoebox.

'Surely not,' I said. Kate turned a knob and the projector sprang to life, film spooling upwards with a jolt. Kate groaned and quickly turned it off.

'Wasn't expecting that,' she said as she threaded the projector properly. I moved to the battery pack and took photos. 'How old is this?' I asked.

'No idea,' replied Kate.

'Surely it would be drained after all these years?'

'Not if it's been recently charged,' observed Kate matter-of-factly. 'Okay, here goes.'

I slumped into a comfortable chair, ignoring the oily texture and fishy smell as a beautiful, leafy summer's day blasted onto the screen. It reminded me of where I grew up in Melbourne, although this was set during the Cold War in the 1950s. The childhood games were menacing and by the mock hanging at the end I was glued.

'Why would they be watching this in particular?' asked Kate.

'How fresh was that popcorn?'

'Very.'

'They're brazen if they've come while I'm doing my report.'

'Unless they thought you wouldn't be in here again because of the seals.' Kate stared at me intently. 'Maybe they spiked your drink so you'd feel scared and wouldn't look around down here as thoroughly as you might otherwise.'

A shiver ran through me. 'Well, they got that wrong.' I paused, straightening my back, willing myself to stay strong. 'Let's go into some more houses. There might be something else you can eat.' I sounded more upbeat than I felt. My nerves were jangling. I took one last photo of the projector and the battery. The film was an odd choice for a group of men – I would have expected Hollywood fare, not a dark film about childhood.

The sun seared my eyes as we emerged back into the street. I quickly put on my dark glasses and again had the sensation of being watched. I turned abruptly and looked everywhere.

'What's wrong?' Kate followed my gaze.

'I get the feeling someone's watching us.'

'That's funny – me too. I thought I was just being paranoid. Do you think the man's here?' Kate shuddered.

'If Connaught's given permission . . .'

'But why would he? It's obvious when we take the Hägglunds, there's all that paperwork. They could just wait till we're not here and do whatever they want.'

I walked over to the building opposite, which was brick with a tin roof, and stared up under its eaves. 'Or they could have cameras here and are watching us from Alliance.' I realised, perhaps too late, that if I was right, it wasn't wise for me to be talking about it. 'Then again I doubt very much that's the case.' I opened the door of the building and peered inside.

'I don't know. Sounds plausible to me,' said Kate.

I shrugged and kept quiet. I'd be saying more to her once we were away from Fredelighavn. I shone my torch around the interior, filled with large old brick ovens and stacks of wire racks piled on top of each other.

'Wow,' said Kate. 'A bakery.'

We investigated, finding sacks of flour at the back behind the ovens. There were stainless-steel basins where the bread must have been mixed, and sinks and stools. A large marble bench still sported wooden rolling pins, laid neatly in a row. I took photos and added to the growing folder of notes on my tablet. As I named it *Bakery – Well-preserved*, I thought again of Pompeii, a town that bristled with the ruins of tiny bakeries.

We left and marched up a street that swung back towards Alliance Point. I kept looking up, trying to find cameras, questions rushing through my mind. Why would there be cameras? Why had the man been here the other day, for that matter, and come back and picked up that piece of red fabric? And what about the film in the cinema – was it just scientists letting off steam, excited by the forbidden, or could it be more?

The buildings creaked and groaned in the cold as Kate voiced my next thought.

'I still feel like I'm being watched,' she said.

'Do you?' I said, trying to sound light.

'If you're not worried, then I'm not,' she replied.

I stopped by a much smaller brick structure sitting between tin-clad sheds. It was different from anything I'd seen. I opened the door and whistled: it was full of shiny banks of electrical meters and three giant generators. A power station. I poked my head back out and looked along the street. Up the hill, a distance away, was a cluster of round oil tanks. There must be underground pipes for the oil to feed the generators, which in turn would have distributed the electricity around the plant. It made sense that the powerlines were also underground, out of the wind and ice.

I photographed everything, then went back outside. We were in what seemed like an industrial area. I walked to the nearest shed. The doors were closed; Kate stood back, rubbing her arms. 'I don't like the vibe of this one,' she said.

Kate took another step away.

'Feels okay to me.' I tried to open the doors. They were stuck. 'It's locked,' I said, surprised.

'Give it here.' Kate moved me out of the way and pushed her full weight against the doors. Nothing happened. 'Well, that's interesting. First building that's locked. Or did you see some the other day?'

I shook my head. 'This is the only one.'

Kate peered hard at the space where the doors joined. 'We need a jemmy bar.'

'Let's see if we can find one.' I led the way to the next shed, which had a huge blue timber door. I turned the handle and it flung open. There was rusted equipment: large harpoon heads – which would have been fired from the harpoon guns into the whales – stacked neatly in wooden crates; huge knives, and coils and coils of thick rope. There were also stacks of boxes, some of which we tentatively opened: reams of blank paper, pens, tinned fruit and vegetables. Supplies for everyday life.

'Toilet paper,' called Kate. 'Totally preserved.'

I inspected cans of smoked haddock, or so I thought from the image on the box. The writing was in Norwegian.

There were huge bags of flour and sugar. They must have divided them up into smaller portions for the residents. It was like a quartermaster's store.

Kate pulled out a box containing cartons of cigarettes in silver packaging. There were only a few left. 'Reckon someone's been here?'

I walked over and took a closer look. 'Hard to tell. Travis and his mates could have taken them,' I said, annoyed. 'Or I guess supplies could have just been low.'

'But everything else – there's so much of it. And why *did* they leave here, Laura? It's like a ship had just come in with everything they needed for the whole year.'

'I thought it was because they hunted the whales to near extinction. But I'm not certain.' I really needed to find this out. Not knowing was starting to gnaw at me.

The next two houses were empty apart from beds stripped down to mattresses, and a couple of old sofas.

Kate stood frowning. 'It's like some people knew they were going, were organised and packed things. While others didn't.'

I started to wonder whether the House of the Carvers might be an oddity.

The third house, a vivid red, took us by surprise. It was full of boxes of cigarettes stacked high in the lounge room and ground-floor bedroom. They were covered in Norwegian writing and sported an image of a slick man puffing away in a suit that looked very much of the 1950s.

'How completely odd,' said Kate. 'Why did they leave them?'

I took photos. 'Maybe they were selling them illegally and couldn't take them on the ship back to Norway?'

It was yet another Fredelighavn mystery. A village that made less sense the more we looked around.

Upstairs were two more bedrooms, one with two single beds, the other with a sagging double bed, all with exquisite bedspreads of embroidered wildflowers.

'The smuggler had a wife,' I said.

'I still think it's strange he left it all.'

'Perhaps it was the wife doing the smuggling and someone clamped down.' I thought of Ingerline, who had organised the building of the church steeple as well as the cinema. Perhaps she needed extra funds? 'Or maybe they just quit smoking.'

We smiled, but neither of us felt like laughing. The place was draining us.

Downstairs in the kitchen, light streamed through a large window onto a table set for ten people, with beautiful navy and white plates, crystal glasses and silver cutlery. There was a large copper pot on the coal-burning stove, but it was empty.

'This looks set up,' I said, my neck stiffening as it occurred to me that someone could be playing a game with us.

'Like a dinner party before they started cooking,' said Kate.

'I mean rigged up. For us. It just seems too weird.'

'It's no odder than anything else,' shrugged Kate as she looked into the cupboards, which were neatly stacked with food, beautiful copper cookware and more cigarettes. 'Perhaps this was the house of a whaling captain?' she said.

I photographed the kitchen, with a growing unease that someone could have set it up just for me. Could they have come down and done it while I was passed out after my drink was spiked? But why?

Next door, the house was painted russet red. Long icicles glinting with rainbows hung off intricate white fretwork around the porch. We headed inside.

And stopped short. It could have been in a current architectural magazine. The floorboards were the colour of rich honey, their wax looked fresh. In the lounge room, the furniture was whitewashed: two wooden, beautifully carved miner's couches, an antique coffee table, a small white piano. Sunlight filtered in through fine lace curtains. The fireplace had been set with coal. 'Is this new or old?' whispered Kate in awe. 'It's amazing. Scandinavian chic.'

I led the way down the passage, which had whitewashed walls that glowed in a pearly hue. There were four bedrooms, two on each side. Everything was white and beautiful; each held a single bed. Paintings of ships hung tastefully. The bed linen was all white and smelled of the sea.

'I could have a beach house like this. Or even a main house,' said Kate as we entered the kitchen. Light flooded in through two colonial paned windows. A whitewashed wooden table sat in the middle of the room with nothing on it.

I flung open a cupboard, eager to see what was inside. And screamed.

There was a dead Adélie penguin.

'How did it get in there?' said Kate, concerned. The penguin was lying with its eyes shut like it was asleep. There was no sign of deterioration, and when I moved closer it smelled oily and salty and fishy like an average Adélie penguin.

I took copious photos.

'This is fresh,' I said.

Kate came up close. 'Someone's killed it and put it here,' she said fiercely as she went to touch it. I pulled her arm away and led us both into the middle of the kitchen. 'Jasper said they're researching viruses up at Alliance. What if they're doing something with the penguins? God knows what this poor fellow died of,' I warned, a wave of horror rippling through me.

'If they're capable of doing that, they're capable of doing anything.' Kate's face pinched up.

'And don't care about the law.' I could barely contain my anger.

'But they knew you were coming. Wouldn't they have removed anything that could implicate them?' Kate pointed out.

'Maybe they're so arrogant they didn't want to disturb their experiment.'

'We couldn't catch anything from it, could we?' Kate wrapped her scarf around her nose and mouth. 'I'm terrified of viruses,' she said in a muffled voice.

I stepped forward tentatively and opened all the cupboards along the wall, and stopped, surprised. There was a gaping hole to the exterior up one end. And no partitions internally between cupboards. A sick penguin could have made its way in and died of natural causes.

'Oh,' said Kate, seeing what I'd just discovered and pulling down her scarf. 'I guess it mightn't be that odd.'

I took more photos. 'Let's explore all possibilities. I'll request a response kit and a lab to carry out tests.'

We knew the drill: if there was ever any uncertainty about a wildlife death in Antarctica, there were strict protocols to follow. We went outside, scooped up snow and cleaned our boots. Then we went straight back to the Hägglunds. We could walk nowhere else today at Fredelighavn. If the penguin had died of disease, we couldn't risk spreading germs to any further wildlife.

Kate slept as I drove back through the icy terrain. Normally the landscape would be exhilarating, its blue–white vista opening my soul with its space and beauty, but now I felt only a low-level dread at things being amiss and what that might mean. What had caused a penguin to end up dead in a cupboard? Was it part of an illegal experiment? Or were the scientists at Alliance targeting me, knowing I was aware of their virus research? Perhaps it was another thing they'd deliberately placed here when I was sleeping off my spiked drink to intimidate me. But it could also be merely death by natural causes.

I pondered whether my Spanish compatriots, the Argentines and Chileans, could have come in and rearranged the houses at Fredelighavn, perhaps to evoke a feeling of mystery that might excite a scientist carrying out an Environmental Impact Assessment. After all, they had the most to gain in opening up the area – getting tourists near the secretive Alliance Station and annoying the British, a plan they would love. It would be a relief if that's all it was. Games and politics. Although not if they'd upset the wildlife. Could the red cloth have had Spanish writing on it that would have given them away?

It was conceivable they could have come by boat to Fredelighavn at this time of year, just as the whalers and supply ships had done for decades. And they were expecting the report; they were the ones who'd asked for it. There was a plausibility to it that reminded me that, as with any scientific investigation, I must keep an open mind.

The more I chewed on it, the more possible it seemed. I sighed loudly, and Kate woke. I told her my latest theory.

'But did they hurt the Adélies?'

'I don't know. It could be two different things. I still want to go diving, tracing what Travis and his mates did.'

To my mind, Travis wasn't off the hook yet.

7

Our room was warm and welcoming, in contrast to the way we were feeling about the scientists at Alliance. Kate and I bagged our boots and clothes. They would have to be sterilised before we could wear them again around wildlife.

After a hot shower I emailed Connaught, copying in Georgia, to report the incident and request the kit and lab facilities. I also notified him that the Hägglunds would need to be sterilised. Then I went to find Travis.

He was sitting alone having a pre-dinner drink in the dining hall, and was eager and helpful about the diving gear. Travis was the sort of guy who liked to say yes.

'But you can't tell anyone. Even Moose.'

Travis hesitated. 'Okay.'

'Does that really mean okay?'

He bit his lips and nodded.

'Travis?'

'I'm not great with secrets.'

I gazed deep into his eyes. 'Could you make an exception for me?'

He visibly melted and I felt a twinge of guilt. And I couldn't help noticing how black his irises were, and the blue, a rich cobalt, surrounding them. Travis had beautiful eyes. I tried not to get distracted.

'I'd make an exception for you any time, Laura.'

'You're one in a million, you know that?'

Travis blushed.

'Thank you,' I said. 'And now I have to go and get ready for dinner.' I was getting wafts of a fishy, oily smell that seemed to have sunk into my face. 'I fear I might still stink of seal.'

Travis grinned. 'I didn't want to tell you.'

We parted laughing but as soon as I was out in the icy street, all I could think of was whether I'd just done a deal with the enemy – the person who had caused the trouble with the wildlife.

And somewhere deep inside me was a little voice saying I hoped Travis wasn't guilty.

Via Skype, Georgia reluctantly agreed to the dive and wanted to hear more about the penguin. She was growing increasingly concerned about Fredelighavn.

'Check and triple-check the equipment. I don't want to see a diving accident tricked up to seem accidental,' she said firmly.

'Georgia, don't scare me.'

'If you'd seen the things I've seen . . . There's an element of gangland down there, from what you're telling me. And that spells trouble.'

I pretended she wasn't unnerving me.

In the morning, Kate was huddled close, her red hair sprawled across both our pillows. I chuckled and she sat up with a start.

'Time to go.' I hauled myself out of bed. Through the window the sun was shining and the sky was deep blue. 'It's going to be a perfect day.'

As we were finishing breakfast, Jasper came over and placed an Unusual Wildlife Death Kit on the table.

'For the penguin. Connaught's asked me to look after you in my lab. After-hours access. We'll have to work the graveyard shift.'

A thrill ran through me: I'd be seeing inside the main building. But why had Connaught chosen Jasper?

'I volunteered for it,' he said, as if reading my mind. 'No one else put their hand up. The scientists down here are a pretty selfish lot and not happy about you coming in. So, you'll have to do exactly what I say. I don't want to sound bossy, but they're the rules.'

'No problem,' I said. 'We'll have the poor bird back tonight. Can we go in then?'

'At eleven. There'll be no one in my lab but us by then.'

'I appreciate it, Jasper.' I opened the response kit and checked everything was there: a blue body bag for the penguin, disposable overalls, gloves, surgical masks and overshoes, alcohol-based hand wipes and a bottle of bleach.

Travis approached, hovering nearby.

'Well, a favour given might need to be returned one day,' said Jasper as he turned and walked away.

Kate glowered. 'Since when's protocol a favour? He's as bad as the rest of them.'

Travis plonked down beside us. 'Everything's ready,' he said in a soft voice, his blue eyes bright. His face was so open and honest I couldn't believe he'd be responsible for anything bad. 'What's this for?' he asked, picking up the body bag. He looked completely innocent when I explained, not like a penguin-tormentor or a person who hid birds in cupboards.

Near the Hägglunds, Travis had assembled drysuits – which were like heavily insulated full-body wetsuits with attached hoods and booties, to keep the body dry and protected while swimming in icy water – and scuba gear. Kate and I methodically checked the tanks and breathing apparatus. All seemed in order.

We tried on the drysuits and chose our gloves.

'Good to go,' I called when we were ready, and Travis bounced over from where he'd been discreetly waiting in the corner of the shed, his back turned to us.

'I won't forget this,' I said. 'And remember, not a word to anyone.'

'You'll get me into trouble one day, Doctor Alvarado.' He was beaming.

We headed off, waving goodbye to him.

*

Fredelighavn sparkled in the sunshine. The air was fresh and clear and there was no wind; it was silent as our skis whooshed along the icy road to the sea – Kate towed a sled, on which our scuba tanks and gear were strapped. The House of the Carvers glinted with icicles dangling from its eaves and windows, like it was winking to me.

When the harbour came into view we both stopped. It was the most intense blue I'd ever seen and it was glass calm.

'Wow,' said Kate, dumping her backpack on the ground, extricating herself from her skis and ripping off her clothes. 'Super wow. That's the best sea ever. Let me in there.'

I grinned from ear to ear as I stripped off too, hoping there were no surveillance cameras on this stretch of beach. The water lapped quietly along the rocky shore. Further up the coast the Adélies were screeching happily, thousands of little black and white birds going about their business. In the other direction, near the hulking skeleton of a ship, elephant seals basked lazily in the sun, taking no interest in us.

With tanks in place, we both checked the quick-release latches on our weight belts. If we got into trouble we'd need to come up fast. They were working smoothly.

We carried torches and cameras in bags clipped tightly to our belts.

At the shoreline we put on flippers and gloves, and spat into masks that would cover our faces, dipping them in a little seawater and swirling the mix around to ensure they wouldn't fog up underwater.

'Ready?' I asked as I fitted the breathing apparatus into my mouth and bit down on the rubber ends, taking a deep breath that felt easy and clean like a fresh breeze.

Kate gave me two thumbs up.

Checking our masks were firmly attached, we walked backwards into the sea and submerged once it was deep enough. The feeling was sublime. The water was crystal clear and visibility stretched for miles. Colours were vibrant. The rusting hulks of nearby ships were brilliant orange, the water a translucent blue. Our drysuits blocked any sense of how cold the ocean was, although I knew from experience it was freezing. Once a season, in a popular Antarctic ritual, we would cut a hole in the ice, strip off our clothes, tie a rope around ourselves and run like mad from the hottest building to leap into the water like maniacs. Then we'd scramble out as fast as we could. The water was truly frigid – and without protection, you could go into cardiac arrest and die in minutes. Which is what made the Polar Plunge such exhilarating fun.

I signalled with my hand to move off. Kate took my other hand and we swam away from shore. I checked my watch and I could see Kate doing the same – we had air in our tanks for two hours. Long strange fish darted about us: mackerel icefish. As we swam further out, huge submerged icebergs came into view, their sculptured, multifaceted walls glowing eerily, like deep green glass and blue quartz. Their jagged, pointed bases, the inverted image of the smaller above-water shape, were hundreds of metres below us, engulfed in shadow. I glanced down and experienced a dizzying vertigo at the upside-down mountains of craggy ice; we took care to keep a wide berth. Suddenly the water churned into millions of swirling bubbles as we were bombarded by Adélie penguins jumping from the nearest iceberg into the water, propelling themselves at speed out to sea. Kate tapped me on the arm and gave a thumbs up, grinning. These penguins weren't remotely interested in us, which was as it should be. Their little black and white bodies shot past, some turning and giving a fleeting look as they pelted through the water. On land, the Adélies could seem awkward as they waddled about. Down here, they were graceful and strong, sleek bodies cutting through the sea like bullets.

I felt weightless, the sound of my breathing was loud and rhythmic as I relaxed into the dive. As we headed out into the bay a huge elephant seal surged past, making me jump and let go of Kate's hand. I could see her eyes wrinkled in laughter as she took my hand again. More Adélies swam past, untroubled. There was nothing amiss, no sign yet that Travis and his friends had caused any damage to the wildlife underwater when they dived.

I signalled to Kate to turn right. I wanted to head up the bay towards the Adélie rookery. Sunlight pierced the water in light green shafts. Two huge Patagonian toothfish swam towards us, and we let go of each other to let them pass between us.

Suddenly I was surrounded by a pod of humpback whales, their song rising and falling, a high febrile sound, soulful, vibrating through me. I grinned, treading water, flapping my hands gently around, a surge of happiness rising as I inspected their tail flukes to see if I recognised any of them. These were new to me. I hooked out my camera and photographed. A large mother humpback with a baby in tow looked at me. I tipped my head to one side and she swam closer, doing the same. I reached out and touched her as she moved past, wishing I could take off my glove and feel her silky black body. Her calf swam past and nudged me playfully, and I was reminded of Lev. The mother swam to the surface and broke through, her back twisting above me as she rolled, then her white belly flopped back into the water.

I watched mesmerised as she rolled again, putting on a show. The baby came back and looked at me. I reached out a hand as he swam past, and he rubbed his body against it. The mother was still rolling above me, breaching the surface and flopping around. Bubbles shot everywhere, like the sea was boiling. Sunlight shone through, giving the feel of a magical forest.

As the mother swam off and the calf followed, I turned to Kate – but she wasn't there. I looked around. Somehow we'd become separated. I tried to keep calm. I swam on, turning three-hundred-and-sixty degrees as I searched the water. There were bubbles from the retreating whales, and more Adélies torpedoing past. But Kate was nowhere to be seen.

I stopped, treading water and telling myself not to panic as I fought an adrenalin rush of fear. A diver must never lose their buddy underwater; it was the first and most fundamental rule of diving. As I swam on I tried to ascertain where I was. Everywhere around me were the sleek, inverted mountains of blue–green icebergs. I had come to a channel and there was only one logical way through. I swam much closer than I would have liked, knowing the underwater mass of icebergs could move rapidly, even in this calm water.

As I swam on, I realised I was heading towards a wall of ice along the shore. I decided to go up to the surface, to get my bearings and to see if Kate had done the same. I was about fifteen metres down and had to rise slowly so that I wouldn't cramp.

Eventually I broke through the water with ease. I was a distance from land and although the water was still calm, a wind was rippling tiny waves into small white peaks. I looked everywhere, visibility perfect. But no Kate. I went under again and began to swim down, wanting to retrace where I'd been, but I hit a current. I tried to swim against it. The rip was too strong; I had to swim across it instead. When I looked around, nothing seemed familiar. I kept treading water, bubbles blowing frantically from my mouthpiece, echoing in my ears, rising to the surface in a thick chain. The current was pulling me along and for a moment I didn't fight it. I was tiring quickly. A white mass of ice came into view: I was rushing towards it. With all my strength I swam to the surface. Further up I could see the jagged outline of a cave in the icy cliff. I waited until I was close and then swam into the broad entrance.

A whole new world opened up. Thousands of icicles dangled from the clear white ice of the ceiling. A vivid blue light emanated further back in the cave. There was a thick layer of ice around the seawater, forming a ledge. I hauled myself up and looked around in wonder. It was the biggest cave I'd seen in Antarctica, stretching far into the distance, its roof undulating with soft, sculptural folds of ice. It was easily high enough for me to stand up in. I took off my flippers and laid them down carefully, then pulled off my mask, mouthpiece and tank, trying to calm down, trying to catch my breath. I placed the tank so it was clearly visible in the cave entrance, and peered out to sea, desperate to find Kate. The air in the cave was cold but not freezing, naturally insulated by the dense blanket of ice. I was warm in my drysuit and my face tingled. I took a step back and glanced into the cave. Somewhere deep inside there must be a funnel travelling up to the surface, because light was pouring in. I stopped in shock.

Behind an icy wall, clear and translucent, stood a boy, tousled dark hair, huge brown eyes, skinny arms raised high. He was calling to me through the ice, trapped like an insect in amber.

All I could hear was the gentle splashing of waves, but I could see his mouth open wide in a yell. '*Help me!*' He pounded his hands against the ice. '*Help!*' Then, as quickly as he appeared, he was gone.

I blinked, stunned, and quickly made my way along the ledge to where he had been. But there was no sign of him, and the ice looked a clear white–blue. Confused, I pulled out my camera and photographed the wall, replaying the images, not trusting my eyes. There was nothing in the ice.

A voice roared behind me. 'Thank God you're here!' I dropped my camera in fright and turned to see Kate hauling herself up out of the water, taking off her tank and putting it beside mine.

'I've been looking for you everywhere,' she said. 'What's wrong, you're as white as a ghost.'

'This is going to sound crazy, but I thought I saw a boy.' I looked around again. 'In the ice. Just here.' I walked right up to the wall and slapped my hand against it, then put both hands against the ice and peered in. There was just more ice. But as I looked further I thought I could make out the form of a ghostly cavern, a mirror image of the one we were in.

Kate hurried up beside me. 'You're right, that's crazy.' She put her face close to the ice and sucked in her breath, surprised. 'Is that a cavern back there?'

'He was calling for help. He was desperate.' I shivered, remembering his face filled with fear, the urgency of his movements.

'But what would a boy be doing down here?' said Kate. 'It's unlikely. If not impossible.'

The ice wall was metres thick, and now just translucent white, with hints of blue. I couldn't get the image of the boy out of my head. His huge brown eyes, dark hair framing an impish face. I knew who he reminded me of. My first husband, Cameron Stewart.

'Alvarado, do you think you might have a case of Toast?' said Kate.

Perhaps I had been down in the ice too long and was getting ice fever – growing increasingly removed from the world, spending too much time in my head, starting to imagine things.

'How old was he, this boy you claim to have seen?' Kate walked around, checking to see if she could find a way through the ice into the cavern.

'About twelve,' I said and my voice cracked. The age my boy would have been; the baby I'd lost. If Hamish had lived, he would have looked like that. I broke into a sweat. My mind must be playing tricks. It had been a strange time at Alliance and Fredelighavn and I'd been unnerved, separated from Kate. And I *had* been down in Antarctica longer than usual.

'There's no way in,' said Kate. 'And now I'm not even sure there is a cavern through there.' She took out her torch and swung it around. Reflections bounced everywhere. 'Do you think it might have been your own reflection? An optical illusion. The more I look, the less I think that is a cavern. It's just thick ice, Laura.' Kate paced along the ledge, bending down and rising up on her toes, trying to view the ice from every angle.

I took more photographs, then turned to movie mode, recording everything again. 'It's so weird. I could have sworn there was a boy.' Why was I even saying it when I knew that it was so unlikely?

Kate stared at me. 'How did we get separated, anyway? One minute you were there, the next you were gone. I was going to scream the crap out of you for heading off without me. Is this just a ploy so I don't get angry?'

'It was the whales.'

'What whales?'

'Humpbacks. A mother and her calf came really close to me.'

'I didn't see any whales,' said Kate, her voice a mixture of concern and impatience.

My head started to spin. I took deep breaths as images of the boy flashed faster and faster in front of me. It was Hamish. My little son. Grown tall and strong with his father's face.

I rubbed my eyes. Hard. Trying to concentrate. Trying to pull myself back to reality. I had never, in all these years, let my imagination run this far. Grief poured through my body like a rushing tide. Everything I'd held back surfaced in a howling yearning.

The boy's face swam before me. The dark eyes. Hamish, my Hamish, had come back.

'Laura?' Kate's voice sounded far away, as if she were calling down a well.

I leaned against the ice where I'd seen Hamish in the white-blue cavern. Was it his ghost, starved of oxygen? I slapped the stupidity of the thought away. I was losing my mind. Panic bubbled up. We were in an ice cave far away from land. Or was there another way out? I suddenly raced towards the back, to the light. I heard Kate following. She had no way of knowing what I was thinking – I'd never told her about Hamish.

The opening high above was tiny. The light expanded as it filtered in, forming a pool of phosphorescent blue. I walked through, watching the skin on my hands turn a lurid sapphire colour. I couldn't remember taking off my gloves. My heart raced in lunging bursts. I peered up through the jagged shaft and could just make out the sky far above.

'There's no way out here,' said Kate, resting a hand tentatively on my shoulder. 'Are you okay? Do you feel up to swimming? We should get back.'

'I'd like to stay here a while,' I said, my voice breaking. How could I tell her that I couldn't leave? Hamish might return. I knew my thoughts were irrational but they kept pouring in. My Hamish. Down here.

Ignoring Kate's worried face, I strode back to the wall where I'd seen him. I shone my torch through. There was nothing but ice. And now I couldn't discern a cavern. I slumped down on the ground, exhausted and confused.

'If there was a boy,' I mumbled, 'he needs our help.' Tears pricked my eyes and I started to weep, gasping sobs like hiccups as I struggled to take in air. *Calm down*, I told myself, to no avail.

'Laura, get a grip. You're scaring me.'

I nodded, 'I'm sorry, I'm really sorry.' The sound of my own voice, distant, foreign, made me cry more, thoughts of the birth drowning my mind. Blood everywhere. Hot, boiling. A vivid scarlet, so red it looked unreal, like jam. Thick blood, viscous and flowing. Washing my tiny baby into the ice in Antarctica.

Kate sat beside me and put her arm around me, wrapping me into her warm body. 'It's okay, you're just a bit toasty,' she said gently. 'Deep breaths. It'll pass. Just let it pass.' I could feel her intake of air, rapid but steady. I tried to think of that and not Hamish. I pushed Cameron's face, puffed and swollen with grief, out of my mind.

Finally, my breathing started to slow. I blinked at the wall of ice. It was just a solid white wall, tinged blue, with a layer of pale mint-green.

'Ok-ay,' said Kate slowly. 'Shall we head back? Do you think you're up to it?' She looked deep into my eyes and I could see her fear.

'Yes,' I said reluctantly.

'And this time we keep hold of each other, no matter what,' she said firmly. I murmured agreement as I picked up my camera and took several more shots of the wall and the cave. I found my gloves further along the ice ledge and put them on, realising my hands were frozen, even though the rest of me was hot and clammy in the drysuit.

At the water's edge we put our tanks, flippers and masks back on, bit into our mouthpieces and submerged into the sea. I tried not to notice the weightlessness that now reminded me of Hamish in my womb. Panic rose, but I fought my fear. I wasn't going to drown out here. What if there had been a boy, in spite of the odds? He needed my help. The boy the same age as Hamish, who had his face.

8

O n the beach we stripped off our drysuits, towelling
sweat from our bodies and putting on warm clothes.
There was a slight wind that chilled bone-deep as soon
as it came into contact with bare skin.

'How are you feeling?' Kate's face was full of concern.

'Fine. Thanks. Let's dump the gear in the Hägglunds and
then get the penguin.' I quickly helped Kate pack the sled, then
put on my skis and left. I didn't want to talk about what had
happened. I was still lost in my own world, and my feeling
that I had seen a boy calling for help was growing stronger.
I would have expected, now I was back on land, that I'd be
even more certain I'd imagined it. Yet I still felt I'd seen him.
My mind raced with possibilities as to who he was and what he

was doing there. Argentinians brought families to their Esper-anza base, in Graham Land on the Antarctic Peninsula; so, too, did the Chileans, at Villa Las Estrellas – *The Town of Stars* – a research station and civilian settlement on their President Eduardo Frei Montalva base on King George Island. Unlike the British, Australians and Americans, they were keen to normalise existence in Antarctica and for years had experimented with having children accompany their parents down here. Both bases were relatively close to South Safety Island, the Chileans to our west, the Argentinians to our south-east. Perhaps I'd been right that the Argentinians were coming into Fredelighavn. Or the Chileans. Maybe there was a way down into the ice at the end of the village near the Adélie rookery. It would explain the behaviour of the penguins if children had been allowed to play there.

But the boy didn't look like he was playing a game. He was crying for help.

The image was seared into my brain. His open, screaming mouth. His hands slapping against the ice. Was there terror in his eyes? I shut my own, trying to remember.

I could see it. His eyes frantic. In the glimpse I'd had, I'd seen a boy scared for his life. I needed to go to the cliff top near the rookery and look for an entrance down into the ice, just to double-check. Because if I hadn't imagined it, the boy was out there somewhere.

'Laura?' We had arrived at the russet house with the whitewashed furniture, and Kate was standing waiting for me to open the response kit. We put the disposable overalls over our clothes, covered our boots with the disposable booties, and slipped on the gloves and surgical masks. I knew that if I was near the dead penguin now, I wouldn't be able to go back to the rookery today. Even with the disposables, I couldn't risk passing on infection. I looked at my watch. It was growing late. We needed to get the bird, and head back to base.

But the boy's image burned my eyes. 'What if the boy had come over from Villa Las Estrellas or Esperanza? You know they have kids on those bases,' I said. My rational mind kept telling me I'd had an hallucination, but my voice kept speaking. 'I want to go and look for him. Try to find an entrance in the ice near the Adélie rookery.'

Kate swung around. 'That's insane, Laura. We have to get back to Alliance. The lab's booked for us. I need to know what happened to this poor bird.'

'What about the boy? There's a slight chance he was really there.'

Kate sighed. 'I don't think there was a boy down there. It was thick ice, there couldn't have been. It was just a trick of the light.'

I planted my feet firmly in the snow. 'I need to go. Now.' Was I losing all scientific process and self-control? But there *was* logic. He *could* have come over from another base. Maybe he'd arrived with his parents and something awful had happened to them.

'You can't. It's a wild-goose chase,' said Kate.

'Why don't you take the penguin, and I'll stay here overnight? You don't need me in the lab, you're more than capable.'

'As if I'd leave you alone. This place, this whole area, Alliance and especially Fredelighavn – it's unsettling. Think about it. It's so completely unlikely. We can all have hallucinations down here, it's no big deal. How about those guys at the South Pole who just walk off into the ice, convinced they've seen angels or bears or giant Hershey's bars? Or the ones who sit weeping into their dinner for no reason, and can't remember they've done it. You're toasty, my dear – admit it.' Kate punched me in the arm.

'What if the boy was with his parents? Or separated from—'

Kate cut me off. 'And when we looked hard, there wasn't even a chamber there for him to be in. It really was just ice. Now, I'm getting this penguin and you're coming back with me. Before you go really bonkers and start attacking me with a screwdriver.'

That was a legendary occurrence. A few years ago at our base, a carpenter who was usually a gentle giant had gone off the rails because he didn't like the gravy on his steak. He attacked the cook with a screwdriver and nearly killed him. A bad case of Toast.

I didn't move. All I wanted was to run in the other direction and go up to the cliff and start looking for the boy. I slumped down, my head in my hands. He'd seemed so much like Hamish would have looked. I tried to think rationally. Kate was right about the ice. It was thick. There was no sign of any space where a boy could have been.

Was I just getting toasty? Separated from Kate, I'd panicked.

But a compulsion to search fired up in me. I tried to push it away, but it kept coming back; I felt like a madwoman.

I stripped off the disposable overalls and booties. 'Sorry, Kate, I have to go.'

When I was halfway to the rookery she joined me.

'I'm not leaving you alone. You really are the most annoying person I've ever met.'

'Blame my Spanish mother, she made me stubborn. Thank you. We'll have a look around, and if we can't find anything, we'll go and get the penguin.'

Kate sighed. 'We're going to be very late back to base.'

'So we miss dinner. We'll still get to the lab. Lucky it's the graveyard shift. Connaught's done us a favour.'

At the rookery, tens of thousands of penguins were hunkered on their nests. We gave them a wide berth as we headed towards the ice cliff by the sea. I photographed everything, just in case my eyes missed something.

There were crevasses in the ice filled with deep green shadows, but nothing that looked like it could be an entrance down. None was wide enough, even for a slender boy. As we walked along, the Adélies watched from a distance, honking and crying and making an ear-shattering racket.

I moved to the water's edge and peered down. I couldn't see any cave entrance from this angle, so I walked on the top of the cliff, up the coast. After an hour of searching, Kate grabbed my shoulder.

'Time to go,' she said. 'We've done what you wanted. There's nothing here.'

*

Again we donned our protective gear. I went to the cupboard while Kate prepared the blue body bag. The penguin lay as before, but this time I could get closer, and when I did I stepped back in shock. I looked at the head, eyes shut like it was sleeping; at its black and orange beak and little black wings; at the angle of its flippers. 'It's different,' I said, anger surging through me. 'This is a different penguin.'

Kate shot forward and took a look. 'It's the same one, Laura.' Her voice was sharp, her expression fierce. 'Keep it together. I can't afford for you to lose the plot down here. That is the *same penguin.*'

I grabbed my camera and took photographs, then compared them to the originals. They did look exactly the same. I bit my lip. I could tell this penguin was different. I didn't know how, but every instinct in my body was saying it. The head looked the same, the body looked identical. But I'd been in the field long enough to know to trust my instincts. Somewhere, something was different.

Kate pushed past me and picked up the penguin with all the tenderness of a mother with a baby. She placed it gently on the blue nylon and zipped up the bag.

We scrubbed the cupboard and table and benchtops with bleach.

'We're out of here,' Kate said. At the front entrance we took off our protective gear and sealed it in a plastic bag. Then we headed off through the icy streets, Kate carrying the blue body bag that I tried not to notice looked the size of a small child.

*

I found Jasper in the dining room, eating with a group of scientists.

'You took your time,' he said. 'We were just thinking of sending out a search party.' By the looks of his friends I doubted it. They didn't even bother to say hello.

'Where can we put the penguin?'

'I'll open up. Then we can go back later at our allotted time.'

I thanked him as I trotted after him. His long legs meant that even his slow walk was rapid.

'We left the penguin in the Hägglunds.'

'Well, off you go.'

By the time I arrived at the shed, Kate had put our diving gear away. She picked up the body bag carefully and we walked to the main building, where Jasper was waiting outside the entrance. He put his eye to a camera and his right hand on a pad, and the heavy door swung open.

'Sophisticated,' said Kate.

'Saves a lot of time and messing around,' replied Jasper. 'No keys or codes.'

We went to follow him in, but he held up a hand. 'Uh-uh, you need to do the same.'

Even though the door was open, we followed suit. 'But how could it recognise us?' I asked. 'We haven't been here before.'

'It will now. You won't be able to get out otherwise.'

'Wild,' said Kate. 'I've never been to a British base before. Are they all like this?'

'No,' said Jasper moving off, the door swinging tightly shut behind us. 'They're all different.' He didn't elaborate further.

He strode down a long neon-lit corridor, its floor polished linoleum like those in a hospital. We passed closed, windowless doors. I longed to know what was inside them.

Rounding a bend and walking up another corridor, Jasper stopped mid-way. Again he put his eye to a tiny camera and his right hand on a pad. The door swung open. The lab looked like any typical one I'd been in. A clean white examination table stood in the middle of the room; microscopes sat on sterile benches around the edges, and there were computers at one end. At the back, there was a door with a window into another lab, where two men were working, looking through microscopes.

'What are they doing?' I asked.

'You know I can't tell you that.' Jasper grinned. 'Nice try, Doctor Alvarado.' He indicated the examination table. 'Leave the penguin here in its bag.'

Kate placed the Adélie down carefully.

'Now you go and have supper. You must be famished?'

Kate agreed enthusiastically. I wasn't hungry at all.

At both the door to the lab and the main entrance, we had to stop for the retina and hand scan to be allowed to leave. The hair on the back of my neck rose. I wasn't used to being locked in by security.

Travis sat with us as we had dinner, and Jasper joined us too. I kept thinking about what had happened in the ice cave. Could it have been a boy?

'I'm amazed you don't have rules about that down here,' said Kate, indicating Jasper's bottle of rough white. 'Drinking while on duty?'

'Connaught's pretty easy in that department,' replied Jasper. 'And I have the constitution of an ox. Not to mention, this wine's as weak as tap water.' He downed another glass to prove his point. Travis poured another beer for himself.

'So, I wonder what killed that penguin, eh?' said Travis and I found myself hoping he had nothing to do with it.

'Find anything interesting at Fredelighavn today?' asked Jasper casually.

'No,' Kate and I replied simultaneously and Jasper raised his eyebrows. 'Well, that *does* sound interesting,' he said. 'Tell all.'

'Nothing to tell,' I said. 'Just a routine visit, to collect the penguin.'

He gave a sly smile and lowered his voice. 'I'm looking forward to seeing what we can see on that penguin front.'

Suddenly I wondered who Jasper really was. Had he volunteered to help tonight, as he claimed?

At eleven o'clock we made our way to the lab, saying goodbye to Travis as we arrived at the main building. Despite Jasper's assertions about his constitution, the bad white wine had lent a slight sway to his walk.

We each placed our eye and hand in position and entered. There was no noise at all apart from our boots making soft squelching sounds on the linoleum. At any other laboratory I would have found the mood peaceful but here it was unsettling to feel so alone.

ANN TURNER

Jasper stopped outside his lab door. 'Let's try and make this quick, I'm knackered,' he said, before gaining entry. As the door swung open he stood back to let us go in first. The body bag was where we'd left it on the table. We donned protective gear – eye goggles, disposable overalls, face masks, paper booties over our shoes, and finally thin latex gloves. Kate unzipped the bag and together she and I lifted the penguin onto the table. Jasper adjusted a lamp to shine brightly on the bird and brought over a tray of sterilised instruments.

Kate chose a scalpel and proceeded to make a long slit down the Adélie's chest and stomach. She worked fast and confidently. 'She's a young female,' she observed.

I documented everything, visually and with notes, which took my mind off worrying about the boy. There were small fish and tiny krill in the penguin's stomach. Everything looked normal.

Kate bagged the contents. We spent the next few hours going through them, placing smears on glass slides and viewing the slides under a microscope.

Jasper yawned and slumped onto a stool. Every so often he'd stare at me with a bored expression, which I found distracting. Kate took blood from beneath the penguin's skin and we moved on to analysing the blood, skin and feathers under the microscope.

We could find nothing out of the ordinary. Black circles were forming under Kate's eyes and my own were gritty and dry.

Kate frowned down at the Adélie. 'It would seem she died of natural causes but I have no idea what. She didn't starve. And if there'd been unusual heat we would have seen more corpses in the rookery. We'll need to keep looking.'

We put more samples on slides and kept analysing. Jasper groaned. 'Enough. It's six-thirty. The morning shift will be arriving and I'm meant to start work in two hours. I'm sorry I volunteered for this rubbish. I thought you two were experts.' He peered hard at me and my blood flushed as his insult stung.

'We've just not seen this before,' said Kate firmly. 'Maybe you could tell us why, Jasper?'

'Perhaps we should go back to our own base and do this there,' I said. 'At least everyone would be onside.'

'Cheers. Thanks a lot. I've just wasted my entire night for you,' retorted Jasper.

I turned to him. 'I'm wondering if you really volunteered. Did Connaught put you up to this?'

'You're full of crap, Laura. And you should learn manners. Come on. Out. Both of you. Time's up.'

'And we *are* grateful to you,' said Kate, giving Jasper a little smile, trying to calm the waters.

Jasper gave a half-hearted acknowledgement. 'Put the bird – or what's left of it – back in its bag and I'll put it in an isolated freezer. I'll give you a container for your slides. And then you have to sterilise the lab.' A grim smile split his lips. 'See you later.'

'You're leaving us alone?' I asked hopefully.

'Don't do anything stupid. Everything, and I mean *everything*, in these labs is filmed. Smile and look pretty. You're being recorded for eternity.'

'Then why did you have to stay the whole night?' I said, unnerved.

'Standard procedure. But I have no intention of watching you clean up. If there's anything out of place, you won't want to be alive, I promise.'

'We're professionals,' I said. 'Give us that.'

We set about disinfecting everything and by the end, Kate and I were so exhausted we could barely move. We didn't speak to each other, knowing we were being filmed.

Once we'd completed our chores, we dumped our protective clothing in a bin and headed out. The doors we passed were so tempting but I knew I couldn't get through them. The place was impenetrable. I thought of the chamber that went down into the ice. Could there be an underground network that stretched all the way to Fredelighavn? But the distance was surely too far – it was about twenty kilometres.

Back in our room, Kate let out a long groan. 'I hate this place. Why did you bring me here?'

'I'm sorry. For what it's worth, I hate it too. Do you think they swapped that penguin?'

Kate made no reply. Frustrated by her lack of response, I flipped open my computer and started to look at the photographs, blowing them up larger to compare the penguin we'd initially found in the cupboard to the one we'd retrieved today. They looked identical.

'They could have changed my images,' I said tiredly. 'They went through all my devices on the first day.'

'Mine too,' said Kate.

'So, they can probably get in and do anything they want. And before you say it, I know I sound paranoid.'

'Quite the opposite,' Kate replied. 'I think it's the sanest thing you've said all day.'

I turned, amazed, and Kate produced three small vials of blood in a sealed bag from her pocket. 'I didn't want to analyse these there. They need to be left for twenty-four hours and I wouldn't trust Jasper not to fiddle with them if they showed something the creeps down here are trying to hide.'

'Kate, we were being filmed – they would have seen you take those!'

'Don't sweat, I'd already noticed the cameras.' She wiggled her hips. 'So I *dids my moves* and covered my handiwork. And Jasper was too bored to notice how many vials I'd filled.' Kate pulled out a portable analyser from her bag. 'I brought my field centrifuge.'

She put it on the desk. I'd seen her use it many times to analyse her penguins' blood, but I wasn't keen on her using it here in our room with this Adélie sample. 'What if there are cameras here?' I looked around the ceiling and walls; they were smooth and bare.

'I don't think so,' said Kate with certainty. She proceeded to carefully place the vials in the machine. 'Everything's sealed,' she reassured me. 'If there's anything infective in the blood it won't leak. You know I'm more paranoid about viruses than you.' She dialled up specifications for each blood sample and then pressed the on switch.

'You're absolutely sure nothing can leak?' I asked nervously.

'There's no choice but to do it here. And anyway, I'm meticulous.' She disappeared into the bathroom and had a quick shower. I stood over the centrifuge, reassuring myself it was working properly and praying nothing went wrong.

Kate came out and hopped into bed. 'And now, I sleep.' She yawned. 'We can talk more in the morning. Oh, it *is* morning. Don't wake me for many, many hours.'

Before I could reply, she was asleep, snoring quietly. I longed to join her but instead I went through everything again. The penguin still looked like the one bird. There was nothing in the ice cave that looked like a cavern, and no sign of the boy. I pored through the photos for hours, examining each one multiple times.

Finally I showered, changed into my pyjamas and lay down beside Kate, grateful for her warmth. My mind kept obsessing on the boy: his brown eyes, his hands pressed against the ice. His screaming mouth. I reminded myself it wasn't Hamish; that was an impossibility. I'd lost my baby at birth. He hadn't gone missing. Tears misted my eyes.

Now the boy wasn't in the cave, but in my old childhood home by the sea at windswept Grange. He was looking out the window at me. I was on the beach, but there was water around my feet. He raised his hands and pressed them against the glass. I tried to walk through the water but it was thick red toffee, sticking hard. It started to weep blood, pouring everywhere until it was a tide. Running down my legs, hot and red, joining the pool that was as vast as the ocean. Bubbling red blood like a cauldron. 'Hot jam donuts! See them being made, cooking, cooking, cooking all the time!' a voice cried to carnival music.

I must free myself. Now I was swimming through the scarlet water. Fake blood, make-up-department blood. Special effects.

Drowning me. Going under. Can't breathe.

I woke gasping for air, thrashing out my hands trying to swim. I touched Kate's warm skin. She was snoring gently.

Tomorrow, I promised myself, trying to calm my breathing, I would return to Fredelighavn and see if my mind had turned to toast, or if there really was a boy – who I could find.

9

The weather had its own ideas. Later that day we awoke to the rocking, howling chaos of a blizzard. Kate lifted her head briefly off the pillow. 'Looks like we won't be going anywhere.' She plonked down again and snored loudly.

I checked my watch – 3pm. Outside was a whiteout, visibility zero. I hauled myself up and Skyped Georgia, but found there was very little I wanted to tell her. I let her know the results of the penguin autopsy.

'That's odd. No cause at all. Even natural causes would show something, wouldn't they?' she said, her face drawn and strained.

'Exactly, that's what makes it so unlikely. I still think they're doing something.'

'Could it have died of fright?' she asked.

I stopped. In my exhaustion yesterday, that hadn't occurred to me, and yet it was so obvious. 'Perhaps,' I said. 'It would fit with the behaviour of the penguins at the rookery, if someone had gone down and disturbed them. But then, why weren't there more who'd died? And why was the penguin in a cupboard?'

'I don't like what you're reporting at all. The sooner Professor Koch arrives the better. Not being sexist, but I think having a man there with you would make me feel better.'

'That *is* sexist. But having another ally would be good. When's he coming? I've not heard from him.'

'Not for another week, unfortunately. There were a few problems with the second operation. He's having to recuperate in hospital.'

'Poor guy. Will he be up to it at all?'

'According to him, yes.'

'Georgia, I don't suppose you could come down? You could fingerprint around Fredelighavn.' I knew she always brought her fingerprint kit to Antarctica, just in case she needed it in an investigation as Station Leader. Several of us joked about it but last summer there was a kleptomaniac glaciologist and Georgia had actually used it, with its portable ultraviolet lamp, fluorescent powders, and lifting tape for prints.

'That's *dusting* for fingerprints.' Georgia corrected me.

'Exactly. To see who's been down there – in the cinema and the other buildings. And also,' I paused, and Georgia leaned forward in anticipation. 'I was wondering if we might be able to put up some small surveillance cameras?'

Georgia sat back. 'Whoa. This is an EIA, not a criminal investigation.'

'Except if people have been going down there unauthorised.'

'Cameras? No. As to the fingerprinting, let me think about it. We'll see.'

We'll see. That didn't leave me hopeful. It was a phrase my mother used that inevitably led to permanent deferment of whatever had been asked.

Georgia signed off, warning me to stay vigilant. I hadn't told her that I might have seen a boy in the ice cave. I knew it would sound too strange and unbelievable.

Which proved I wasn't too toasty.

Hunger stirred but I didn't want to leave the warmth of my room and brave the blizzard. I spent the next few hours writing notes on everything, all the while wondering if Connaught was hacking into my computer and reading these too? That would be a violation of my Antarctic Council-endorsed mission. Surely Connaught wouldn't risk it? But then, if he'd switched my photographs . . . The idea filled me with a deep weariness.

I lay down quietly beside Kate and thought about Hamish: the terrible day I'd lost him, and the unconditional love that had swept through me as I held him and bathed him. The unconditional love I still felt. I acknowledged his birthdays, and every Christmas I imagined him. But in my mind he was blurry: changing from a newborn to a child, to older – it was more a sensation of love. To suddenly imagine him so vividly and concretely was different. Surely it made no sense?

Except, as odd as it seemed, if the boy in the ice was real.

*

At 9pm I woke Kate and we battled through the blizzard, holding on to guide ropes, slung from building to building, until we reached the mess hall. There was no one sitting at the tables.

'Damn, I'm starved, there'd better be something left,' said Kate as she lurched towards the heated food stand. There were two tiny plates of roast of the day, whatever it was – just the same grey meat slathered in gravy. I could see Guy cleaning dishes in the kitchen, his skinny body bent over a sink as he scrubbed vigorously. He was alone.

'Guy?' I called. 'Speak to you for a moment?'

He jumped and came over.

'That night of the fancy dress – did you serve me enough alcohol to get blotto?'

He stood mutely. Kate turned and stared at him. He flushed a deep scarlet.

'So?' said Kate firmly.

'Not really.' He turned on his heels and fled.

'Wow,' said Kate.

My mouth went dry.

'So you probably did have your drink spiked,' said Kate. 'My guess would be by Jasper, because he's the one you were with. And I bet it's not the first time he's done that to a woman down here. Lucky he didn't fancy you, and was only trying to make you look like an idiot.'

Goosebumps rose up my legs at the thought of Jasper spiking my drink and then helping us in the lab.

'But his story matched Travis's.'

'Hate to tell you, but Travis might not be a friend either.'

My face burned. I didn't want to believe that.

We sat down and ate our meals in silence.

Kate stood over the centrifuge, checking the blood samples. She peered at the vials and pressed a button. On the desk, a small battery-powered printer started to whir, and the results were spat out. Kate grabbed them, studying the figures.

'Damn. All completely normal.'

'Well, that proves the point – the penguin was switched. Or it died of fright.'

'Well, it died of *something*. As soon as this blizzard's over I want to go back.' Kate's freckles stood out in her pale face, which had tensed up. 'I want to go through every single house and shed down there. See if they've hurt any other wildlife and find out what they're doing,' she said with fury. 'Because that penguin didn't just crawl into that cupboard and die of untraceable natural causes. And they know we'd know that. They're laughing in our faces, Laura.'

She looked at the results again. 'Anyway, at least we know now. I'd bet my life that Connaught's up to something at Fredelighavn. And it's such a horrible, sexist base, he probably thinks we're just stupid girls who'll never find out.'

Three days later the blizzard was still raging and Georgia was still deferring an answer on the fingerprinting equipment, worried about jurisdiction. In the meantime I'd come up with an alternative plan. I walked down the passage and knocked on Travis's door.

'Who is it?' he called blearily.

'It's just me. Laura.'

The door opened with lightning speed. Travis stood grinning, wearing blue-striped flannel pyjamas that matched his eyes. With his tousled hair, he looked dangerously cute.

'Come in,' he said, standing back. 'What can I do for you?'

I made small talk about the blizzard as he poured us both a strong coffee, and then I told him about the fresh popcorn and film in the cinema. His eyes widened as I outlined my idea. Travis gulped his coffee then poured another cup before he spoke.

'We'd be breaking safety protocol.'

'Will you do it?'

He sighed. 'You know I will. But if anything happens to you down there . . .'

'It won't, I promise. I'll find a way to repay you someday.'

'No need.' He smiled. 'We're friends. And I'd like to know what happened to that poor penguin as much as you do.' He poured a third cup of coffee and blushed. 'I've been meaning to ask . . . Do you think when Moose and Simon and I went diving, we could have hurt the penguins?'

I stiffened. 'Well, that depends on what you did there.' I held my breath, desperate to hear the answer, and praying it wouldn't destroy my trust in him.

'Like I told you, we went diving and looked in a few houses.' Travis grew sheepish. 'And when we were on the beach, after our dive . . .' He glanced out the window, to the white cloud of lashing snow. I waited, tense.

'We walked up to the rookery.' His eyes shone. 'And the penguins attacked us.'

'What did you do to provoke them?' I asked sharply.

'That's the thing, nothing. I swear. Absolutely nothing. We just walked up to them and they attacked. We felt really bad. And they bit deep into our hands and legs.'

I tried not to show my relief. Not only was it exactly what had happened to Kate and myself, it formed a pattern of behaviour.

'And, now we're having this heart to heart, did you really not touch anything in the houses?' I asked.

'A few cigarettes. Well, more than a few. They were really good.'

'Where did you find them?'

'In a shed.'

'I think I know the shed. Like a quartermaster's store?'

Travis nodded guiltily.

'Was that box full when you found them?'

'Yes, it was. I'm really sorry. Are you going to report us? If you are, can it just be me? I don't want to rat on my friends.'

'Don't worry. As long as you tell me everything, I won't say a word.'

'I have told you everything.' His jaw was set tight. 'So that's it?'

'For now.'

He grew even more concerned.

'Forever,' I smiled. 'You're off the hook. You shouldn't have done it but, on a scale of badness, it doesn't seem too awful.' Knots loosened in my shoulders. My better instincts about Travis seemed to have been right.

He started to relax too, his face opening up again.

'Where did you smoke the cigarettes – down there or back here?' I asked.

'Neither. We smoked them when we went across the island to Baldwin Glacier and camped out. It was incredible, they weren't even stale. If you hadn't come, we were going to go back and get the rest.'

'You can't do that.'

'I know. Of course I know. I'm a reformed man.'

'I hope so.'

'Except, I'm about to break the law for you.'

I reached up and kissed his forehead. He smelled like salt air. He went to take my shoulder but I swivelled away.

'You know, I don't think my mother would like you,' he joked. 'She raised us boys to be honest.'

'I'm almost old enough to *be* your mother and I'm giving you a free pass on certain activities for the greater good.'

'Don't say that,' Travis pulled a face. 'You're not old enough to be my mother. You're being grotesque.'

'See you soon. And thanks.'

'Just don't say you're like my mother ever again.'

I was laughing as I shut the door. The innocence of Travis's confession gave me a sensation of lightness. And I didn't know why I'd let down my guard and kissed him but it felt good. *Careful, Alvarado*, I told myself. *Don't go being a fool.*

The next day the blizzard stopped. Kate and I were careful as we packed food, water and emergency flares from the store.

We didn't want anyone to see us, even though the supplies weren't very different to those I took every trip to Fredelighavn. There were just greater quantities, and we would actually be eating the food.

We signed out the Hägglunds. Kate and I sat up front as Travis put in a sick-leave application, claiming his lower back was playing up and he needed to rest. Then he grabbed a jemmy iron, leaped into the back cabin and hid. I drove out onto the icy road, pure white and pristine after the storm, as my plan started to unfold.

10

Light was playing on the houses, icicles glistening in fairy rainbows as they dangled from roofs and windows. Today Fredelighavn appeared like a magical wonderland.

I had fourteen hours before the sun sank low on the horizon, plunging South Safety into the deep blue of astronomical twilight. I would have liked to go straight up to the ice cliffs and look for signs of the boy whose face haunted me, but I couldn't with Travis here. Instead I would search in houses, checking for recent habitation and the possibility of an entrance that led underground to the ice cave.

I was glad to have Travis with us; it made me feel safer. I led my troupe down to the bay, where Travis looked nervously up towards the Adélie colony. More penguins had arrived from their winter seas, and there were hundreds of thousands of birds nesting up the hill. The noise was even more deafening and a light breeze carried with it a strong fishy smell.

Adélies torpedoed out of the calm blue ocean onto the ice, and further out in the harbour they were plummeting from icebergs into the sea. Elephant seals sunned on the beach, and Weddell seals popped their heads out of the water. A pod of orcas – black and white killer whales – swam a little way out. I dropped my bag, pulled out my camera and started to film, soothed by the sight. Kate grabbed her camera and followed suit. Travis stood beside me, entranced.

Down the coast, in the opposite direction to the Adélie rookery, about a hundred more gentoo penguins had come ashore and thousands of chinstrap penguins had arrived. As the season was swinging into shape, it was apparent why Fredelighavn had been designated an Exclusion Zone for its extraordinary wildlife.

I was eager to head to a clutch of large houses on a rise towards Alliance Point, closest to the ice cave.

We moved up the hill and stopped outside a grand pink and blue two-storey house with a sharply sloping roof. Although the paint had peeled, the building was still attractive. I could feel Travis shifting from leg to leg with excitement as we turned on our torches and I flung the door open. A wide corridor greeted us, with immaculately waxed wooden floors. To the right was a magnificent lounge room, four times the size of those we'd seen to date. My heart was thudding. Could there be an entrance here down into the ice?

We walked into the room and I studied the floor. All the boards were consistent. There was no sign of a trapdoor.

Comfortable sofas were upholstered in pale blue fabric. A round coffee table was immaculately decorated in pink and silver. An elaborate ashtray on a stand was in Art Deco style. Above a grand fireplace, a convex mirror in Regency design – gilded, with small round balls dotting its circumference – made me jump when I saw our reflections. Then I froze as I glimpsed a fourth person. A tall, blonde-haired woman in a stylish 1950s woollen dress, blue with white bands, hurried past in the passage. I turned sharply and stuck my head out – but there was no one there. She'd vanished into thin air. I turned back to the mirror: only our reflections. My mind was playing tricks again. Was I coming down with a bad case of Toast?

Travis and Kate were bent over an old wind-up gramophone with a pile of thick seventy-eight records stacked on a table beside it. 'These are from a much earlier period. Classical,' said Kate, pulling a record from its slip, to Travis's scowling disapproval.

I walked out, my pulse quickening, and headed along the corridor. The next room was empty. The room after that, the kitchen, had simple cupboards and a table with six chairs. I checked the cupboards. Empty. There was nothing on the scrubbed-pine benches either, and no sign of anything that could lead underground. The woman couldn't have been real; there was nowhere for her to go. I wasn't just toast – I was *burnt* toast. Yet I felt completely normal. I'd never experienced anything like it.

The whine of a thin violin drifted into the air, joined by a cello and oboe. A thrill slipped up my spine. The music fitted gloriously. It was sparse and serene. I imagined the living room full of people, the fire blazing and wind roaring outside, the gramophone turned up loud.

With effort, I slid a rusty bolt and swung open the back door, which clearly hadn't been used in years. In an enclosed porch was a tiny bathroom and toilet, untouched for decades.

Upstairs all four bedrooms had been stripped of possessions. Only the empty beds with delicately carved bedheads remained, looking sad and abandoned. I took photos, and then went back to the lounge room, filming the furniture while Kate recorded details on my laptop, placing the house within my mapped grid and putting in GPS coordinates. The music swirled around us.

When the record ended we went next door, to a house that was even larger and just as pretty, painted a deep rose. But as soon as I entered I felt it – someone had been here recently, perhaps was even living here. The lounge room was filled with blond wood furniture, neat pinstriped cushions scattered about. There were two coffee tables and ashtrays brimming with cigarette butts. I inspected them closely, taking photos.

'Do you think someone's been here smoking?' said Travis.

I peered again at the butts. These had no lipstick on them. They smelled stale and rank.

'Maybe,' I said, trying to think rationally. If someone was here, there were no tracks in the ice outside, and today with the sun the streets were softer, and there would have been. I walked back and checked. I could see our three sets of footprints, but no other signs of disturbance.

I ducked inside again and collided with Travis who was coming out. 'Follow me,' I whispered and went quickly upstairs, taking care to make no sound. All the doors off the corridor were shut. I stopped, making sure Travis was behind me. I whipped open the first one. The bed was fully made up with pillows and a thick blue and white eiderdown. I strode across and pulled open the covers. The sheets looked clean and had a pleasant scent of fresh air tinged with salt. 'Good enough to sleep in,' I mumbled and walked out. There were no wardrobes or cupboards, nowhere to hide.

The next room was similar: a single bed with sheets and blankets that smelled fresh and inviting. On a freezing day in a blizzard, I could imagine curling up here myself.

The third room had a double bed, again comfortably made up. There was a huge wooden wardrobe. I flung open the door and stepped back, alarmed. It was full of clothes.

Carefully I went through them, coathangers clanging quietly, matching my rattled nerves. The clothes were boys' outfits: woollen trousers and thick woollen shirts in a checked pattern. The size of a teenage boy. They would fit the boy I thought I saw in the ice, the boy who looked like Hamish. I shivered, hoping I wasn't going mad. These clothes were from decades ago. Why would a boy be down here wearing them? Now I wasn't even making sense to myself.

Travis stepped forward. 'Vintage 1950s,' he said. 'They'd sell for hundreds.'

'Don't get any ideas,' I warned, but my mind was already far away, trying to remember what the boy in the cave *had* been wearing. Was it a checked shirt or a T-shirt? I shut my eyes, trying to visualise, but all I could see was his face, screaming for help.

I pulled out a shirt. It was a pale lemon check pattern, 1950s-style, heavy and warm. Two more were checked in red and blue.

I took out hand-knitted woollen jumpers and thick coats. They were also vintage, from the days when Fredelighavn was alive. On a top shelf in the wardrobe was a row of woollen caps.

I hadn't found any other clothes in the houses I'd seen. *Was this whole thing staged? A show village, just for me?*

Although, if the boy existed, he hadn't been acting. I had seen – or *imagined* I'd seen – real fear. But if it was all in my head, why? We were tested for psychological health before we came to Antarctica, and were briefed to tell our Station Leader if we had problems. I didn't want to confess anything – certainly not to Connaught, who probably thought all women were crazy anyway. Not even to Georgia. I determined to keep my thoughts to myself.

I went to the door of the fourth room and stopped abruptly as I heard a faint trace of movement. Travis nodded – he'd heard it too. I turned the carved wooden door handle and could feel Travis tensing his muscles behind me, flexing up ready to defend. The door swung freely and we looked in. The entire room was empty. Sunlight beamed through a window onto the floorboards, cutting a rich yellow swathe of light.

'That's odd,' said Travis, looking around everywhere. I did the same: up and down, across the smooth, timber-lined ceiling with no manhole, no break. Along the white walls, and the floor. There was nothing.

We retreated downstairs to the kitchen, where Kate was checking through cupboards: some were empty, some were full of canned food. There was no sign of an entrance above, or below. Nothing to explain the rustling.

The bathroom hadn't been used for decades and had no trapdoor or manhole.

Frustrated and perplexed, we moved on to the house opposite. It was huge, the largest of all, painted the colour of a ripe orange, with beautifully carved white fretwork on its porch covered in long, delicate icicles. The lounge room was first off the passage – it was almost the size of a ballroom. Its floorboards were waxed and mellow, the wide planks wafting a delicious honey perfume. On the walls hung portraits, and one in particular drew me towards it. In a huge gilt frame, a woman with piercing blue eyes and long blonde hair swept up in a bun peered down sternly. She wore a simple white cotton blouse fastened at the neck by a carved brooch of a whale. Beside her hung a portrait of a serious-looking man, fair-haired, blue-eyed, in a navy sea captain's uniform, his face etched in deep ridges from sun and salt and life on the wild ocean. Around them were paintings of their children – three snowy-haired boys.

Ingerline? I studied the woman. It was hard to tell her age, but she might have been close to forty. The painting was perhaps from the 1930s. If it was Ingerline, this was not what I had expected. Having built a cinema, I'd imagined her to be fun loving, but this woman looked strict and humourless. Maybe it wasn't Ingerline – there must have been other captains and their wives running the whaling station after Lars Halvorsen. Presumably Ingerline didn't stay until the demise of the place in the 1950s. How many years had she been down here? How could I find out?

Travis was gazing at the wide blue eyes that sparkled as if the woman were alive, and the full red lips beneath her pert nose.

I found it hard to envisage this beautiful woman living here in this harsh environment. 'She was good looking. Who is she?' said Kate, and I jumped.

'Steady on,' said Travis, taking me by the elbow. 'Are you okay? You look like you've just seen a ghost.'

I laughed. 'Do I?'

'You know this woman?' said Kate.

'I think she's Ingerline Halvorsen.' I shuddered as I heard myself say the name out loud. My nerves really were stretched. 'Although perhaps not.'

I strode out of the room and down the hallway. Children's bedrooms were on both sides, with little carved white beds, fully made up with pillows, white sheets and thick blankets. Colourful childlike paintings covered the walls on yellowed paper, the edges curling up.

The kitchen was large, with an enormous table. I counted ten thatched chairs placed neatly around it. There was an electric refrigerator, pale pink, 1950s style, in one corner. Its door hung slightly ajar. There was nothing inside.

I opened a corner cupboard. It was lined with empty shelves.

There was a pot on the elegant coal-burning stove. I opened the lid and saw frozen water.

Cups sat face down on the bench beside the kitchen sink, as if they'd just been cleaned.

Other cupboards were full of bags of tea, coffee, flour and sugar.

I pulled down the stove door and smelled inside. The air was stale. It didn't seem like it had been operated in a long time.

'I'm sick of nothing adding up,' I said. 'This room looks like it's just been used but then it seems it hasn't been. This place is doing my head in.'

'We need to find someone who knows about Fredelighavn,' said Kate. 'Aren't there Norwegian scholars who've studied it?'

'Not that I know of. It's been an Exclusion Zone for years, so no recent study.'

'There must be records. Shipping records, that kind of thing,' said Travis.

'Do you know where?' I asked.

'Sorry. I'm just an electrical engineer. But my father's an academic, a history professor at Harvard.' He blushed. 'He left when I was thirteen. But I remember Dad researching through the night in his study. Sometimes I'd sneak in and watch until he'd look up and kick me out.'

'Do you still see him?' I said, surprised that he and I had a similar background.

'Unfortunately no,' said Travis, with a tinge of anger and sadness that I recognised.

'What was his area?' asked Kate.

'American naval history. That's why I know about the shipping records. They go way back.'

'I'll try to put out a few feelers in Norway,' I said. 'I don't know anyone there but I'm sure I'll find a way.'

'I could help,' said Travis. 'I've got plenty of spare time.'

'They don't work you hard enough,' said Kate and Travis laughed, his white teeth bright in his smooth tanned face. He caught me looking at him, and turned to me keenly. I turned away and headed upstairs, feeling myself blush. 'Let's see what's up here,' I called, floorboards creaking underfoot.

The first rooms had single beds with white sheets and floral eiderdowns. The master bedroom was at the end, stretching wide across the whole building. It was sunny and airy, the bed made up with pink sheets and a thick pink eiderdown. There were two large wardrobes, and photographs on a small table. I peered at them and reeled back in alarm: there was a photo of an older Ingerline – or the woman in the portrait downstairs, whoever she was – now in her fifties. And she was wearing a dress, blue with white bands, 1950s-style, exactly like the one worn by the woman I'd glimpsed in the mirror in the pink and blue house. If I was seeing ghosts I really was losing my mind.

'Let's go,' I said, over-loudly. 'I want to open that shed we couldn't see inside the other day.'

I turned on my heel and fled.

'But we haven't looked in the wardrobes,' Travis called as he flung one open.

Kate followed me. 'What's wrong, Laura? You're scaring me again.'

'Absolutely nothing,' I said firmly and rattled down the stairs. Someone was messing around with me, was my scientific view. I didn't believe in the supernatural.

Out in the street we waited for Travis, stamping our feet against the cold. The day was turning icy.

Kate scrutinised me but I remained silent. I had no intention of telling her what I thought I'd seen.

Travis came barrelling out. 'Lots of old clothes. Men's and women's. Beautiful quality suits. Thick wool. And before you say it, no I didn't touch them.' He grinned. 'Still, it's a treasure trove. This place will make a phenomenal museum.'

Was that what whoever was behind this was hoping? Or were the clothes simply original and left here like so many other things? I'd have to go back and take a closer look. I quaked at the thought of being near Ingerline again – the portrait or the ghost. And why, if I *had* seen her ghost, was she haunting someone else's house – assuming this place, with the portraits and photographs, was hers?

'You brought the jemmy iron?' I asked Travis as I headed off.

'Sure. It's in my backpack.'

I was beginning to know my way around. I took only two wrong turns before I found the locked shed.

Travis wedged the jemmy iron between the doors and crunched them open. We shone our torches inside through the darkness – there were no windows – and saw nothing but a few old mattresses piled in a corner, with blue and white ticking stripes.

'Check the floor,' I said, entering. 'Look for anything that could lead underground.'

'Why?' asked Travis, puzzled.

'Because I say to,' I replied. 'If the shed's locked, something must be here.' I pulled the mattresses out from the corner and Travis helped. There was only concrete floor underneath.

I walked around the shed, thinking about the massive building effort required to construct the village. Timber, concrete, corrugated iron and brick – it would have taken a lot of men to put Fredelighavn together each short summer, when the weather was warm enough to allow them to work. Which led me to a realisation: perhaps they left everything in the houses because they were certain they were coming back next season. They were used to doing that. Packing up and heading back to Norway in March each year, then returning the following summer. But if it was the whalers who locked this shed, and not Connaught, what were they trying to protect?

Travis was casting his torch around the floor, following my instructions, searching for a trapdoor down into the ice. He shuffled with his boots, attempting to feel a ridge. Kate and I started to do the same.

'What do you think is underground?' he asked.

'A tunnel to the sea. Through an ice cave.'

Kate tensed and pursed her lips, clearly thinking I was off on another wild-goose chase.

'Like smugglers,' said Travis. 'But why would they bother?' He frowned. 'There were no real laws when they were down here, were there? They could do whatever they wanted. So why would they hide anything? Or are you saying they were building underground for the weather, like at the South Pole? But it's so much more benign here on South Safety, they wouldn't need to.' He walked close to me and stood studying my face. 'So, will you tell me what this is all about?'

Kate looked across, shadowy in the torchlight, waiting for my answer.

'Not yet, Travis,' I said. 'Can we just do this. Please?'

Disgruntled, he moved off. I hoped I wouldn't lose his trust, or help. But I wasn't going to mention the boy yet. Particularly not after I'd just felt I'd seen a ghost.

'I think people may be hiding down here. It's part of my job to find out,' I said.

'You think the guys in the cinema are living here?' Travis whistled. 'I thought they were just men from Alliance. Who the hell are they, then?'

'I have no idea. But it's possible they could be from another base like Esperanza, or Villa Las Estrellas. Argentinians or Chileans on orders to set this place up for my benefit, to make it more likely I recommend it be opened as a museum.' Even as I formed the words, my mind butted up against the possibility. They wouldn't need to stay here if they'd already set it up. It made no sense. I was clutching at straws because of the boy.

'Unless,' I said slowly, 'Connaught's conducting some experiment at Fredelighavn and they have no intention of stopping just because I'm here.' I stared at the roofline, dashing my torch around, searching for cameras. 'Did you get that if you're listening?' I called loudly.

'Yeah, of course I'm listening,' said Travis.

'I didn't mean you. Or Kate,' I added quickly.

'What, you think Connaught's got this place under surveillance?' asked Travis. I shone my torch over to him and his face was full of alarm. 'I'm in deep trouble if he has,' he said, his panic quickly turning to hurt and suspicion. 'You know I'm not meant to be here. Why didn't you warn me? What else aren't you telling me, Laura?'

I cringed. 'I don't know for sure. It's just one theory.'

'What are your others?' asked Kate stonily.

'Nothing I'm clear enough to talk about, yet.'

Travis leaned against a wall. 'I need a cigarette.'

'Well, you can't unless you brought your own.' I hauled the mattresses back into the corner and took photos of them.

'Oh come on, just one packet, please?' pleaded Travis. 'If Connaught's watching I'm in for it anyway.'

'No,' I replied seriously. 'The EIA prohibits anything being touched.'

'Kate played that record.'

'And put it back just the way I found it. That was research.' She walked up to him. 'Travis, do you think Laura's right? You've been at Alliance for a year. Does it seem possible that there's an experiment going on down here?'

Travis was silent for a moment, frowning. 'If there is, they don't come often. I'd know from the Häggies' mileage.'

'Unless they adjust it. That would be possible, wouldn't it?'

'Not really. Tampering with the speedometer? Unlikely. Anyway, if this place is bugged or on film or whatever, why are we talking?'

He marched out. Kate and I followed and I drew Travis close. 'There may be cameras in the streets too,' I whispered. He pulled away and shook his head.

'You're not straightforward, are you?'

'Sorry,' I said, and meant it.

'Where next?' said Kate.

'Let's go shed by shed.' I started to walk off down the street towards the harbour, until I heard Travis call after me.

'I need to eat!'

Kate glanced at her watch and did a double-take. 'It's seven o'clock!'

'No wonder I'm starving. You girls are slave drivers,' said Travis. 'Let's go into a house with some decent furniture.' He strode off.

'Which one?' asked Kate. Travis turned up another street and stopped outside the russet house with the whitewashed furniture inside. Where we'd found the dead penguin in the cupboard.

'This one's my favourite. I could live here,' he said.

Kate glanced at me.

'So you've been in?' I asked evenly.

'Yeah. Absolutely. It's beautiful. Have you not been? Wait and see.'

He bounded up the stairs and swung open the door. Kate came close to me. 'I know,' I whispered, 'but why would he lead us here if he'd killed the penguin and left it? It wouldn't make sense.'

'Just strange that of all houses . . .'

'Travis,' I called, 'wait up.' But he was already far down the passage. By the time we got in, he was sitting at the kitchen table, his food unwrapped in front of him. 'What's wrong?' he asked as he bit into a thick biscuit layered with cheese.

'This is where we found the dead penguin,' I said, and he stopped chewing.

'We laid her out on this table,' said Kate, and Travis stood abruptly.

'Don't worry, she died of natural causes,' I said.

'Are you sure?' asked Travis, placing his biscuit down on the table, pushing it away.

'Do you promise me you didn't have anything to do with that penguin?' I asked.

Travis frowned, indignant. 'Of course not! As if I'd come here if I did. And I certainly wouldn't be eating in the kitchen.'

'If it was natural causes that killed the Adélie, what's your problem?' said Kate.

Travis looked sheepish.

'Travis?' I tensed – he *did* know something.

'Just . . .' He stopped. 'Could we visit the rookery? Come on.'

I frowned and followed; Travis was afraid of the rookery. Was he more afraid that Connaught had bugged the houses and was listening in?

Kate and I crunched through the ice on either side of him and none of us spoke.

At the rookery the penguins were screeching happily, hundreds of thousands of pairs stretching as far away as the eye could see. Mutualling, white chests pushed together, beaks to the sun, tiny black wings flapping. New arrivals kept pouring in, waddling up the rocky hillside to join the throng, while others streamed down towards the sea, tobogganing on their bellies once they reached the ice.

We didn't go into the rookery, but we stood nearby. In the ear-shattering racket we could barely hear Travis. He'd chosen the perfect spot.

'I didn't want to say back there,' he shouted above the din, 'but you've got me worried about whether there *are* experiments down here, or one experiment, or whatever.'

'Why do you say that?' I shouted back.

'The Häggies. You're right, they could adjust the speedometers. But they mightn't even need to. Where they say they're going and where they end up – I wouldn't really know. And they could easily wipe any digital record they want.'

'So they could come here all the time?'

Travis nodded. 'Connaught could be supervising anything. And I'm as suspicious about that penguin as you are.'

'Wouldn't we see tracks, though?'

Travis paused. 'Not if they're living here. Living here since you arrived so they wouldn't have to drive down and risk the ice revealing that a Häggie's been. And most of the time the ice is too hard to leave footprints.'

I shivered. It would make sense of a lot of things.

'But where do you think they are?'

'There are so many sheds and houses. They could be anywhere. Can't I stay with you? I don't think it's safe on your own.'

'No, you have to go. They won't do anything to us.'

'How can you be so sure?' he asked worriedly.

'Because they'd have the wrath of my Station Leader, and I can't see how that would help their cause.'

'Not if they made it look like an accident.'

I glanced at Kate, who had turned ashen.

'Remember the penguin,' I said to her above the Adélie din. 'You want to find out what happened.'

'I'd like Travis to stay,' she replied.

'That would defeat the whole plan.'

We went around in circles until our throats were hoarse from shouting. Finally, we were all so cold and exhausted, I won.

We went back into the village and searched through houses until the sun flared the horizon a blazing orange and the air thickened to a deep blue. There was nothing different to what we'd already seen: some houses were fully furnished, others partially. Many kitchens held supplies, but others didn't.

'Maybe not everyone thought they were coming back,' I said, as we found another completely empty house. 'Perhaps some had moved out, and others were going to arrive in the next season.' The more I thought about it, when people had a holiday home, they probably left it somewhat like some of these houses through the winter until they returned in summer. It reassured me that Fredelighavn mightn't be as odd as I'd first thought. The decision to stop whaling could have been made by the Norwegian company between seasons and those expecting to return hadn't been able to come back to collect their belongings. It was completely logical.

As the twilight turned a thicker indigo, stopping clear visibility between the dark spaces of the houses, we all climbed into the Hägglunds. Birds – skuas and albatross – could be seen flapping across the sky, but the streets were shadowy. As soon as Travis fired up the engine, Kate and I hopped out and ran quickly towards the purple house, carrying our bags of supplies. The Hägglunds roared off, lights blazing. Hopefully if anyone was watching, they'd think we'd all left for the night.

As we entered the purple house, it was pitch black and freezing.

'It's much darker on the inside,' hissed Kate. 'I don't like this at all.'

'Sh,' I said, closing the door and feeling my way, running my hand along the icy passage wall.

'I still think we should have come earlier to check it out. We don't know what's in here,' whispered Kate fearfully.

'If they've been watching, they know we've never been in this house, so they won't suspect us here now,' I said.

'Because it's so completely illogical and dangerous to be doing what we're doing.'

'Exactly,' I said, putting a hand on Kate's shoulder. She yelped.

'Sh!' I hissed.

'Don't do that again,' she said. 'You'll send me straight to my grave.'

I was wondering if the house was furnished. We couldn't risk shining a torch anywhere. I touched a door and it creaked loudly. Kate groaned. I took her hand. 'It's okay, we're the only ones here.'

'And if they've got a camera inside they'll hear us even if they can't see us,' said Kate.

'I know. I'm just hoping they haven't.'

I knew my plan was full of holes but it was the best one I'd come up with. Up ahead was a doorway into the kitchen, and I could just make out the dark shadows of a long table with chairs around it.

'Perfect.' We sat down and Kate pulled her chair close to mine.

'Can we sit around the other side?' she said. 'If someone comes in, they're likely to come through the front door.'

'I don't know about that.'

'Well, that makes me feel a whole lot better. Not.' Kate moved to sit at the head of the table so she had a view of both front and back.

'Good idea,' I said as we slipped into our sleeping bags for warmth. I broke open the food, handing Kate chocolate and biscuits slathered with thick butter and jam for energy, and a bottle of water.

She pulled out a hipflask and took a deep swig. 'That's better,' she sighed, holding out the flask to me. I took a small sip, and brandy shot heat through my body. I took another, bigger gulp.

'Steady on.' Kate snatched back the flask. 'That needs to last all night. Unless you brought one too?' 'I have whisky.'

She chuckled. 'Knew there must be a reason we're friends.'

We chomped in companionable silence. After half an hour it was time to venture out.

'Ready?' I said.

'No,' said Kate. 'But do I have a choice?'

'You could stay here. I'll come back.'

'You've got to be joking. Do *not* leave me alone at any time, Alvarado, is that clear?'

'Promise.' I took her hand and squeezed it. I shouldered my bag, which still held the rusty knife, and kept my camera out as we headed into the thick twilight. In just over an hour it would be daylight again, but for now the houses, deep shadows in the gloom, creaked and groaned in the cold. The day had been warm and now it was well below freezing. The timber was adjusting. I kept my mind ticking over logically. I hadn't imagined how terrifying it would be out here, in the middle of nowhere, suspecting that men might be hiding nearby. Or not hiding. Going about their business.

Men who would be unhappy to meet up with us.

But my plan was to witness, not to interact.

We went slowly over the ice, careful to make as little noise as possible. Kate's breathing was raw with nerves. I wished she could be quieter.

At the House of the Carvers we turned right, heading towards the large houses on the rise near the Adélie rookery. In the dark, everything felt different. I was glad I knew my way around as well as I did.

Kate took my hand and clung tightly. I pulled her on. She was shaking, but now was not the time to feel guilty for bringing her.

We turned up the icy street towards our goal, and I stopped in shock. Kate gasped. Up ahead, light was blazing through the windows of the huge orange house. Heart thumping in my chest, I approached and moved down the side nearest to us. Kate followed, breathing hard. Outside the first window, we crouched down. I indicated for Kate to stay where she was, and then slowly, so slowly my limbs ached from the cold and strain, I rose to peer in.

There was no one in the room. The portrait of Ingerline stared from the wall, eyes flickering in the light. I was unable to see the source but guessed it was a kerosene lantern. The sofas were empty. I waited, hoping someone would enter. I took photographs, turning the camera in all directions in case it captured something I couldn't see. No one came in.

Taking Kate's hand, I moved towards the warm glow in the kitchen at the back of the house. I rose up and looked in, anticipation building. But again it was empty. Two candles sat burning on the kitchen table. A chill ran up my spine. Someone had lit them. Someone was here. The shrill creak of the front door made me duck down. Footsteps crunched out onto the ice, heading towards us. A beam of light from a torch played in front of a large, thickset man. Was it the same man I'd seen on my first day here in the blubber cookery? This one seemed taller. As he came closer, Kate rose like a shadow and fled. I was tempted to wait, to confront the man. I could hear Kate running away. In a split second it would be too late for me to leave, he'd be too close. I pointed my camera and snapped off several shots as I stood, then I ran as fast as I'd ever gone, my boots slipping and sliding over the ice as I cursed myself that I hadn't stayed. But every instinct in my body was telling me to get away.

I saw Kate disappear into the purple house and I followed. It was already getting lighter. We ran to the kitchen and hid under the table, behind chair legs. I looked at my watch. Travis was due in ten minutes. Would that be soon enough? My ears were attuned to the slightest sound. I found the knife in my bag and gripped it. The wind was strengthening and the house was groaning and wheezing in a full vocabulary of unearthly howls. I waited, terrified, for the creak of the front door opening. After what seemed like an eternity but must have been minutes, the roar of the Hägglunds sprang out of the dawn, growing louder. We raced out, jumping in before Travis had stopped.

'Drive!' I cried and he turned the large cabin around and accelerated away.

'What the hell happened?' he asked, horrified. 'I knew I should have stayed.'

'Someone's here,' I said.

'And they knew we were,' said Kate. 'They knew *exactly* where we were.'

'But they didn't follow us,' I said. 'Maybe they didn't know for sure. Perhaps they just sensed something.' I wasn't even convincing myself. Did they have thermal imaging? Deep down I knew Kate was right – they seemed to have known precisely where we were when we crouched outside their house.

11

I looked at the images on my camera as Travis took us back to Alliance. The torchlight pierced the darkness, and behind was the unmistakable figure of a thickset man; he was shrouded in black and could have been anyone. There were no features visible at all. My flesh crawled, but at least I had incontrovertible evidence that someone was down there, unauthorised. It was a breakthrough. Adrenalin surged.

'Stop,' I said. 'I want to go back.'

'No way,' said Kate.

'With Travis we'll be okay. Won't we?' I looked at him.

'Are you sure?' he replied. 'We don't know who that was.'

'Are you saying you won't do it?'

He slammed on the brakes and turned around, roaring the Hägglunds back towards Fredelighavn.

I smiled. He said nothing. Kate gazed furiously out the window.

As the village came into view, the sun was already fully in the sky. It was another beautiful day.

'Just for the record, I think you're mad,' said Kate as Travis parked by the purple house. 'And we could all be killed.'

'Don't be so dramatic,' I replied, hopping out. I marched off, slinging my bag over my shoulder. Having silenced my initial fear, I wanted nothing more than to come face to face with whoever was down here. I was the controlling person at Fredelighavn. They were accountable to me. I was, however, more than grateful to have Travis walking briskly at my side.

When we reached the orange house I looked down the side and at the front. The ice was hard; there were no footprints. I raced up the stairs to the front door and barged in. Travis was so close behind I could feel his hot breath on my neck.

The lounge room was empty. Ingerline stared down from the wall; the sea captain scowled from his portrait.

The two bedrooms on the ground floor were empty. We arrived in the kitchen. There was no one there, and the candles had been taken.

'We're here!' I yelled angrily.

Silence.

Travis leaned against the table and Kate settled in the far corner of the room. 'We're alone,' she said.

'*Now*,' I replied furiously. 'They were here and they've gone.' I strode down the passage and went up the stairs at the front of the house, two at a time.

In the first bedroom, I hurled off the bedclothes. The sheets smelled freshly laundered, but there was no indent, nothing to indicate anyone had lain there recently.

In the master bedroom at the end of the passage I tore off the pink eiderdown and top sheet – and stopped. Between the bed linen, a small brown T-shirt lay stranded. Left behind. And on it was a logo for Stands, a popular sports product. A brand that only started in the last decade.

Travis whistled. Kate grabbed it and looked at me.

'Hey, you're not to touch anything!' said Travis. 'Someone really *has* been here. Sleeping here.'

There was no indent in the bed, but they could have straightened the sheets. Goosebumps pricked my arms. If a boy had been here, then it was possible he'd been in the ice cave too. As I took the T-shirt from Kate and put it back where it had been found, I could see she was thinking the same thing. The T-shirt was too small and narrow for a man, and too large for a child. I photographed it from every angle, and then picked it up myself. Holding it in the air, I could see that it was the size of the boy I'd seen. Suddenly my knees were wobbly and I sat down on the bed. If the boy had been here recently, then hopefully he was all right. If he'd rested in this bed just hours before, at least he wasn't trapped in a cavern in the ice cave. Lifting the T-shirt to my nose, I smelled a faint, sharp odour of sweat. Recent sweat. My heart was beating so hard it pounded in my ears. I looked at the label: *Made in USA*.

But what was the boy doing here? The man who'd come at us was tall and thickset. Was that his father?

I wanted to discuss it immediately with Kate, but would that be wise in front of Travis? There was a strong possibility that the boy in the cave was real, but my instincts warned me not to talk about it just yet. I glanced up at Kate, relieved she wasn't mentioning him either. The scientist in me was already processing the idea that there could be more than one youth down here, as unlikely as that seemed.

A teenage boy had been in this room, that much was certain. The sweat was fresh. The clothing brand was not available until this decade. They were the facts. The screaming face of the boy in the cave burned in my brain.

I pulled a clean plastic bag from my backpack and placed the T-shirt into it.

'Are you taking that?' asked Travis, confused.

'This is modern. It's evidence someone's here,' I said.

We went downstairs and looked around the house again but found nothing more.

I was exhausted but I was determined to go through every house in Fredelighavn; I would find whoever was here. I was about to share my plan with Travis and Kate when a static crackle made me start. Travis took out his satellite radio and Moose's voice rang out. 'Hey, man, where are you?' Travis reacted, alarmed, but before he could talk Moose continued, 'Everyone has to report for duty. Don't know why yet. Gotta go.'

Travis, clearly concerned, turned back to us. 'Sorry, guys. You heard Moose.'

'I'm staying,' I said.

'Under no circumstances, absolutely no way. Even if we have to carry you out,' said Kate. 'We need sleep. We need to think about what to do. We could walk straight into real trouble. Georgia needs to know.'

'There's no way anyone's staying here without the means to get back,' said Travis. 'I have to take the Häggie, so you've got no choice, Laura. We're all leaving together.'

'Since when do you order me around?'

'Not an order. Standard protocol. You can't be left in the field without transport.'

'Please, Laura?' Kate tugged my elbow.

'We can come back soon. I promise,' said Travis. 'Now I really have to go.' He walked off. Kate gripped me and pulled. I felt like a stubborn mule as I planted my feet.

'Come on, Laura. I don't want to stay here any more.'

'I can be on my own.'

'Don't do this,' said Kate. Travis came back, his face flushed.

'I've helped you,' he said. 'Now return the favour. I have to be at base. You don't want to blow this whole thing out of the water, do you? If Connaught gets wind you had me here, it won't be good for any of us.' My little brother made a potent argument; I hated losing family fights.

As Alliance appeared on the horizon, it was immediately apparent that something was different. Skidoos were roaring around like stung bees, speeding in and out of base. As we drove up to the Mechanics' Shed, there was a hum in the air.

'What on earth's going on?' said Kate. 'It's like the whole place just had an adrenalin shot.'

170

I sat mutely, fearful it was something to do with us and our presence last night at Fredelighavn. Beside me, Travis was as tense as a clenched fist.

'What is it?' I asked. 'What's wrong?'

'He's here,' said Travis. 'Much earlier than usual.'

'Who?'

'Our Chief Scientist.' Travis stopped.

'Does he have a name?'

'Andrew. Or Snow. His nickname's Snow.'

'And a surname?' This business of first-names-only had run its course with me.

'Sorry,' said Travis apologetically.

'Come on, you're one of us now.'

He sighed. 'It's for your own benefit. You might slip if I told you. I'm not allowed.'

'You weren't allowed down at Fredelighavn,' I pointed out helpfully.

Beads of perspiration sprouted above Travis's upper lip. 'Truly, it's better you don't know.'

'And how's that?' said Kate. 'Honestly, Travis, don't go playing games with us now.'

'I can't, I'm sorry,' he said firmly, parking the Hägglunds and jumping out. 'See you later.'

'Well, your boyfriend's had a change of heart,' said Kate, gathering our gear.

'He's not my boyfriend, but he's frightened of something.' Whoever this new arrival was, Travis was far more terrified of him than he was of Connaught. And he hadn't expected whoever it was to be here. What did that mean?

Kate and I trudged through the ice back to our room. Moose ran past us towards the Mechanics' Shed, but didn't say hello.

'That T-shirt,' said Kate. 'You think it's the boy's, don't you?'

'Don't *you*?'

'I didn't see him.'

'It's the right size.' My shoulders tensed. 'I think he was real.' I could barely believe it.

Kate frowned. 'So you think they've got a chamber into the ice?'

'They must have. But how will we find it?'

'I don't get it,' Kate said, perplexed. 'We searched in that cave for a long time and couldn't see anything. How could a chamber appear and disappear like that?'

'The light?' Truth was, I couldn't work it out myself, no matter how hard I tried. 'It's possible it was an optical illusion. Just the other way around from what we thought: the boy was real, and not seeing the chamber afterwards could have been a trick of the light. It was a wall of thick ice that he was behind.'

'Maybe. I guess,' said Kate, unconvinced.

As soon as we were in our room I tried to Skype Georgia but it was early and she didn't respond, so I phoned her instead. After three tries she finally picked up, groggy with sleep. I explained what had happened, including seeing the boy in the ice cave.

'Why haven't you told me about the boy before?' said Georgia, voice rising in frustration. 'I wanted to know *everything*. What else have you kept from me?'

'That's it.' I wasn't going to tell anyone about the ghost of Ingerline, not that I believed it was a ghost anyway. 'I'm sorry,

Georgia, but I thought he must have been an hallucination. We couldn't find any trace of the boy after I'd seen him in the ice. I thought I was just getting toasty; imagining things, you know what it's like.'

'I do.' She sounded concerned. 'Okay, you're off the hook with that.' She paused, thinking. 'I'll need to speak to Connaught. If he denies their presence down there, then I'll have to come over. Because it could be anyone. And I don't want you two on your own any more.'

My body went limp with relief. Georgia was an experienced detective. With her help, we'd surely unravel what was going on. 'You're not to go back to Fredelighavn until I'm with you or have given you permission,' she said. 'Is that clear?'

As she hung up, my mind was full of the boy. Was he really all right now? I couldn't get his distressed face out of my thoughts. He'd been calling for help. A boy shouldn't be down there. He was no older than twelve, thirteen at most. My chest tightened. What if the man last night wasn't his father? What was he doing with the boy? I needed to get back to Fredelighavn as soon as possible.

I was exhausted, but also curious to find out more about the arrival of Andrew – or Snow. At Antarctic bases nicknames were common, but no one used a nickname for Connaught. This made Andrew–Snow intriguing. At one level there was less formality – and yet Travis and Moose seemed terrified of him. He'd certainly swung the base into action.

Kate emerged from the bathroom, wet hair hanging around her face, steam following her. 'What did Georgia say?'

'Hopefully she'll come over.'

Kate flopped on the bed. 'That is the best news I've heard in a very long time. Does that mean I can go back to my penguins?'

'We'll see,' I said, feeling like my mother. *We'll see.* The standard response that meant no without saying it. Kate closed her eyes and fell instantly asleep.

I turned up the heating, worried that she should have dried her hair. Then I crept out.

People were in the mess hall, hurriedly gulping down breakfast. Snow seemed to have the whole base in his grip.

'So who is this bloke anyway?' I asked Guy as he poured more porridge into the bain-marie at the servery.

'The professor oversees the research down here,' he replied, lowering his voice and looking around.

'I thought that was Connaught.'

'Nah. He's just an administrator. Snow's the man. And he likes to run a tight ship, so watch yourself.' Guy gave a feeble smile and hurried back into the kitchen.

I took my porridge and sat at an empty table. I'd given up trying to make friends with the ghastly scientists and there was no one I knew in the room anyway. I hooked out my phone and started to look through emails from friends back in Australia, replying as I went. Bending the truth, pretending I was having a great time down here. I attached a few cute photos of penguins. The internet age. Easy lies. I found a breathless message from my mother, saying how lonely she was and complaining about changes at her university. I scrolled through quickly – if she was lonely that was her fault, and if the university wanted to push her out, I was with them. She'd stayed too long; younger people needed jobs. But I slowed to read how she was lobbying her local member of parliament to pressure the Prime Minister to take more refugees. She'd attached images of desperate families in overcrowded boats braving the Mediterranean Sea, heading to Italy. I was pondering how many to open, reluctant to fill my head with confronting pictures of people I couldn't help, who I felt concerned for. It was so typical of Mum, pushing more troubles onto me when I was struggling to cope with my own. And never asking me about my life. I heard a chair scrape out. Looking up, a tall man in his mid-fifties, blazing blue eyes, hair greying at the temples but still mainly blond, sat down. He was tanned, youthful and fit, like an athlete. He wore a white T-shirt and his muscles bulged neatly. A fizz rippled through me. He was just my type. I hadn't seen him before. I warned myself to steady on, as the far-too-familiar attraction to a good-looking man bubbled up. I had to perpetually re-learn to take my feelings more slowly.

'Hi,' he said in a cultured American accent, his voice deep and resonant as he reached over the table. His grip was strong and straightforward as we shook hands. 'I'm Snow.'

I struggled to contain my surprise. That this man, with his congenial smile and easy manner had sent the base into a frenzy didn't add up. He seemed laidback, curious, attentive – and nice. Had I misheard?

'I'm Laura,' I said. 'And you are?'

'Snow. Well, Andrew, but everyone calls me Snow on account of that's my middle name. My mother was having an English phase. Andrew Snowden Flynt. Snowden for Lord Snowden, though goodness knows why. Never could get any sense out of her on that.' He laughed a full, wholesome roar. I thought he

175

might lean over and slap me on the back. But here was a surname at last. Professor Andrew Flynt.

'I hear you're down doing an EIA on the abandoned whaling station. How's it going?'

'Pretty well,' I replied.

'Are you going to open it up?' he asked curiously.

'I can't tell you that, and it's not up to me anyway.'

'I guess not. Still, I'm sure your opinion counts for a lot. I looked you up before I came. Your research on whales and penguins is impressive.' He leaned forward, as though about to exchange a confidence. I could smell his aftershave; it was fruity and exotic.

'I would have loved to be a marine biologist,' he said. 'But it wasn't the way my mind worked.'

'So, what's your area?' I was surprised he'd given me an opening.

'Clinical research. Viruses.'

'Down here?'

'Yeah, down here.'

'What in?'

'You know I can't tell you that, Laura.' He grinned, his blue eyes twinkling.

'At other bases they're usually more than keen to share their research,' I said.

He winked. 'You might get lucky.' He stood. 'Hope to see you round, Laura. Good talking to you.'

As he sauntered off, I found myself blushing. People were looking at me. I'd just spoken with God.

Snow shrugged on a thick coat and opened the door. A blast of freezing air rushed in. The sun was blazing outside, and for a moment he was silhouetted. My blood ran cold. He was exactly the same shape as the man last night. I tried to think clearly: could he have been down there all this time? Had he arrived today by air, as I'd assumed, or had he come up from Fredelighavn?

I hurried out of the mess hall and back to my room, where I phoned Georgia to tell her my fears, my hands shaking uncontrollably.

'I'll be there tonight,' she said.

My body tingled hot and cold. I was desperately in need of sleep. I changed into my pyjamas and lay down beside Kate, who was snoring peacefully. But my mind wouldn't switch off. I tried to visualise the person I'd seen last night. He was tall and thickset – but the thickness could have come from his coat.

I hauled myself out of bed and opened my laptop, studying the photographs of the man with the torch, enlarging them until they disintegrated into digital noise.

There was just no way of telling if this man and Snow were the same person.

I closed my eyes and tried to remember everything from last night. Had the man had a smell? Was he wearing aftershave?

I could remember Snow's aftershave – fresh and strong, with the promise of mysterious lands. Moroccan perhaps. Or somewhere from the Middle East. It spoke of the Silk Road. But it wasn't cloying. It was exotic but enticing.

No scent had drifted through the air from the man last night.

I looked up Professor Andrew Snowden Flynt online, my fingers flying over the keyboard. He was at Harvard and held more science awards than anyone I'd ever known. The only one he seemed not to have garnered was a Nobel Prize. Was that what he was chasing down here?

An eminent virologist, he was playing a significant role in developing a cost-effective treatment for the Ebola virus, the African monster that killed over half the people it infected through haemorrhagic bleeding and massive organ failure. I shuddered. Surely they weren't testing such a deadly virus in the pristine environment of Antarctica?

There were hundreds of papers in leading scientific journals that outlined Snow's work. I glanced through a few and was intrigued to see that there were certain areas of overlap with my father. Could they know each other? They would certainly be aware of each other's research, and it was even conceivable they'd met at a conference somewhere.

Snow's main area of work at the moment seemed to be investigating a gene that exhibited qualities in an extraordinarily complex mathematical sequence, that was so robust and different to any other known gene that he and his team had named it *Superstar*. The research was sophisticated and specialised and I struggled to understand it. They seemed to be searching for other Superstars that had similar properties.

I read page after page of dense material: Snow was brilliant, top of his field. I began to understand why he could be so approachable. Just his presence would inspire loyalty and respect. The base had swung into action not because they feared him, but because they were in awe of his work. They probably all wanted to prove themselves to him.

I'd come across it before at my own university. The professors who were world standard were always kinder and more helpful than those struggling to make their name, or those whose best days were behind them. I swatted back the memory of the professors I'd blown the whistle on: little men who had never achieved anything of substance. Fabricating results because they weren't up to working the long hours and delving into material that would allow them to make real discoveries. Men who weren't brilliant.

I was eager to spend more time with Snow. And then I remembered his silhouette in the mess-hall doorway – how much he looked like the man at Fredelighavn. But Snow was an esteemed international scholar. I couldn't imagine him hiding out at an abandoned whaling station.

I stood stiffly – I'd been online for hours. I went to my backpack and took out the brown T-shirt. I held it up and pictured the boy in the cave. Had he been wearing it? Try as I might, I couldn't conjure the image of what he'd had on: there had been too many reflections through the white–blue ice.

I smelled the bitter sweat on the T-shirt again. Could the boy be part of an experiment? Personnel at Alliance had a habit of thumbing their nose at the law, but human testing was well beyond the boundaries even for them. And Snow would be bound by strict ethics – a top scientist like him wouldn't be compromised. Especially if he was after the Nobel Prize.

I put the T-shirt carefully away, went into the bathroom and washed my hands. I couldn't stop. I used all the liquid soap in the bottle until my hands were red and raw. I knew I had to sleep, otherwise paranoia would truly set in. It was ridiculous to think the boy would be part of an experiment. It was far more likely he had nothing to do with Snow and that the man I'd seen at Fredelighavn was intent on setting up the abandoned whaling station to make it attractive as a tourist destination.

I lay down on the bed, promising myself that Georgia would be here later, and everything would change.

12

Propellers roared overhead. Kate sat up blearily. I jumped out of bed and looked out the window to where a Twin Otter plane with skis beneath its wheels was descending on the outskirts of Alliance.

'Let's hope it's Georgia.' Excitement bubbled through me as I flung on my jeans and jumper. Kate leaped up, throwing on clothes, brushing her flaming red hair so that it shone like silk, and applying lipstick.

'I want to look my very best when I ask to go home to my penguins,' she said.

'What about the penguins here? I thought you wanted to protect them.'

'They'll be in safe hands with you and Georgia. And with whatever's going on – she'll be so much better at dealing with it than me.' Kate blushed. 'Sorry, Laura, but I'm not cut out for this. I'm an ornithologist. Now you'll have a real detective.'

'I would have liked a real friend as well.' I moved to hug her. 'I didn't mean to drag you into all of this.'

'I know. Anyway, Georgia's a mate too, isn't she?'

'Not like you.' I wanted all three of us here. My only hope was Georgia would say no to her leaving. I knew I would. Even if I was being objective, which of course I couldn't be.

'Okay, enough emotion, you dag,' said Kate. 'Let's go and meet her.'

We put on coats, scarves, gloves and dark glasses and crunched through the ice. It was 9pm but the sun was still blazing. In the distance, the mountains glinted an icy blue. There was not a breath of wind.

'I hope we can go down to Fredelighavn tonight,' I said and Kate groaned.

'Not with me, babe.'

'Well, maybe just Georgia and me. I guess Travis will be too busy.'

The plane was a red blotch in the ice. Its occupants had already disembarked and were walking towards us: tall, Australian Simon – the good pilot; Stan, his co-pilot, who I recognised from the mess hall; and a fair-haired man about six feet tall who strode purposefully along. There was no sign of Georgia.

'Laura, here's your partner,' called Simon and I could see from the other man's features that this was the colleague I'd been waiting for: Rutger Koch. He had thick, healthy fair hair, with a fringe that dropped over one eye that he kept brushing away. When he smiled he revealed straight white teeth. His skin had no blemishes, and he was fit and well-toned. He was about my age but appeared younger. He was far better looking in real life than he'd been in his photograph.

Kate visibly melted as I introduced him to her. Here was her saviour. Now she would be allowed to go home.

'Georgia's not with you?' I asked. Rutger looked confused.

'I'll be picking her up tomorrow,' said Simon. 'There's a Dash 7 from McMurdo, stops at Rothera. That's where she'll spend tonight. We've done our flights today – Professor Koch slipped in courtesy of the Argentines, so we diverted to Esperanza to pick him up. We can't take off again now without ten hours on the ground, and our offsider Reg is busy on other assignments. Not that you'd want him to fly anyone you care for.' Simon winked and grinned. 'We're off. Can you bring Professor Koch up to speed?' He shook Rutger's hand and hurried off after his co-pilot. Kate and I helped my new partner with his luggage and we traipsed across the ice towards the main street of base.

'Laura, did you get my message that I was arriving?' asked Rutger in perfect English, with just a hint of German accent. 'You seem surprised.'

'No. Did you email?' I was sure I'd checked all emails and texts every day.

'I let Professor Connaught know and I thought he'd pass it on.'

'Well, that'd explain it,' said Kate. 'Connaught would have delighted in not passing it on.'

'I see,' said Koch, a little coldly. I was reminded how much men stick together.

'How are you feeling?' I asked. 'All well from the operation?'

'Operations,' he corrected. 'Yes, thank you. I don't ever want to see a South American hospital again. I hope they got all the instruments out and didn't leave some behind,' he finished dourly.

'Gallstones can cause trouble once they play up, I've heard,' I said.

'Hmm. So where shall I be sleeping?'

'You can have my room,' said Kate. 'Well, it was actually your room in the first place. I'll just clear a couple of things out. I haven't been in there much.'

Rutger nodded and strode ahead, staring at the Alliance buildings, taking them in. They gleamed in the light, reflecting the mountains.

'It's very beautiful,' he said approvingly.

Kate pulled me close. 'I've left the bathroom in a pigsty. Take him for a drink or something. I'll need time.'

I suggested to Rutger I show him the mess hall. 'Let's eat while Kate gets your room ready.'

'If we must,' said Rutger.

I had the feeling he wasn't going to be a barrel of fun.

The dining room was buzzing, men talking loudly in a dull roar. I looked around for Snow but couldn't see him. Connaught sat at his usual table, so I took Rutger up and introduced him. Connaught stood and shook his hand.

'Very pleased to meet you, Rutger,' he said warmly and then introduced Rutger to the other scientists at the table. Still first names only, but the tone was genial – and Connaught and Rutger seemed almost familiar.

It made me sick; the world of men at Alliance. I left them bonding and went to get food. Travis called me over as I walked past.

'Keeping your seat warm, Laura,' he smiled. 'Who's your friend?'

'Professor Rutger Koch has finally arrived.'

'That so?' Travis looked crestfallen. He lowered his voice. 'I guess that means you won't need me at Fredelighavn any more.'

'My Station Leader Georgia's arriving too. So there'll be a bit of a gang.' I felt a pang of sadness that Travis probably wouldn't be coming again.

'You better get some food before it's all gone,' he said. 'Everyone's working so hard they're eating like maniacs.'

I went across and filled my plate with the usual colourless roast and gravy. I sat back with Travis, and Moose joined us. I ate rapidly, hungrily.

'You know, this is the worst food I've had in Antarctica,' I said as I finished the plate, wiping bread around the gravy.

'It's all I've known down here,' laughed Travis. 'I thought that's the way it was.'

'Wish it would stop me eating it,' said Moose, knocking back a beer. 'I've never been so fat in my life.'

Kate joined us and ploughed into her food like she hadn't eaten in years. After a few minutes I caught Travis staring at me. I looked at him directly, and barely perceptibly he cocked his head, indicating for me to leave with him. 'See you back in the room,' I said to Kate, and bid Moose goodnight. Both were so busy eating and drinking they just mumbled.

In the icy street, a thin blue twilight was starting to fall. Travis walked so close our shoulders were touching.

'Now Snow's here a lot will be different. Everyone will be working shifts, the base will run twenty-four hours a day.'

'Why?' I said. 'Why's it so different?'

'It's always been that way since I've been here, and word is since before that. And people either don't know why or won't say. We just ramp up to full capacity. He usually comes around December when the base would probably be doing that anyway. But this time he's early.'

'Travis, do you think he's got anything to do with the people at Fredelighavn?' I asked.

'Anything's possible down here. You know that. I wouldn't have thought there'd be a kid's T-shirt in a bed at Fredelighavn. A modern T-shirt.'

'That brand's been around a few years, so it doesn't actually mean someone was there yesterday. Well, someone that size.'

'But I know you think there was.' Travis held my eye.

I shrugged. 'Nothing's certain until we sight the person.'

'Laura, you seemed to almost expect that T-shirt. Like you already thought there was a boy down there. I saw the way you looked at it.'

'It could be a girl. Why do you say boy?' I tried to sound casual but I was immediately suspicious.

'I don't know.' He smiled. 'Just not that many girls down here.'

'Would you tell me everything you know, Travis?' I asked him slowly.

He was silent. The snow crunched underfoot. The air was freezing.

'Does that mean no?'

'Part of my job is confidential – I had to sign a National Secrets clause. There are certain things I can never tell you. I'd be sent to prison if I did.'

He stopped and looked at me intently. 'So, no. As much as I've got your back, I can't tell you everything I've seen down here.'

Was he trying to tell me something in code?

'Your Georgia,' he continued, still watching me carefully, 'she's a cop, right?'

'A detective,' I replied.

'Make sure she thinks of everything, like she would in any major investigation.' Travis leaned close, and for a moment we were both fixed to the ground, like a net had come down and trapped us. His blue eyes shone, he looked vulnerable, and I was reminded of how his father had abandoned him when he was young, like mine. Was that bringing us together? Or was it the bond of Antarctica, a place we both loved so deeply?

'Come and see me in my room if you need anything,' he said and strode off, turning at the first street, towards the Mechanics' Shed.

Travis had definitely been trying to say something but I had no idea what it was. My heart was racing. I needed to walk. At one level the base seemed inviting with so much activity in the streets. Skidoos were still zipping in and out. New faces had arrived, coming in from the field. The adrenalin rush was contagious.

As I walked past the main building I was drawn to the inner part that went down through the ice, glowing a deep blue. Again I found myself wondering: was it possible they'd dug underground channels to Fredelighavn? It *was* at least twenty kilometres away, which was why I'd initially dismissed it, but they'd been down here for years. And the Americans had built tunnels at the South Pole. With sophisticated machinery, perhaps it wasn't as unlikely as I'd first thought. And if there were tunnels, people could come and go unseen between Alliance and the old whaling station. Instinctively, I still thought the distance was too far. The temperature dropped. I shivered as I stood gazing at the building, wondering how I could get in.

I walked on, doing a lap of the base and taking in the frenetic energy before going back to the warmth of my room. Kate was already in bed, laptop computer propped against her knees, watching her Adélie colony through the camera we'd installed.

'I want to be rested for my Adélies,' she said.

'How are they?'

'Much better than the ones here.'

I felt a surge of anger, wondering who had put fear into the Fredelighavn penguins, as I stripped off my clothes and changed into my pyjamas. I tried to force myself to fall asleep quickly because I wanted to be fresh for the morning, but thoughts of Travis swept me up. What had he been trying to tell me?

My mind turned to Rutger, who seemed very tight with Connaught very quickly. Could they already know each other? I wasn't looking forward to working with him at all, and I knew I could never assume Rutger was on my team, which wasn't a good start.

*

At breakfast, looking out through the picture windows, we saw Georgia arrive: roaring up to the mess hall on a skidoo, her black hair flying. With dark goggles and a bright red jacket, she looked like a fiery superhero. Mine. She alighted and disappeared from sight.

Kate chuckled. 'Always one to make an entrance.'

The door opened and Georgia yelled across the room. 'Here you are! My girls!' I stood and she flew into my arms. Men at the tables around us stopped eating and stared. Georgia ignored them as she gave me a bone-crushing hug.

'It's so good to see you,' she said, letting go and hugging Kate. 'You've had me worried,' she added quietly.

'Where are your things?' I asked.

'Travis dropped them off so I could come straight here. I'll be sleeping in the same building as you. I'm starving.' She walked off to the servery and Kate and I followed like puppies.

'What are you doing?' she said and we laughed.

'We'll have more coffee,' said Kate.

Guy watched us curiously, and I introduced Georgia. He welcomed her and brought out a fresh container of porridge, even ladling it into her bowl.

'Rutger arrived yesterday,' I said, and Georgia turned.

'I had no idea. How is he?'

'Seems fine.'

'Why didn't you text me?'

'I'm sorry, I assumed you'd know.'

'Connaught should have said something,' she muttered. 'Where is he? And point out Rutger while you're at it. I'm surprised he didn't have the courtesy to tell me himself.'

I looked around and couldn't see them. 'Not here yet.'

Georgia checked her watch. 'Eight o'clock. Surely this is breakfast time?'

Back at our table, Georgia took out her phone and sent a text to Rutger. 'I'll get him over. Then I'll outline my strategy.'

'Are you going to tell Rutger everything?' I asked, alarmed.

'Why not?'

I shrugged. 'I had the sense last night that maybe he and Connaught know each other.'

Kate raised her eyebrows but didn't say anything.

'Well, we're going to need him to help us,' said Georgia. 'I'll go through the protocol with him first. Like you, he reports to the Antarctic Council, not to Connaught. But are you saying we shouldn't tell him about the boy?'

I nodded. 'It's just instinct . . .'

'Instincts are valuable,' said Georgia. 'Okay, we'll search through Fredelighavn in two teams. I'll be with you, Laura. Kate, you can be with Professor Koch.'

Kate's cheeks blazed and suddenly she looked thunderous.

'What's wrong?' said Georgia. 'Do you hate him that much? He only arrived yesterday.'

'I want to go back to my penguins. I thought that now you and Rutger had arrived . . .'

Georgia reached over and squeezed Kate's hand. 'Sorry, mate, we're going to need you here a bit longer. And just to bring you up to speed: Connaught's denied any knowledge of personnel down at the whaling station or anywhere near Placid Bay and Alliance Point. He said he'd never let anyone into an Exclusion Zone.'

'Except people diving and watching movies,' I said.

'Exactly,' said Georgia.

'Did you tell him about those things?' Had I got Travis into trouble? 'Did you mention names?'

'No, I didn't give him any detail other than to say there seemed to be activity down there and people had been sighted. I left it vague. Connaught said he had no idea what I was talking about. Put in an attack on you while he was at it. Said you should have reported it to him.'

'No I shouldn't, should I?'

'No,' said Georgia firmly. 'I pointed out you report solely to me.'

'Which he already knew,' said Kate.

'He seems to have it in for you though, Laura,' said Georgia.

'For no reason at all,' I replied.

'You sure?' Georgia gave me a piercing look. 'Seemed personal.'

'Absolutely not!' I said loudly, my body flaring with heat. If there was one thing I hated more than anything in the world, it was being accused of something I hadn't done. Over the years my mother and I had huge fights if she ever did that, and I wasn't happy to take it from Georgia.

'Okay, calm down,' said Georgia. 'Just had to check. I believe you, for what it's worth.' She grinned, her face lighting up, making it impossible for me to stay angry.

'I'm very glad you're here,' I said.

Kate slumped in her chair, chewing her bottom lip. Later, I'd hint to Georgia to let Kate return to her penguins, but now wasn't the moment.

Suddenly a blast of icy air entered the room as Connaught, Rutger and Snow walked in. Georgia stood. 'That's Connaught, isn't it? I recognise him from Skype but he's taller and thinner than I expected.'

'Yeah, that's him. The big guy's Snow, and the other one's Rutger,' I said.

'Good-looking bunch. Well, not Connaught but the others.' Georgia went over to greet them. The conversation seemed convivial, but Connaught's body language was stiff. Rutger appeared polite but cold, but maybe that's the way he always was with women.

Snow beamed and wrapped his hand around Georgia's, then brought his other hand to rest on top. He looked into her eyes, smiling and chatting. Men at surrounding tables watched – as they always did with Snow – and so did I.

'I can't believe I have to stay,' said Kate. 'And I certainly don't want to walk around Fredelighavn with Rutger. Can't you help me?'

'I'll try,' I said. 'But Georgia seems in a fairly intense mood.'

'Cops. I never trust them.'

'I thought you liked Georgia?' I said, turning to look at Kate.

'Not now she's trapped me here. Whoo, they're coming over.'

Moments later Snow was introducing himself to Kate, sending out his usual charm, chatting casually about her work.

'I'd really like to get back to my Adélie colony,' she said pointedly.

'In good time,' said Georgia. 'We'll be a lot faster now that there's four of us on the project.'

'So why did things change?' said Snow.

Georgia took a step back, surprised. 'Didn't Connaught tell you?'

'We're a little busy down here,' snipped Connaught, 'and the EIA at Fredelighavn has nothing to do with Alliance.'

It was an obvious lie and I could see he immediately regretted it. He would, of course, have told Snow.

'There are reports of people being in the whaling station,' said Georgia to Snow. 'As you know, that's illegal. I'm here on behalf of the Antarctic Council to supervise a complete search of the area. Professor Connaught's assured me it's nothing to do with Alliance personnel. So, our thought at the moment is that there's been a possible breach of protocol by Argentina or Chile or any other countries that have bases on the Antarctic Peninsula or nearby islands. I've checked with the Base Commander at Rothera – it's no one from there.' She smiled at Connaught. 'You Brits seem clean.' He gave a string-lipped smile in return.

'With the harbour accessible at this time of year someone could have come in by Zodiac,' continued Georgia, looking at Snow, appraising him. 'Don't worry, we'll get to the bottom of it. And when I can, I'll report back to you.'

'To Connaught,' said Snow, 'as Base Commander. It's an administrative issue. As Chief Scientist it's not my area, but I appreciate being kept in the loop.'

'Of course,' said Georgia. 'Okay, gang,' she turned to us. 'Let's go and organise our provisions while Rutger has his breakfast.' She swung back to Connaught. 'I'm assuming we can have a Hägglunds?'

'I'm terribly sorry, but no,' he said, clearing his throat. 'Full capacity, I'm afraid. I've authorised four skidoos.'

'Great,' said Georgia, sarcastically, and it was clear that Connaught realised he'd met his match.

Out in the street we walked in thoughtful silence, carrying our supplies to the Mechanics' Shed. A cold wind was blowing, making the day unpleasant. It was going to be uncomfortable on the skidoos.

'Change of plan,' said Georgia. 'It's not good weather for travelling, so I think we should camp down there rather than make the trip back tonight.'

'Please, no,' said Kate, 'I couldn't bear it. That place is scary, Georgia.'

'Safety in numbers,' she replied. 'Where do they keep the tents?'

13

Georgia hammered in the steel pegs with gusto, the sound echoing down the icy street as we set up camp near the purple house. I'd advised we stay as far away from the Adélie colony and harbour as possible, to have the least impact on the wildlife.

'So, Rutger,' said Georgia, 'how do you know Professor Connaught?'

Rutger stopped hammering, and blinked. Kate and I, busy on our own tent, turned. The silence was deafening.

'I, I . . .' Rutger stuttered, cheeks flushing a strange shade of pink. 'We worked together several years ago on a project.'

'And what was that?' asked Georgia. Rutger glanced my way, knowing he'd pretended only last night to meet Connaught for the first time.

'I'd forgotten, you know,' he said, smoothing over the cracks. 'He looked familiar and then it came back to me. It was a minor project, we had very little to do with each other. But when I started talking, after a while I thought, *I've met you.*' Rutger smiled, flashing his perfect teeth.

'I get that all the time with other cops,' said Georgia. 'When I was young I had a memory like a steel trap. But since having kids,' she rolled her eyes. 'Mind you, I blame my little monsters for everything.'

Rutger laughed and seemed relieved. Kate and I went back to hammering the tent pegs, and I wondered if it was coincidence that Rutger had been chosen for this project or if Connaught had influenced the Council. Either way, we would have to be careful with him.

Once our tents were secure, we headed into the village in our two teams. In the first stage, we would be documenting and numbering the buildings in grids, and looking for signs of entry by unauthorised personnel. Later, in a second, much longer stage, Rutger and I would go through every structure in greater detail.

I'd assigned Kate and Rutger the end of Placid Bay furthest away from the Adélie rookery. Georgia and I were going to the orange house, where I'd found the T-shirt and photographed the man. Georgia carried her fingerprinting kit in its aluminium case as she walked beside me.

As soon as I was away from Rutger I felt more relaxed. His energy was depressing; he was tense, cold and aloof – everything I hated. And then I felt guilty because Kate had no choice but to be with him.

Arriving at the orange house I showed Georgia where we had crouched outside by the windows. The ice was so hard, there was no sign we'd been. I flicked up my photo and Georgia studied it closely. The beam of torchlight, the silhouetted figure behind.

Inside, the rooms were still and empty. Georgia looked curiously at the portraits of Ingerline and her family staring down at us, then methodically dusted for fingerprints. She found nothing. Kate, Travis and I had been wearing gloves when we'd been in the house; the intruders must have done the same. In the kitchen, there was no trace of candle wax on the table.

Georgia turned to dusting for footprints. One lot were clearly mine, the others looked like the size of Kate and Travis.

'But the man was definitely in here,' I said.

'Did he walk on thin air?'

I led Georgia upstairs. In the room where we had found the T-shirt, she studied the timber floorboards. 'There are smudge marks,' she said. 'They could have put disposables over their boots, or simply worn socks.'

'Why do you think they're here?' I asked.

'Well, it's odd, isn't it,' she replied matter-of-factly. 'Several theories. One, they're from another base, and I agree that means Esperanza or Villa Las Estrellas, because they're the ones with families. They could have just been looking around out of curiosity, and weren't expecting to encounter anyone. It's November, they can get in by Zodiac. Could have been dropped off here by a bigger ship and are waiting to be picked up. Of course hiding from you, so they know they're not meant to be here. Two, they're a family in a yacht – tourists, adventurers.'

'But where's the yacht?'

'Exactly. So less likely. But only some of the family might have come ashore – say, Dad and his son. Mum could come back for them after sailing around with other family members.'

That hadn't occurred to me – I *supposed* it was a possibility.

'There are families who do that. Rip the kids out of school and take off,' said Georgia, seeing my scepticism. 'Or three,' she continued, 'the man and the boy are somehow connected to Alliance. And beyond that, it would be mere conjecture. We need to find more facts.'

'The boy was upset. Really traumatised. Calling for help.'

'Which could mean anything. My kids get upset all the time. And a young teenage boy, let me tell you.'

'It was more than that,' I said firmly.

'And it seems likely he slept here after you saw him. With, perhaps, his father. I hope his father, in any case.' Georgia turned away and continued to search for clues.

A chill ran through me at the way she said *hope his father.*

After filming the house, we went back into the street, where Georgia turned her attention to hidden cameras. She looked around, dark eyes hawk-bright. 'If the men at Alliance are up to something down here, they could have removed any cameras, of course,' she said. 'It was hardly a secret that I was coming.' She strode down the street, calling back. 'It's a remarkable village, by the way. Highly suitable for opening up to tourists.'

My heart sank.

'I hope you'll put that in your report,' she called.

'Would you like to see the Adélie colony?' I said, catching up with her. I needed to show her the importance of keeping tourists away.

'Not yet. We'll stick to this part today.'

We moved through house after house, methodically numbering, photographing and noting GPS coordinates. There was nothing different to what I'd seen before: some places were furnished; a few were empty. There were no trapdoors down into the ice.

I didn't run into the ghost of Ingerline. Or anyone else.

We had dinner in the purple house: dehydrated meat and vegetables that we boiled up on a tiny paraffin camping stove, biscuits, no alcohol. That night we slept on the ice. Our tents of reinforced fabric would keep us warmer than if we were in a freezing house, and with four of us, I'd felt it less disruptive. Georgia and Rutger were in separate tents; Kate and I were together. I was glad for Kate's body heat but she was in a foul mood.

'It's bullshit she won't let me go back. And Rutger is the most boring handsome man I've ever met.'

'So you find him good looking?' I tried to make light, but I was in a bad mood myself.

'Not any more,' she said. 'If you have a bland personality and bond with men like Connaught, you can't expect women to find you appealing.'

'Does he have a wife? Kids?'

'You've got to be joking. Rutger Koch is married to his work. Which he takes very seriously, from what he's bored me with all day. He loves Antarctica. That's about the only good thing about him.'

'Does he like penguins?'

'No.' Kate shook her head emphatically. 'He finds them stupid.' She hunched down into her sleeping bag and closed her eyes. 'I hate my life.'

I leaned over and massaged her shoulders, which were rigid with tension. 'I'm sorry. We'll have you with your Adélies soon, I promise.'

The tent was flapping wildly in a vicious wind, pelted by powdered ice that, from the shadows inside, I could see was piling high. I hauled on my coat and trousers and peered out. It was a horrible day. Our skidoos were already encased in drifts of snow that had been hurled off the ground.

'This is crap,' said Kate. 'I'm staying here.'

'Suit yourself,' I said, irritated and impatient. Of course the weather would turn just when we were camped down here.

'Grub's up,' said Georgia, appearing through the flap of the tent. 'Breakfast's in the purple house.' She disappeared.

I pulled on my boots. 'Coming?'

Kate sighed deeply.

'The sooner we're through here, the sooner you can go home,' I pointed out. She pulled herself out of her sleeping bag, emerging like a butterfly from a chrysalis, as I headed into the freezing air. Tiny pieces of ice pelted my face as I pushed against the ferocious wind into the house. I could smell oats cooking. When I entered the kitchen, Rutger looked up briefly from his bowl of porridge. He may have grunted hello but I didn't hear it. He ate sloppily. No wonder he was single.

'So how did you sleep?' Georgia asked as she dished up my porridge and poured a cup of steaming tea from a huge blue and white teapot.

'Did you bring that?' I looked at the teapot.

'Found it. Don't worry, I'll put it back just where it was.'

'Make yourself right at home,' I said disapprovingly.

'Always do,' Georgia replied cheerfully. 'So, up to venturing out?'

Rutger put his bowl down with a thump. 'I'll catch up with my notes. I can't go out in this, particularly after my operation.'

Kate clambered in. 'Me neither.' She rubbed her hands over the flame of the camping stove, and then moved to inspect the oven. 'What does this run on, anyway? Can we get it going?'

'No,' said Rutger, 'that would be dangerous, even if we had fuel. It runs on coal. The electricity at the station was saved for the whaling operations and lighting.'

'It's probably warmest in the tent,' I said supportively.

'Is it okay, Georgia, if I stay back with Rutger? I can't go out alone,' said Kate.

'That's fine,' Georgia replied. 'But Laura, you'll come with me? I thought we might go up to the church?'

I paused, looking out the window at the weather. I hadn't been to the church, and I wanted to see it and check for an entrance underground.

'Okay,' I said.

'Good girl.' Georgia's face lit up as she poured me another cup of tea.

The wind was howling. We strapped on skis and headed along, bent forward, trying not to be blown backwards. I had a waterproof fleece hat with ear-muffs, my scarf was wrapped tightly around my mouth and I wore dark goggles, but still the needle-sharp ice found a way to pelt my face.

I led the way, Georgia behind me getting a little shelter from my body like the pageboy who followed in the warm footsteps of Good King Wenceslas. The thought of protecting Georgia spurred me on through the foul weather.

Visibility was poor in the streets between the houses, but once we reached the bay it was a complete whiteout. I couldn't even see my hand in front of me; space was disoriented.

'You sure we should be out in this?' I screamed above the wind.

'We don't know how long it'll go for and I don't want to waste time,' shouted Georgia. 'Since when have you been soft?' She belted me on the back and I headed off to the right. If I followed the bay and then went up the slope at the far end, I'd be to the left of the Adélie rookery, and heading straight for the church.

But it was hard to sense where the water was to get my bearings. Georgia was being impatient and foolish: it paid to wait when the weather turned. I suspected that being out in the blizzard made her feel like a true Antarctic explorer. I chuckled to myself and kept going, hoping it was the right direction.

The shriek of the wind was so loud I couldn't even hear the penguins, who would be hunkered down on their nests. They knew what to do, even if we foolish humans didn't.

I listened for the sea but it was drowned out. My lungs were burning. I wanted to turn back but I was so bitterly cold, it was probably closer now to get to the church and have shelter and rest before facing the elements again.

I felt the ground slowly incline upwards and I knew I needed to be careful with the skis – the hill was rocky. But snow seemed to cover everything now. As it became steeper I had to lift each ski up, dig in my poles, and step up slowly. By the time the church loomed close, my eyes were painfully dry and sore from the cold and the impenetrable white. I climbed up a snowdrift in front of the entrance, pressed myself against the door and fell in, dropping a couple of feet to the ground, and feeling it. Georgia almost landed on top of me.

'That was great,' she wheezed.

'Crazy woman.' My voice sounded harsher than I felt – it had been an exhilarating journey, like doing an extreme sport. The sensible part of me thought it was unnecessarily dangerous and we were lucky to have arrived in one piece.

I looked around. Windows high up illuminated everything in a white light. It felt heavenly, eerie. Timber pews lined both sides of the room, and we were close to a stand with a stack of neatly piled hymnbooks. I took off my skis, pulled out my camera and went to investigate.

The hymnbooks were in Norwegian, with beautiful gilt-edged, wafer-thin paper.

Georgia walked up the aisle to the font and I followed, filming. Sound was muffled, the wind now a dull throb. I scanned the floorboards, searching for an entrance underground but the boards were all smooth and consistent, with no unusual breaks.

It was a Lutheran church, simple and austere. There was a pulpit with a minimum of carving, on which was propped an immense, heavy leather-bound Bible the length of my arm. Had Ingerline organised to bring such a massive tome here? I looked back and visualised the congregation listening to the sermon. The church would fit about a hundred people. Whalers and their families, led by Ingerline. Who was the minister? Or ministers. Through the years, there would have been a number of them. It was frustrating how much about Fredelighavn I didn't know. I longed for historians to be let in, to trigger research, to unearth records. It was as though Ingerline's ghost were whispering for me to do it. *What are you waiting for?* She seemed to say. *Get them down here.*

Georgia opened a door on the right that led to a tiny room, where the dark shadow of a minister's robe hung on a hook, and a huge book lay open on a small wooden table. A registry. I peered over Georgia's shoulder and took photographs. There were dates and names; details were in Norwegian. The last date entered was *15.3.57.* Was that when the place had closed? Or perhaps just when the last sermon had been given.

I leaned past Georgia and turned the pages to the front of the register. It began on *3.1.38.* It must be a second register, as the church had been built around 1910. I searched the bare timber walls looking for the first one but there was nothing. Georgia moved off and I heard the creaking of a door being opened. I followed to the back wall, where the door was swinging shut.

Entering the room behind the chapel I stopped, astonished.

I was in a library. Books lined every wall, rows and rows sitting at right angles on low-slung shelves around the room. There were thousands of leather-bound volumes and also hardbacks and paperbacks. A vast collection. I filmed the room, careful to record everything, and then turned off my camera and

picked up a few books. They were in Norwegian. And then
I came to several in English. The whalers must have also come
from America: Nantucket, judging by a leather-bound biogra-
phy written by Captain Erling Halvorsen, who had dedicated the
book to his father Captain Lars Halvorsen and mother Ingerline.
I flipped through, entranced. It was a history of Fredelighavn,
as well as Erling's exploits on the high seas and his emigra-
tion to Nantucket. I sat on a small wooden chair and was
quickly absorbed.

The book had been published in 1954. And to my astonishment,
Ingerline was still coming to Fredelighavn at the time. Another
son, Olaf, was running the whaling station. The Halvorsens were
a dynasty, the directors of Larvik Fishing Company, who owned
the entire operation. Here was the history that I'd craved.

'What's the book?' Georgia leaned in close.

'A history,' I said, unable to wrench my eyes from the book.

'Fair enough.' Georgia walked away.

I flicked through the chapters, searching for photographs.
In the middle was a glossy page of black and white images. At
the top, Ingerline stood with her sons, both in neat captain's
uniforms – Erling, the proud author, and Olaf, whose caption
read, *Fredelighavn Station Manager, Larvik Fishing Company.*
Ingerline was older, stouter, and the photo had made her eyes
eerily pale. Her sons were upright and handsome with neatly
clipped beards. Their eyes, too, were pale and seemed to look
right through me. A shiver ran down my spine. I couldn't resist
looking around, in case they were all here.

'You okay? You look like you've seen a ghost,' said Georgia
from across the room.

I grinned. 'Nah, we're the only ones here.' But I couldn't shake the feeling that wasn't true. Thankfully all I could see were the mellow-coloured books lining the walls of this most inviting library.

'We should be heading back,' said Georgia. 'The wind's letting up.'

'Just a little longer,' I implored.

'Take the book. You can put it back later.'

She was practical as always. I was keen to see what else was on the shelves before we left, so I placed the book in my backpack and went quickly in search of others while Georgia jittered from side to side to keep warm.

The books in English were mainly novels and hobby titles, from knitting and cooking to building kit ships.

There was a swag of books on Nantucket, Erling's adopted home when he wasn't stationed on South Safety Island. I wanted to sit and look through them.

'We're out of here,' said Georgia. 'Now.' She hauled me off by the elbow, just as a scrap of blue material caught my eye. It had been shoved between books in one of the smaller bookshelves in the middle of the room.

'Hang on.' I went over. Carefully parting the books – two nameless, leather-bound volumes – I lifted out a cotton T-shirt. It was plain and worn and sported no manufacturer's tag. It could have been here from the 1950s. But it was an odd place for it to be. A thought occurred with such force sweat pricked my brow: was the boy leaving a trail for me? Like Hansel and Gretel?

'What is it?' said Georgia.

'A boy's T-shirt.' I laid it out on the library table. 'About the same size as the other one.'

Georgia grabbed it up, inspecting it closely. She held it to her nose. 'Sweat. I don't think this is old.'

'Do you think he's deliberately leaving them for us?'

Georgia nodded slowly. 'I wouldn't discard that theory.'

'What are we going to do?' I desperately hoped Georgia could find an answer.

She sat heavily, her face lined with worry. 'I hate it when kids are involved.'

I felt a sudden, deep yearning. This boy could have been Hamish. 'We must find him,' I said.

'I just have no idea how. They could have already left by boat.'

'Or be underground. If he's leaving a trail, maybe he's written something somewhere.' I went to the books where the T-shirt had been. The first was a diary, hand-written in Norwegian in loopy writing. On the front page the author's name was proudly stated: *Ingerline Halvorsen*. My heart thumped against my chest. I flipped through the pages but nothing fell out; no loose note from the boy. I couldn't understand anything, other than dates, and *Lars*, *Olaf* and *Erling* – and more names that were perhaps other children of Ingerline, or just people at Fredelighavn.

The second book was another diary – also by Ingerline. I checked the dates. The first diary went from 1915 until 1938, the second from 1946 to *29.3.57*. Ingerline had been here seemingly until the end, with a large gap during the years of the Second World War. Or perhaps there was another diary. I looked around but couldn't find one.

Without understanding the content, I could see that Ingerline only wrote occasional entries each year, and all from November until March – the months when the ships were able to sail into Placid Bay after the sea ice had broken up.

I longed to have the diaries translated, but foremost in my mind was why the T-shirt had been left here. Why did the boy think I'd be looking for Ingerline? Or was it just coincidence, a random space where he could tuck his T-shirt when the man wasn't looking? My stomach twisted into a painful knot. What was the relationship between the boy and the man?

Georgia dusted the shelf for fingerprints, but there were none. This made sense: I was wearing gloves in the freezing air; it was logical the boy – if it was the boy – had done the same.

Georgia then dusted for footprints, and found my boots and hers – and smudges.

'Someone's going to a lot of trouble to leave no prints. I don't think it's a coincidence,' she said grimly.

'Do you think Connaught is involved?'

'Or Snow,' she replied firmly.

'But the more I think of Snow, I don't think he could be involved,' I said, wanting to defend him, feeling guilty I'd placed him as a suspect in Georgia's mind. 'He's an internationally renowned scientist. A top one.'

'That doesn't put him out of the picture. The whole base is in awe of him and I'm guessing would do anything for him.' She sucked in her breath. 'And our mate Rutger could well have been sent to watch over us. Well, you in the first instance, and now me too.'

I shuddered, wondering if Travis could be part of whatever was going on down here.

I forced the thought away and went to the bookcase where I had found the T-shirt, and pushed with my full weight.

'What on earth are you doing?' said Georgia.

'Seeing if this is concealing a way down.'

The bookcase was on coasters and after a moment's resistance moved easily. The boards beneath were smooth and unbroken, like everywhere else. 'There must be an entrance somewhere,' I muttered as I put Ingerline's diaries in my backpack. Georgia came over to look, and as the wind moaned outside we spent the next hour covering every square inch – and found nothing. Georgia stood with her hands on her hips, glaring at the room, deep in thought.

'Time to head back,' she said.

In the church, we picked up our skis and hoisted ourselves up the pile of ice to the gap in the doorway. The wind had dropped: it was an acceptable gale now rather than a blizzard. We tossed our skis onto the snowdrift and jumped after them. I found the blast of salt air soothing, and there was a great deal more visibility. A wild sea heaved in the bay, and to my left the penguins hunkered, draped in snow, on their rocky nests.

We put on our skis and whooshed off down to the bay. A glimmer of sky was peeking out, pale blue against the grey. I was warmed at least by the weight of the book and diaries in my backpack. The history of Fredelighavn. Perhaps somewhere I might find a record of tunnels built when the whaling station was operational. Tunnels that were now hiding a boy.

14

In clear morning light we set off investigating the village, looking everywhere for an entrance underground, and for more signs of the boy and man. I tried to stay focused, but my mind was full of awful possibilities of what could be happening. Could there be more than one boy down here, and more than one man? The man I'd seen in the orange house, and the one I'd seen in the blubber cookery, had seemed different heights, but I couldn't be sure. If they were connected to Alliance, what was Connaught's involvement?

Kate had gone off with Rutger, and on Georgia's instruction wasn't mentioning either the tunnels or the boy to him, although Kate herself was looking for anything leading down beneath the ice.

I noted everything on my tablet, in a grid, and filmed the sheds and outbuildings, and the houses with their possessions. The lives of vanished whalers.

I showed Georgia the cinema, where a drift of snow lay through the doorway and seals were again in residence, sleeping, sprawled on chairs and the floor. The film looked the same, but I didn't dare go in to make sure. Georgia stared at the screen, and then cast her eyes down to the stage.

'Did you check under the stage? It could hide an entrance.'

'I didn't.' I tried to think back. 'I saw the boy *after* we'd been in the cinema.'

'Can we go in now?' asked Georgia.

The seals were in deep and comfortable slumber. Several were on the small stage, that I now noticed was about two feet off the floor.

Carefully I took a step inside. And all hell broke loose. The huge bull elephant seal awoke and bellowed, and younger seals leaped to attention. I backed out quickly and headed towards Georgia, who had already shot to the opposite side of the street.

'The seals come and go,' I said. 'We can check back tomorrow.' I was burning to take a thorough look around the stage, but for now I had to settle for taking Georgia to the blubber cookery and showing her where the red T-shirt – I was now certain it had been a T-shirt – was sighted.

'Do you think there might be more than one boy?' I asked fearfully.

'Yes,' she said, and turned away, leaving my mind churning at greater speed, with ever darker thoughts. More than one man; more than one boy. What could a group of men do to a group of boys? I couldn't think of anything that wasn't deeply traumatic. I wanted to air ideas with Georgia, but she was giving the distinct impression that she didn't want to talk at the moment.

The rusty knife was still in my bag, and I was near the wall where it should hang. With Georgia by my side, I felt I no longer needed it, and it had been troubling me to have taken an artefact. Georgia caught me as I put it back, and I explained how I'd picked it up the first day I'd seen the man.

'What were you planning to do – give him tetanus?' she commented drolly, trying to make light, but neither of us was in the mood.

We picked our way through the shed at the back of the flensing platform that, on its upper loft, revealed a vast array of rusted saws that would have been used to cut the bones after the whale skeleton – its head and spine – had been winched up. Below lay a double row of vats. The bone cookery.

The shed behind was a vast space where giant steel driers rose from the floor. After the oil had been separated from the whale blubber, meat and bones, any solid material left was dried, then ground up to make whale meal, or what was called guano, and used for protein in animal food, and as fertiliser. There were still sacks of powdered guano lying around.

We inspected a laboratory where the whale oil had been graded, the equipment still sitting in rows on bench tops. But there were no T-shirts, or entrances underground.

On the far side of the village, away from Alliance Point, we found an old bakery that, from its basic equipment, seemed to have been abandoned long before the 1950s. There was a large brick building that had housed pigs, and another building where they had kept chickens. A long, dilapidated shed – a barracks – had two rows of single beds, their mattresses long gone. Two adjacent buildings of communal bathrooms stood beside it, and a timeworn mess hall. A distance away, there was a butcher's shop with a slaughter room, with all its tools in place, and a little further on a two-storey clapboard building sat alone. The hospital, its beds and equipment untouched, like the staff had just walked out for a break. Were back injuries common among the whalers? I looked at the old 1950s X-ray machine and imagined men lying in pain, and flinched knowing what they'd done to the whales to hurt their own bodies.

Near the water, there was an area where the whale catcher ships had been repaired. It was a self-sufficient settlement.

Georgia and I investigated scientifically and forensically but there were no more clues. The trail of T-shirts had ended, and there was no sign of a way underground.

In the following days the four of us mapped Fredelighavn. What had been mysterious was now being reduced to statistics and facts. The seals didn't leave the cinema, and so, much to my frustration, we couldn't search there again.

In my downtime I read Captain Erling Halvorsen's book, which gave an insight into the design of the whaling station and the frantic work that had gone into constructing the village each year in the short summer seasons. But there was no mention of tunnels or anything underground.

Erling spent far too long outlining the whale hunts at sea,

casting the murdering whalers as heroes and the whales as prey to conquer. He had complained bitterly when, in 1937, the International Agreement for the Regulation of Whaling had been signed by nine nations, placing a much-reduced quota on the number of whales slaughtered. And then he had crowed valiantly when, in the following year, more whales were killed than ever before, a fact also lauded by his brother Olaf. I could only imagine the celebratory dinner that Ingerline had put on for them.

Ingerline's diaries made no sense; I could see nothing more than a pattern of names and dates. I would have to send them to a professional translator as soon as I could.

With Georgia, I returned to the pink and blue house, where I had seen the ghost of Ingerline in the mirror. The lounge room looked exactly the same, the convex mirror reflecting light on a shining day, but with no ghost in sight. We searched thoroughly around the floors and walls for an entrance into the ice. Had Ingerline been sending me a sign?

There was nothing. Fredelighavn was making me feel claustrophobic.

I took Georgia up to the Adélie rookery. The birds were happy on their nests, and no chicks had yet hatched. As Georgia walked through, she was attacked and was forced back quickly.

'What have they done down here?' she asked, ashen-faced.

After five days in the field our food supplies were running low, but between our two teams we had covered most of the village.

We had found no underground entrance nor further signs of recent human habitation. And the seals were still reclining in the cinema, letting no one in.

I wanted to stay but Georgia ordered me back to base; she wouldn't leave anyone down here alone. As my skidoo sped over the blue–white ice, fresh from the recent blizzard, the wind was bitter. It was strange that I now knew so much of the history of Fredelighavn, while its secrets remained buried deep, with the possibility of awful acts going on somewhere under the ice.

I couldn't get my mind off Travis. Did he know what was happening? Could he be involved? He had hinted at something the last time I saw him, the night before Georgia arrived. I wanted to interrogate him, to make him aware it was no longer a game. The stakes were high. If he was on my side, he needed to tell me everything.

Alliance came into view, luminous and perfectly formed. What was it hiding?

Sweet, skinny Guy greeted me warmly as Kate and I walked into the mess hall. 'We've all missed you.' He winked. 'Especially Snow. He's been asking after you.'

'Really?' Georgia mustn't have updated them regarding how long we'd be down at Fredelighavn. Cop behaviour. I was glad she was here. And I was ridiculously pleased that Snow had been asking after me.

I sat down and ate hungrily. Kate wasn't talking, furious to not be going back to her penguins – which gave me time to think.

Snow was older. Not as old as my father, but in that direction. Was that drawing me to him? Or was I impressed with his scientific achievements? There was no doubt I found him fascinating, and his body of research was more significant than that of anyone I'd worked with at my university.

I didn't want to accept Georgia's reasoning that Snow was involved in whatever bad things were happening down here. If he wasn't in league with Connaught, Snow would be the perfect ally. At that moment he walked into the room and looked around. His fair hair shone, and his powder-blue jacket matched his eyes. When he saw me he made a beeline across.

'You're back.' He pulled up a chair and straddled it. 'What have you been up to?' He sat so close his aftershave wafted over – it was a different one, lemony and fresh with a tang of salt. My heart skipped, and I glanced to see if he was wearing a wedding ring. He wasn't.

Kate stopped eating and stared across sullenly. Snow was so focused on me he didn't seem to notice she was there. I looked into his sparkling eyes and tried to imagine him leading something terrible – but it just didn't gel. Connaught, absolutely. But Snow was a very different man. Vibrant, attractive, glitteringly bright. There seemed no darkness within him.

'I've been documenting Fredelighavn,' I said. 'Well, we all have. Do you know the buildings?'

'Wish I did, but no. I'm not *that* ancient, Laura.' He laughed and his face lit up, making him look years younger. 'It was an Exclusion Zone long before I started coming here. So what's it like? Do you have photos?'

'I do but I can't show them to you.'

'Yet,' he said. 'Once your report's in hopefully you can. I'd love to see the place. Tell me about the wildlife? It's meant to be extraordinary. That's the whole point, isn't it, of no one going in?'

Kate's eyes flickered, warning me to say nothing. Georgia sat down with us, busily texting on her phone. Images of her son and daughter were flashing up and she was smiling happily, a world away.

'My lips are sealed,' I said to Snow. I felt someone staring and glanced across to see Travis watching jealously.

'Can I join you all for dinner?' asked Snow.

'Of course,' I replied. 'I'm having seconds.' I scraped my plate clean. 'Never thought I'd miss this food but I did.' As we walked together to the servery I felt eyes following us. Snow's attention was not going unnoticed and I couldn't help but be pleased. If I could grow close he might reveal useful things about Connaught. They had, after all, spent many seasons down here together. And I longed to learn more about Snow's work.

'Do you know my father, Professor Michael Green from Sydney?' I asked, surprising myself. Snow frowned as he slopped meat and gravy onto his plate.

'Green?'

'Yeah. I have my Mum's surname. My Dad's Mike Green. He's a biomedical researcher.'

'Hmm. Doesn't ring a bell, but then my memory's not what it used to be.' He turned. 'I'll give it some thought. Your dad, eh? Then I'd like to know him.'

I blushed. It was ridiculous of me to even raise it – but I was also taken aback. My father was well known. Sure, predominantly in the Asia-Pacific region, but still.

'I guess you've heard of him?'

Snow held my gaze with his blue eyes. 'Should I?'

'He's just . . . a bit of a leader in his field. He's a microbiologist – and he researches in virology too, like you.'

Snow smiled warmly. 'You must be proud of him.'

My cheeks blazed. The abandoned child boasting about a father she hadn't seen in years. What had Fredelighavn done to me?

'I'm more interested in *you*, though,' said Snow as we walked back to the table with our meals. 'Your research. I know you can't talk about the whaling station, but you can talk about whales, surely?'

Sitting down, I found myself launching into great detail about Lev, the humpbacks' songs, and all the whales I'd observed in Antarctica over the years. Snow was a good listener.

'You talk about them like they're your friends,' he said. Kate watched silently. Georgia was still absorbed in her texting.

'I guess they are. Like family.' I shrugged.

He grinned and looked at me so directly I melted.

'It must be a bit boring going through old houses,' he said.

'Not at all. Different sorts of family. Well, families once lived there. Not on the right side when it comes to whales, but it's fascinating to see how they managed. And that's all I can say.' My tone was light, but underneath I was starting to feel a nagging unease. It was peculiar he hadn't heard of my father – although Americans could be insular.

'Nothing more appealing than a secret,' said Snow.

'Speaking of which – I'd love to see your lab. Is there any way you could bend the rules?'

Georgia glanced up.

'Not if I don't want to be arrested,' said Snow. 'Wish I could. But sadly it's impossible.' He pushed his plate away. 'Dessert?' he said.

'Not for me, thanks.'

'I hope you're not watching your weight, you don't need to.'

I could feel the scarlet creeping up my face again.

'We could always work out at the gym. Do you do that?' he asked amiably.

Kate's eyes widened. Georgia focused on her text conversation with her kids, but I knew she was listening.

'It's been a long day,' I said self-consciously. 'Another time?' I stood.

'Good seeing you,' said Snow.

'You too,' I said, bidding goodnight to him and Georgia. Kate came with me.

As soon as we were out in the street, Kate groaned and stuck a gloved finger down her throat. 'That was absolutely nauseating. What on earth were you trying to do?'

'Get close. We have no other leads.'

'He's old enough to be your father.'

I didn't point out that might be part of the attraction. 'He's nowhere near that old!' I dissembled. 'Anyway, I asked him if he knew my dad and he didn't recognise the name. Don't you think that's strange, when they're both big figures in a similar field?'

Kate mulled it over. 'I guess one's in Australia and one's in America – they're a long way away.'

In our room, Kate fell into bed and was quickly asleep as usual, but I stayed up, thinking about Snow. His strong limbs, warm smile. Height; I liked that he was tall, and there was something reassuring about his maturity. Worried about the boy, I yearned for physical comfort, especially if it helped me bond with a crucial ally. It would be so good to be held by a masculine body, to let go. I'd been on my own for three long years, and I felt the urge for an ice-relationship. Nothing permanent, one that stayed here. Snow was the best-looking man at Alliance – if I excluded Travis, who was fast receding into the background. And I liked that Snow was a leader.

But what if Georgia was right that Snow was involved in whatever was happening at Fredelighavn? Another voice nagged, too – his not knowing my father was odd. My heart started to race at the thought that perhaps I could phone Dad. Ask him if he knew Snow. A background check might smoke out something, one way or another. I felt woozy with anticipation at the idea of having contact with my father.

I picked up my phone and dialled Dad's number. I'd left a few messages over the years, and occasionally he had called back, but he always managed to miss me and just leave another message.

My blood pounded as I heard my father's deep, well-spoken voice. 'This is Mike Green. I'm currently overseas, so please leave your number only if it's urgent, and I'll get back to you as soon as possible.' Beep. Disappointed, but not surprised, I asked him to call, knowing it was likely to be a long wait.

There was hysteria in the air. The feverish activity had gone into warp speed.

'What's going on?' I asked Georgia as I sat beside her with my porridge.

'No idea,' she said. 'But I want us to go back to the whaling station and search through everything again. If there *is* an entrance into the ice, we'll find it. I'll be treating it like any crime scene. We'll go over and over the evidence.'

I nodded, but my attention was on what was causing the base to wind up to explosion level.

Travis came bustling in and sat with us. 'Hi Georgia, how are you?'

'Fine,' she replied.

He tried to subtly signal for me to join him elsewhere, but he didn't fool Georgia.

'Whatever you have to say, Travis,' she said, 'you can do it here. Laura will just tell me anyway.'

He looked crestfallen, clearly wanting the intimacy of having me alone.

'Snow's leaving,' he said, lowering his voice and leaning in. 'He's never done this before. Come so early and left so quickly.'

'Where's he going?' I asked, shocked.

'Back to Harvard.'

'Ooh, that's Boston.' On the other side of the world in Massachusetts – *and right near Nantucket.* My mind started to move at the same pace as the base, but Travis merely looked perplexed.

'I wonder if I could hitch a ride,' I said. 'I need to get to Nantucket to research the whaling museum. It would be the perfect opportunity.' *To spend time with Snow.* The boy in the ice cave flashed before me and my stomach lurched. *But I'd be leaving him – in order to find him.*

Georgia tensed but said nothing. Travis turned white.

'Would that mean you wouldn't come back?' he said.

'Not at all. We haven't finished down here, have we, Georgia?'

'Most certainly not.' She glared at me like a cloud about to drop a month's worth of rain. My mother had the same expression when I was a teenager.

'But if I could go with Snow – maybe he's coming back later and I could catch two rides with him,' I said, looking at Georgia imploringly. She stared at me, deep in thought. Travis watched.

'You could ask,' said Georgia suddenly, coming around to my side. I paused to take in what was happening.

'It might be very opportune,' she continued. 'The report does have a tight deadline, and we can keep in touch by email.'

'Does that mean I can go back to my penguins?' said Kate. I was surprised to find her standing behind me.

'How long have you been there?' I asked.

'Long enough to know you're leaving me. Georgia, please?' She sat down close to her. 'Summer's short and I really do need to get back to my Adélies. It's what I've been funded to do.'

'I'll think about it,' said Georgia. 'We'll see.' Poor Kate. *We'll see*. Georgia clearly wasn't about to let her go. But she was letting me. That's if Snow said yes.

I'd shocked myself at how quickly I'd formed my plan. But I knew that I was completely out of ideas about how to find the boy at Fredelighavn, and Snow felt like my best chance. Officially he wasn't going to say anything, but intimately, a little voice kept telling me, he just might. It was the only shot I had. As a scientist, I knew the long shot, the calculated risk, was often the path that found a way forward.

It was an experiment I had to undertake. More days searching fruitlessly through the whaling station held little appeal, and in any event, Georgia was fully covering that. I grew certain my way could be faster in discovering where the boy was, and who he was. And that was the most crucial thing of all.

Snow's sudden exit was fascinating. Had he found something going on of which he disapproved? That he couldn't be involved with or it would sully his outstanding reputation?

If he and I had a romantic liaison, I could get him to trust me. If there was something bad happening, I sensed that Snow would want it fixed. Maybe he couldn't do it himself. Maybe he needed me. In Antarctica, anything can change at any second. If Snow said yes to my accompanying him, what would that reveal?

I couldn't get into the main building to ask Snow in person, so I emailed and asked him to meet me in the mess hall. He arrived, perplexed, and I brought two coffees over to a table in the far corner. There was no one else in the room.

'Is something wrong?' he asked, concerned.

'No, not at all. Particularly if you'd do something for me.'

'What is it?' Often when people are put on the spot they back away, but Snow leaned forward, his smooth hands, neat and strong, resting on the table.

'I need to get to Nantucket for research and was wondering – well, hoping – I might hitch a ride with you.'

He laughed loudly. 'A ride. What sort of Aussie term's that? You want to *hitch a ride*?'

'Yes. Which way are you going?' I grinned, enjoying being with him.

'Well, for you, I might even take the short way. I'll check if there's room on the plane.'

'Really?'

'Yep. But I'm leaving tomorrow.'

'Perfect. I'll organise my things. What time?'

'Hang on, I have to see if it can happen first.'

'Where do you fly into? I'll sort out my onward travel.'

He sat back and shook his head, dazzling eyes creased around the edges as he smiled broadly. 'I haven't said yes yet.'

'Anyway, *if* you agree, where are you finishing up?'

'I can take you as far as Boston.'

'Brilliant.' That was exactly what I'd been hoping. 'So you're going straight back to Harvard?'

He nodded. 'I have a lab to run. And this one down here's going smoothly.'

'Will you be back this summer?'

'That I don't know. Depends how things go at home, and what comes up at Alliance. But for now it's good I can get away. And you, will you be back?'

I grinned again – that sounded like he had already decided to take me along for the ride.

'*If* you come with me,' he quickly added.

'Yes, I will.'

'May I ask, then, why you're not doing this travel at the end of your trip?'

'I was going to, but the person I need to see at the whaling museum is off on sabbatical shortly,' I lied. 'It'll be worth its weight in gold for me to meet up with her and now's the only time. When I heard you were heading that way it seemed to be fate.'

'I didn't think we scientists believed in fate.'

'Well, put it this way, I'm an opportunist, so when the possibility arose . . .'

'I'd do exactly the same in your position,' he said, draining his coffee and standing. 'I'll get back to you.'

I wanted to high five the air. Then I realised I had to set up a real meeting in Nantucket. I raced back to my room and found the details of the person I needed to contact – Betsy Bryson.

My mother always told me it was bad to lie. And today was no exception. My email to Doctor Bryson bounced back: she really was on sabbatical, from last week until March next year. I cursed loudly but Kate, who was sulking and watching her beloved Adélie penguins on computer, didn't even look up.

I quickly searched the museum staff list and found the next most senior person: Alice Hussey. I sent a detailed email explaining who I was and why I needed to come. I added that I would like to explore any archives on the island with the hope of finding out more about Captain Erling Halvorsen and his parents, Ingerline and Lars. I crossed my fingers as I pressed send, praying that somewhere in an archive on Nantucket I'd find mention of tunnels under the village.

I looked up Norwegian staff at Harvard and emailed an academic who had a friendly face – Astrid Bredesen – asking if she might know someone who could translate Ingerline's diaries, which I hoped I could drop off in person.

But my other concern was how I could get to spend time with Snow. After doing what I needed in Nantucket at lightning speed I planned to pay him a visit at Harvard.

After several hours talking to Georgia, mulling over everything, she gave me her blessing for the trip.

'Be very careful with Snow,' she said. 'If he is involved and he senses we're onto him, you'll be in real danger. Tread lightly. He's pretending to be as attracted to you as you are to him, so that does give you an opportunity.'

'What do you mean "pretending"?'

'You might be a few decades too old.'

I felt like she'd just slammed me in the gut. 'Why do you say that?'

'I'm not ruling anything in or out until we know more,' said Georgia firmly. 'But let's just say, if one of my hunches is on the money, there's no way you can get involved in the way you want. You should be able to glean something, though, and that's why it's important to go. Send any information straight back to me.'

A chill rippled through me – I hoped deeply she was wrong. And then an awful thought occurred. 'Georgia, what if Connaught's watching your computer and phone? He could have done anything to your electronic equipment when you arrived, just like with me.'

'Don't worry, I scanned everything as soon as we got back to proper reception. My systems are clean. I'll do yours now. And just to bring you up to speed – last night I phoned the station leaders at Villa Las Estrellas and Esperanza. They're adamant no one from their bases would have come to South Safety, let alone brought children.'

'That's one theory gone, then, I guess,' I said, disappointed. It would have been so much better if that was the explanation. Something innocent. 'Although they wouldn't necessarily know, would they, if some of their own were doing it unofficially?' I added, wishing it could be so.

Georgia nodded, concentrating on running a sophisticated software check on my phone. It hadn't been tampered with, nor, it turned out to my amazement, had my computer, tablet or camera.

'Why didn't you do this before?' I said, shaken. 'You knew I thought they switched that penguin.'

'Well, they didn't. Not the photos anyway.'

She clearly hadn't believed me at the time, either.

'Well, let's see who's right about Snow,' I said, feeling exhausted and worried to be leaving the boy down here.

'Just find out what you can,' said Georgia. 'And look after yourself.'

*

Five am and the sun was already high in the sky as I hugged Kate.

'Next time you ask for a favour, I'll be saying no,' she said.

'Georgia asked you, not me,' I replied lightly.

'Yeah, right. Don't try and squeeze your way out of it. You owe me big time, Alvarado, and I'm not going to let you forget it. And as for abandoning me here with Rutger . . . If I'm not back with my Adélies soon I'll be a madwoman.'

'I promise I'll find a way to make it up to you.' I tucked a strand of red hair neatly behind her ear.

'I'll miss you,' she mumbled.

'Me too,' I said, hugging her again until it hurt.

Georgia and I said goodbye as Travis packed my bags into the Hägglunds.

'Your flights have been paid, and get receipts for the rest of your travel and accommodation.' Georgia looked at me intently. 'Keep your head on your shoulders and your eyes in their sockets.'

'What sort of advice is that?'

'The best, believe me.'

'Greek dag,' I said, and she punched me on the arm. Hard.

I hopped up into the Hägglunds and looked back as Georgia walked out onto the icy road and stood waving as we left, her hair a black mane shining in the sun, her smile broad and caring. A lump formed in my throat – but it was stupid to be feeling so emotional when I'd be here again soon.

I didn't turn around until Georgia was just a speck in the white.

'So,' said Travis, staring straight ahead, hunched over the controls, 'I want to know what the great professor has that I don't.'

I sat back and glanced at him. His jaw was set tight. 'I'm going over for research,' I replied matter-of-factly. 'Nantucket was always part of the plan.'

'Not in the middle of a tour here,' he said tersely.

'That sounds military.'

'Whatever you want to call it, it's very unusual for someone to go elsewhere and claim they're coming back to Antarctica in the same season. I'm afraid I don't believe you. You're not coming back, are you?'

'Travis, I am. I promise. How could I abandon my little brother? You're family.' I desperately hoped that he wasn't involved with the boy.

'Don't say that.' He turned to me, eyes flashing blue. 'You know, Laura, I can be a very patient man.' His gaze was so intense my whole body tingled. I forced myself to ignore it.

'I'll miss you,' he said gently.

'I'm really glad we got to know each other, too.' *But only if you're innocent.* I looked away.

'So what's happening at Fredelighavn? You've gone very quiet since Georgia arrived,' said Travis.

'I wish you'd told me all you knew. It's not too late.' My voice had turned to ice. Travis sat up straight, surprised.

'If you're covering up a crime, you'll be implicated, you know that. Forget Official Secrets Acts. They won't protect you,' I said.

Travis paled.

'You do know something, don't you?' I grilled. 'Are you involved?' I glared at him, wanting and not wanting to hear the answer.

'No,' he replied emphatically. 'No, I'm not.'

'Then tell me what it is.'

I was clenching my fists like I was going to punch him. I'd never hit anyone in anger in my life. My feelings were a jumbled mess.

'I don't know exactly but I think you're right that there's something underground,' he blurted.

'Does it involve children? A boy?'

'I don't know. I don't know what they're doing. You found that T-shirt . . .'

Was he really on my side? Could I trust him? I wanted to, badly. 'Tell me about the underground part of the main building.'

'We can only go down one floor. After that it's restricted. And they're definitely doing something down there.'

'Could they have tunnels going all the way to Fredelighavn?'

'It's possible, I guess, but it's such a long way. But there's something else,' he said quickly.

I held my breath.

'Did you see a generator room down at the whaling station?' he continued. 'I had a good look around it with Moose, the day we went diving.'

'Yes, what about it?' I pulled out my tablet and brought up photos of the room, with its old electrical meters stacked high. Travis stopped the Hägglunds. He took the tablet and inspected the images closely.

'Nothing was moving on the dials, right?'

I nodded.

'But if people are underground, they'd need electricity. I've been thinking about it. I bet you didn't check the oil tanks? The ones clustered at the side of the mountain. See if they were full or empty?'

I sat back, frustrated. 'No. I didn't think to. Do you think they're using them?' My heart beat faster.

Travis nodded. 'I do. They could have diverted the underground pipes for their own use, at the point where they enter the generator room. It'd be simple; just run a connection and take it down. If they had their own generators beneath the ice, we wouldn't hear them. They could easily have them in concrete rooms, keeping the noise in. I want to go back down – with your permission – and have a look around. Check to see how much oil is in the tanks.'

I could barely believe what I was hearing – that I'd missed such a fundamentally important point made me feel stupid and furious with myself, but it also encouraged my faith in Travis.

'Will you do me a favour?' I said. 'Be really careful when you're doing that?'

He looked at me vulnerably and nodded. I wanted to take him in my arms and kiss him. It was a brilliant idea – and not, I believed, the plan of someone involved in the secrets South Safety was hiding. Relief flooded through me.

'Laura, will you have dinner with me when this is all over? I'd like to take you to my favourite lobster shack in Maine.'

I laughed, it was so unexpected. Travis looked mortified.

'I'm serious,' he said. 'It's the best food ever and I'd like to share it with you.'

'Maine?'

'We have a summerhouse in Kennebunkport. It's not that far from Boston.'

'So you're from Boston?'

'Yeah. I grew up there and went to Harvard, like all my family. Will you come?'

I squeezed his hand. It was warm and strong. And Harvard trained. A surge of heat swept through me. *He's your little brother, Alvarado*, I reminded myself.

The plane was waiting on the blue ice runway. Not a Dash 7 that the British flew, but a much bigger bird. I hugged Travis goodbye and then pulled back slightly, looking into his cobalt eyes. His dark lashes were wet. He hugged me again, tightly, and a warm, gooey feeling fluttered through me.

'Take care,' I whispered into his ear, feeling his smooth skin. 'Call me if you find anything.'

Travis kissed me quickly on the lips and my stomach flipped. Then I climbed the plane's stairs as he went to put my luggage in the hold.

Inside the cabin, Snow was waiting. With a flute of champagne. There were four large seats at the front and he was the only one in that section. Behind, about a dozen scientists were crammed into smaller seats. They weren't talking to each other, all absorbed in their computers.

'Welcome aboard,' said Snow, handing me the champagne. I gulped it down, suddenly feeling shy, wondering if he'd seen Travis kiss me, and what he thought about it. But I needn't have worried: as soon as the plane took off, Snow excused himself and started to work on his computer, creating complex mathematical formulas that made no sense to me.

As we arced over Fredelighavn I focused on the cluster of tanks stretching up the mountain on the southern side of the village. Were they full of fuel-oil? I wished I could stay and investigate with Travis. I would phone Georgia and tell her about them as soon as I could.

Near Alliance Point, the Adélies were a black and white mass. In the bay, pods of humpback whales and killer whales swam through the sparkling water. The elephant seals basking on the beach looked like giant slugs, and chinstrap and gentoo penguins were all along the coastline in the other direction.

Icebergs studding the bay shone blue and white, with deep green shadows. Adélies huddled at the edges peered nervously into the sea – then the group jittered and pushed one lone penguin into the water. Checking to see it hadn't been eaten by a leopard seal, the rest followed in a fluid movement.

The plane banked sharp left and headed for South America. I felt a deep pang in my heart as the view turned to endless ocean, shimmering ink blue with waves that seemed deceptively small, but would be high and treacherous.

I opened my laptop and checked my email. Nothing from Alice Hussey at the museum, but there was one new message that pleased me: Astrid Bredesen at Harvard was willing to do my translation. At least I'd achieved something.

As I gazed back at the ocean I could think only of the boy. I promised myself that the next time I flew out of Antarctica I would be bringing him with me.

15

In Ushuaia we transferred straight to another plane. Snow took out his computer as soon as we were on board and again worked the entire way, politely rebutting every attempt I made to talk. When we landed in Buenos Aires and headed for the commercial flight to New York, to my frustration Snow and I parted company: he was travelling business class, while I was in economy.

Fifteen hours later we touched down at John F. Kennedy International Airport in New York at 6am on a cold, grey autumn day. I cleared passport control and found Snow at the baggage carousel. He'd already collected his suitcase but was waiting for me. He helped heft my bag off.

I was trying to adjust to the noise and chaos of the terminal, feeling panicky after the space and serenity of Antarctica as we wheeled our luggage to check in for the next flight. The scent of so many people in close proximity was overpowering, and colours seemed too plentiful, too intense.

When Snow took me into the business lounge as his guest, there were fewer people, and I was grateful.

'Can I see your lab at Harvard?' I asked. 'I have to go to the campus to meet someone.'

Snow paused, and looked at me with interest. 'Who are you seeing?'

'A colleague. A marine biologist,' I lied.

'Unfortunately I'm not going straight to work. I'll be at home for a few days sorting things out,' Snow replied.

'When will I see you again?' I sounded as vulnerable as I felt. I had to get close to Snow – or how would I find information about what was happening on South Safety Island?

Snow, clearly surprised, laughed awkwardly. 'That wasn't part of the deal, was it?'

A burning flush shot from my neck to the top of my scalp.

'It's okay,' he said, softening. 'Give me your cell number and I'll keep in touch.'

I relaxed a little; a smile curled my lips.

'I *would* like to get to know you better, Laura. Rain check on dinner, okay?'

'Perfect,' I said, happier as I pulled out my mobile phone. 'Shall I send you my number?'

'Just say it.' He stabbed in the digits as I recited them, and I tried not to show how annoyed I was that he wouldn't give me his number.

'You could, of course, spend a weekend with me on Nantucket,' I offered.

'A little cold at this time of year,' he said lightly. 'But I would if I weren't so busy. Make sure you see Brant Point lighthouse, it's a beauty. Well, you won't miss it if you go by boat. Or are you flying in?'

'I haven't actually booked that part yet. What would you suggest?'

'Get a car with a driver to Hyannis and then take the ferry. It's the best way to see the island, and flights can get cancelled from bad weather.'

'Thanks,' I said, smiling flirtatiously. 'Any suggestions where to stay?'

'Haven't you organised anything?' He grinned, the old Snow coming back, thawing after the trip.

'I always travel like this.'

'That'd drive me crazy.'

'I could change.'

Snow laughed. 'This time of year, there won't be many tourists, so you should be okay. But be careful, quite a few places might be closed for the season.'

'I'll be fine,' I said, suddenly realising I had been foolish not to have planned more. 'And I'd love to take you out to dinner in Boston.'

'But *I'll* be taking *you*,' he replied, pretending to be affronted.

'Two dinners, one each then.'

'We'll see.'

We'll see. Not another one to use that dreadful phrase – was the world turning into my mother? My neck tensed as I wondered if Georgia was right: Snow didn't seem all that interested in me any more. It was like pulling teeth to make any connection. I gazed into his blue eyes – eyes that still seemed honest and straightforward – as he looked back.

'What's wrong?' he said.

'Just feeling funny being in the real world again. It's loud.'

'And colourful.'

'Well, Fredelighavn was colourful too. It's just that there are too many ugly colours here.'

He smiled. 'You've got that look.'

'What look?'

'Like you're staring right through me into the distance. Like you're a little bit toasty. You were down in Antarctica a while?'

I laughed. 'Over a year. And I don't feel toasty.'

'It happens to us all, you know that. Take care in the next few days while you adjust.'

They announced our flight and Snow headed off into the front of the plane. I was wedged between two huge passengers at the back.

By the time I arrived at the baggage carousel to collect my luggage, Snow had already left. I cursed; things weren't going to plan at all. I grabbed my bag and went out to the taxi stand, where a friendly driver took me over the river to Cambridge.

I found my way across the Harvard campus to the Faculty of Scandinavian Studies and met Astrid Bredesen. She was bright and young and more than happy to contact me if she found any references to tunnels under the ice.

I left feeling that at least Ingerline's diaries were in safe hands. There was an afternoon ferry to Nantucket, and I took Snow's advice. After checking it wasn't too expensive, I booked a chauffeured car to get me to Hyannis. On the trip, I looked up accommodation on the island, trying to keep my eyes off forests of trees whizzing past outside, and an array of picture-postcard townships we drove through. I found the landscape confronting, too complex. It churned me up. There was just too much in it.

Snow was right about Nantucket. A lot of places had shut for the season – or until the Christmas period. I chose the cheapest room in a small inn that promised to be friendly and cosy.

I checked my email. Still no reply from Alice Hussey. The museum was closed weekdays during November and today was Monday, so all I could hope was that my affable inn proprietor could put me in touch with Alice, or at least with the Nantucket archive. This trip, my priority was to find anything I could about Erling Halvorsen. I could always do the museum part later, even if it meant flying back at my own cost.

My driver dropped me at the ferry terminal, where I bought a ticket on the fast ferry due to leave in half an hour. It was a cold, windy day and I stayed in the small, warm ticket office, thankful there weren't many people around because even these few felt loud. City noise was grinding my ears.

*

The water was rough as we crossed Nantucket Sound, the ferry bucking like a horse in a rodeo. Feeling seasick, I went up on deck, where the wind wrenched around my face and bit into my skin and I started to breathe more easily. After fifty minutes Nantucket came into sight – first just a line of buildings clustered on the horizon, and then as we grew closer we passed a beautiful lighthouse, white with a black top, squat but perfectly formed, sitting proud on the point. I was buoyed with anticipation. Here I might discover something more about Fredelighavn. Something that could help.

I alighted on a broad wharf dotted with small shops and was amazed to see a tall, fit-looking woman in her early seventies, with a neat bob of blonde hair blowing in the wind, holding a sign with the name of my lodging – Annie Coffin's Inn. She was well dressed in navy woollen trousers, white blouse and a well-cut navy coat. I walked up and introduced myself.

'I'm Nancy,' she said in a gentle New England accent, covering my hand in a warm, strong grip, and I felt I'd chosen the right accommodation.

'How did you know I'd be on this ferry?' I asked.

'There aren't that many,' she said amiably. 'It was either this one or the next.'

Nancy led me up Main Street, my suitcase wheels echoing on the cobblestones as I hurried to keep up. Trees lined both sides, bare-limbed save for the odd fiery leaf clinging on. The buildings were old and immaculately preserved, predominantly red brick with glossy white woodwork. It was like stepping back centuries in time. Though it was only mid-afternoon, lights were starting to twinkle in the few shops that were open. There was a comforting, homely feel.

At the top of the street sat a sturdy, pillared bank. We veered left and wound further up the hill past houses with startlingly green lawns. They were well kept and led mysteriously down the sides of houses. There was simplicity in the detail, and after so long in the white of Antarctica, their lush colour was riveting and pleasing. Deep emerald, like my favourite Derwent pencil when I was a kid. My eyes soaked them up as I inhaled the moist, grassy odour, mixed with the rich pungency of soil. Fallen leaves were heaped neatly, with their own musty notes of decay. My head swirled giddily; I hadn't realised how much I'd missed the familiar scents of gardens. For a fleeting moment I longed for my family home in Kew.

Nancy stopped at a grey-shingled house with white windows, a wooden sign announcing Annie Coffin's Inn. There was a glossy black door with a brass whale doorknocker and shiny brass lanterns on either side. On the rooftop rose a tiny balcony – a widow's walk where wives had stood and waited for their husbands, captains sailing their whaling boats around the world. Homecoming would have been ecstatic but the seas were unforgiving and some men never returned. I wondered where Erling had lived; he hadn't mentioned an address in his book. It intrigued me that he'd moved here decades after Nantucket had sent out its last whaling ship in the late 1860s. But Erling had been explicit: this island welcomed whalers into its heart. He had come on business in the 1930s and felt so at home he bought a house, and in quick succession married and made it his northern-summer base.

As we entered the inn I drew in my breath: wide pine plank floors had mellowed to the colour of honey, and gold-framed paintings of ships sailing the high seas lined the hallway. To one side, a dining room flowed off with a grand table and chairs and a rich red carpet, and beyond was a lounge room with an elegant white timber fireplace in which a fire blazed, its wood crackling merrily. Above the doors were small windows that let the light shine through; large colonial paned windows lined the walls. Welcoming navy and white curtains hung luxuriously to the floor.

It was similar to the houses at Fredelighavn but like the flipside of a coin. It was so warm and lived in. I immediately relaxed.

Nancy carried my bag up the wide wooden staircase and deposited it in a room on the top floor that had a spectacular view down to the harbour. I could see boats bobbing in the swell and a long flat goods ferry, the *M/V Sankaty*, sliding in. The bed looked soft and inviting, covered in a red, white and blue quilt, thick and handmade. There was a tiny ensuite bathroom off to one side. I sighed – it was perfect.

'Hot chocolate downstairs when you're ready,' said Nancy. 'You're my only guest tonight, so just make yourself right at home.' I struggled to find words to thank her, I felt so over-whelmed. I tried to look directly and smile, remembering what Snow had said about my distant gaze. But Nancy didn't seem the least bit worried as she turned and skipped down the stairs with an energy that was contagious.

I unpacked, wishing I could stay a while; sad knowing that I must be quick. I needed to find everything I could about Erling and the whaling station, and then get back to Snow – and the boy in the ice. I sat on the bed, which absorbed my weight in such comfort I longed to lie and sleep. But instead I checked my email just in case there was a message from Alice at the museum. Still no word.

I went downstairs, wafts of freshly baked cookies drifting towards me.

In the kitchen Nancy was lifting a tray filled with perfect golden orbs dotted with chocolate chips from the oven.

'Pull up a chair,' she said.

I sat down at the scrubbed pine table and Nancy served me hot chocolate and cookies. I almost purred with delight. This was the home I'd never had, my mother always too busy working to bake treats. And she didn't believe in anything containing sugar.

I tried to talk with my mouth full, but had to make a choice: eat more cookies or ask the question. I gulped two more down, took a sip of hot chocolate, and then sat forward.

'These are the most delicious cookies, ever.'

Nancy beamed and pushed the plate closer. 'Have some more.'

I took another, and put it on my little china plate covered in blue hydrangeas.

'I was wondering if you knew Alice Hussey?' I said.

'Why, of course.'

'I need to contact her,' I offered politely.

'Alice is off-island at the moment. She won't be back till Friday night.' Nancy watched me curiously.

'I was hoping to talk to someone at the whaling museum.'

'Well, it's open Saturdays and Sundays at this time of year. And I believe from your booking you'll be here then?'

'Yes,' I smiled. 'I'd also like to go to the archive. I want to look up a Captain Halvorsen who lived here in the fifties.'

'You mean Erling?' Nancy roared with laughter.

'I do,' I said, surprised.

'Captain Halvorsen sounds so formal. Erling would've loved that. Would have made him smile.'

'So you knew him?' I asked, amazed.

'Whole town knew Erling. Mind you, in those days we *all* knew each other. Even now, those of us who stay on-island year-round are a pretty close bunch.'

'Did he have children?' I tried to keep a lid on my excitement. Right here in this warm kitchen sat a woman who'd known Erling. It was more than I could have hoped.

'Of course, my dear. Sons and a daughter. The boys moved to Boston but Helen stayed on the island. Lived here all her life.'

My heart missed a beat. 'Is she still here?'

'Right around the corner. Helen's one of my oldest friends.'

Blood rushed to my face.

'What's wrong, darling?' Nancy reached across.

'I would so like to meet her,' I said.

'Why don't I ring and see if we can go round? Or I could have her here for dinner.' Nancy rose. 'Let's see what suits.' My pulse was racing as I listened to the gentle babble of Nancy's voice from the next room.

Within minutes she returned, chuckling. 'Helen's going to make coffee. Thought you'd probably had enough hot chocolate. And she's putting out her best cookies – but don't you tell me they're better than mine or you'll be sleeping by the harbour.'

Nancy smiled broadly and went into the hallway to shrug on her coat. I followed and hurled on mine, wrapping a scarf around my neck. We marched outside, Nancy as keen as I was to get on with the conversation.

Helen Halvorsen lived in a gracious sea-captain's house on top of the hill, with cedar shingles weathered a silky grey, large white colonial windows, and two attic windows jutting out like friendly eyes from the slate roof. As Nancy knocked on the front door, the colour of deep blue sea, it flung open. The woman standing in the entrance – early seventies, tall and lean – had the same pale eyes as her ancestors. In real life they were grey with a touch of blue, like a far-flung ocean, and almost transparent. A mane of blonde hair perfectly framed a face that was generous and vibrant; full lips had just a hint of pink lipstick. Helen was a beauty like her grandmother Ingerline. They could have been sisters, but Helen was much more relaxed. Time had not worn her down. She was dressed immaculately in a soft blue jumper, camel trousers and matching stylish leather pumps with discreet gold buckles.

Nancy's introduction was short, as she only knew my name and nationality.

Helen reached out and shook my hand with a firm grip. 'So lovely to meet you, Laura,' she said, in a gentle rhythm that echoed Nancy's. I was enjoying the elegance of the Nantucket accent, its soft vowels and tunefulness; the uniformity of the women's voices struck me, after having been around such a cultural mix in Antarctica. 'Come right on in. I've a hot brew on the stove.' Helen led the way down a long, wide passage.

A heavenly mix of cinnamon and almond wafted to meet us. Had Helen managed to whip up a batch of cookies in the minutes it had taken us to walk around?

We entered the kitchen: through huge old windows the manicured lawn fell away, revealing a vista of the entire Nantucket harbour. Sailing boats bobbed about. The *Sankaty* was heading out to sea again.

Helen ushered me to a chair at a long, cherry-wood table in the middle of the room where three mugs were neatly set. Nancy sat up one end while Helen went to the stove nestled in a giant old fireplace, plucked up the coffee and brought it over.

'Nancy tells me you want to talk about my father?' Helen's pale eyes shone.

'I'm doing an environmental study on Fredelighavn—'

Helen gasped and sat down opposite me. 'Fredelighavn? I haven't heard that name in a very long time.'

'I've been down there for the past few weeks. It's a beautiful village.'

'It is.' She nodded but didn't seem certain.

'I found a book in the library written by your father on the history.'

'He was mighty proud of that book.' Helen smiled.

'Have you been down there yourself?' I asked.

'Indeed I have.' She fell silent.

'It's extraordinary to think all those people went each summer. It must have been bustling,' I said.

'Oh yes, my word. It was a bustling settlement.' Helen paused, then sat forward. 'I was eight when I first went. Daddy took me and my two elder brothers while Mama stayed home with little

Peter, who was one year younger than me. Being the baby of the family, Mama over-protected him. He was so dark about not going.' She blinked and I caught the trace of a tear. 'We were a long time at sea. It was an adventure, all right.' Helen glanced at Nancy, who smiled back gently, reassuring.

'I'll never forget crossing the Drake Passage,' Helen continued. 'Waves so high I thought we were gone. My brothers nearly died of seasickness but I managed fine. Uncle Olaf and Granny Inga looked after us like we were the Norwegian royal family itself. But the sight of the poor whales.' She stood abruptly, and moved to pull a tray of golden cookies from the oven. 'Better get these out before they ruin,' she said.

'Ooh, they smell good,' said Nancy. 'But remember what I told you.' She winked at me.

'What's that, Nance?' Helen arranged the cookies around an old creamware plate.

'She's not to like yours better than mine.'

Helen laughed, her skin crinkling. She offered me a cookie. 'Take two.'

I willingly obliged.

'You saw the whales?' I said.

'Yes. It was awful. I knew it was how Daddy and Uncle Olaf and Poppa Lars had made us rich, so I didn't dare say a word. I'll never forget my first whale. I ran away to the pigpens and hugged the little piglets and cried my eyes out. Then I went with the chickens and kept crying. Finally I went back to Daddy's house and Granny Inga put me on her lap and rocked and rocked. She knew exactly why I was upset and said I'd understand when I was older.'

'And now you do,' said Nancy.

Helen drew in her breath. 'I respect it but I never liked it. And I never let that get in the way of my love for my father. Sometimes you just have to let people be who they are.'

'This whole island's descended from whalers,' said Nancy, looking me firmly in the eye. 'Men who risked their lives for our prosperity. And they were true-life explorers, heading out over the oceans. My great-great-grandfather was one of the first to get down over your way, Laura, into the Southern Ocean. How far was that! The other side of the earth. They were explorers, all right, with the American spirit. They made our country great and all from this little sandy spit of an island.' She glowed with pride.

'And I don't disrespect them,' Helen emphasised again as she passed me more cookies. I took three, they were so delicious, and it was also my way of trying to show her support.

'My mama's family were Quakers here from way ago,' Helen continued. 'All sailors. Four whaling captains among them. Mama had two brothers taken by the sea.' Again Helen stopped. 'Anyways, tell us more about Fredelighavn. How's it stood up after all these years? I heard they turned it into a place no one could go.'

'That's right, in the seventies,' I said. 'And it's stood up just fine. It was incredibly well built.'

'Norwegians know how to do that,' said Helen, smiling. 'And the houses were pretty, weren't they?'

'They still are. Magical, actually.'

'Colours like the rainbow in a soap bubble. I went there four times, you know. Daddy and Granny Inga thought it was good for our constitution, and Granny loved having us with her.' This time Helen's eyes did tear up, I figured from nostalgia. I could see that she was growing tired, so I thought I'd better seize the moment and ask what I really needed to know.

'Helen, I was wondering – did you ever go in tunnels under the ice?'

She frowned, her blonde brows knitting together. 'Tunnels? No. Where are the tunnels?'

'I don't know exactly,' I said.

'Well, that's strange,' she replied and looked suddenly so frail and gloomy I wondered what I'd done. 'Laura, why are you asking about tunnels?'

'It's just … I wondered if I saw a chamber behind an ice cave.'

Helen looked at me almost knowingly. I fell silent, thinking how unlikely it would sound to say I thought I'd seen a boy in that chamber.

Helen was paling to the colour of porcelain as she gazed at me intently. She met my eyes, willing me to speak.

'I thought there was a boy there,' I stuttered, against my better instincts.

Helen tensed. 'A boy? What sort of boy?'

To my astonishment Helen didn't seem to think I was making things up.

'How old?' she demanded.

'About twelve. Dark-haired.'

She let out a yelp. I couldn't work out what was happening.

'Why are you coming round saying things like that?' asked Nancy sharply.

Helen pulled out a handkerchief and blew her nose, her pale eyes drilling into me. 'I lost my little brother down there, but you seem to know that already,' she said.

'I'm so sorry, I didn't.' I leaned over and touched her arm, which was as cold as if she were dead. In his book Erling had made no mention of his children.

Helen sat glaring. Nancy did the same. All the warmth had drained from the room. I kept quiet – desperate to know more but cautious not to upset her further.

'It was on my last trip down in 1955,' said Helen. 'I was thirteen and Peter was twelve. There was a whale in port and they were stripping its blubber. I stayed with Granny Inga and read a book. Peter hated what they did to those whales as much as I did and he slipped away. They always said he fell through a hole in the ice and drowned. Died of cold.' Her eyes held a fire beneath their shiny pale blue. 'Now you're telling me there were tunnels. That he fell into a tunnel. That you've seen his ghost in the ice.' She blew her nose again, loudly, furiously. 'What am I meant to believe?'

'No, no, that's not what I'm saying.' I leaned forward but she pulled her arm away. 'The boy I saw. He was alive.' As soon as the word left my mouth I knew it was the wrong one. 'It wasn't your brother.'

'Obviously it couldn't be my brother, he wouldn't still be a boy after more than sixty years,' she snapped. 'Where exactly did you see him?' She blew her nose a final time and slipped the handkerchief up her sleeve.

'I swam in from the ocean, he was in an ice cave. But he must have got down there some other way. We don't know who he is or why he was there.' A pang of emotion swept through me as I remembered the boy.

'Why didn't he swim into the cave like you?'

'He was behind a wall.'

'A man-made wall?'

'No, an ice wall.'

'Where was this again?'

'Up near Alliance Point. Below the cliff.'

Helen's shoulders sagged. 'My little brother fell in the town. Near the bakery. The new bakery, not the old bakery – that was up near the pigs and chickens and wasn't used any more by then.'

It was strange to hear it talked about like a living village.

'Do you think there could have been tunnels?' I asked directly.

She sat back and traced a nod. 'I never believed he fell through the ice. There wasn't that much of it around that summer in the streets. And when Peter and I had explored around those dreadful sheds where they boiled the blubber and made the guano, there were all sorts of nooks and crannies that could have gone underground. Well, there were trapdoors. But we opened a couple and they didn't seem to go anywhere.'

'When you say near the bakery, do you mean by the cinema?'

'That's right. Straight opposite. In the street between the cinema and the bakery, that's where they said he fell through. Froze to death in the icy water, they claimed.' She turned even paler, and her breathing quickened.

A chill crept up my spine. 'Helen, did you ever play around the stage in that cinema?'

'Around it? No. On it, yes. I fancied myself as a bit of an actress and Granny Inga indulged me.'

'Could there have been a way underground beneath the stage?'

'Well, anything's possible, isn't it, but no one told me anything.' Her breathing was growing coarser. I'd taxed her. It was pitch black outside.

'We must be on our way,' said Nancy protectively, rising. I did the same.

'I'm sorry,' I said. 'I've kept you too long.'

'Come back tomorrow, dear,' said Helen, softening. 'You just gave me a fright but I can see you didn't mean to.' She stood stiffly, and Nancy and I followed her out of the room. In the passage I noticed a table of family photographs.

'Peter's not there,' Helen said, catching me looking. 'My mama never got over it. She wasn't in Fredelighavn, see? Didn't like the rough ocean journey even though she came from generations of sailors. Blamed herself, didn't she? It's not natural for a mother to outlive her son, not in this day and age, she'd say. Not in the 1950s.' I felt an awful bond – *a mother who'd lost her son* – as I gazed at the photo of the thin, sad woman, pale-skinned, dark-haired, a thick knot forming in my throat. But Helen was moving away towards the front door and I had to follow. 'Buried all the photos with her. It was Mama's way of being with him.'

I wanted to hug Helen as she opened the sea-blue door, but she stood proud and upright. She looked into the distance as we said goodbye.

'Come back tomorrow, Laura. I'll let you see some things. Maybe you'll find those tunnels if you know where to look.' She shut the door gently and we made our way through the freezing cold back to Nancy's house. I forced myself not to dwell on Hamish – the terrifying emptiness that robbed my own will to live, on the day I buried him. I couldn't afford to lose myself in memories or it would be impossible to think about anything else.

I didn't feel like sitting and eating; I wanted to be alone, to make notes about what I'd just heard. But Nancy insisted, heating up leftovers – an aromatic beef stew. Home-grown carrots, green beans and baby potatoes glistening with butter were dished on the side. They were the first fresh vegetables I'd had in months, and even though I was distracted my mouth watered with every bite, savouring each morsel after such a long absence. We sat in front of television, both only pretending to watch the news. As soon as we'd finished, we went upstairs. Nancy stopped on the landing; her room was opposite mine.

'I know you didn't mean any harm. I just hate to see my old friend like that. Erling never talked about it, you know, the loss of that poor little boy. I'm a year younger than Helen. I was in his class at school.' Nancy went into her room and shut the door.

I felt terrible. It was devastating to think of the death of a child down there. But Helen hadn't dismissed the notion of tunnels under Fredelighavn. She'd embraced it. Clearly she'd wondered all these years about them.

I didn't believe in ghosts. There was a boy down there. One I could save. If I could find the tunnels, I could find him.

16

I woke cocooned in feather-soft sheets that smelled of salt and roses. Sitting up I remembered where I was, and the grief of yesterday's conversation came flooding back: little Peter, his photos buried with his mother who had died of a broken heart.

The friendship between Nancy and Helen was strong. I'd be like that with Kate and Georgia when I was old. Island life had similarities to Antarctica: friendships were more intense, enduring. Creating new memories; protecting us from the abyss of loss.

I hauled myself out of bed and had a quick shower, the steam fragrant from a spiced cranberry soap.

By the time I went downstairs, Nancy was serving up breakfast. Two puffy pancakes smothered in cranberry jam were placed in front of me. As I put the first forkful in my mouth, the cranberries exploded, sharp and sweet. There was a glass of fresh cranberry juice to wash them down.

'Sleep well?' Nancy shuffled back in an oversized fleecy dressing gown and placed another hot pancake on my plate. I devoured the lot and had a fourth, the food so different to the fare I'd eaten in the past twelve months.

'So we'll go over to Helen's and see if we can make head or tail of the papers stashed in her attic. She was going to bring them down herself but I convinced her to let you do it. You're much stronger and younger than us.' Nancy beamed.

I was touched they'd forgiven me so quickly.

'And don't you go listening to my friend about those poor old whales. The men had to make a living. I doubt any of them really liked the killing. It was something they had to do. They were brave adventurers who put this country on the map long before those west-coasters went out into the prairies.'

I thought it best to let the conversation stop there. I didn't want to get into a fight about the slaughter of American Indians on top of what happened to the whales. Yet I couldn't help feeling a grudging respect for the ancestors of Nancy and Helen. It wouldn't have been easy for them. I tried to convince myself that they didn't know that whales had feelings akin to humans. The field of cognitive ethnology had only begun in the 1970s, when scientists put forward the theory that whales could not only feel, but love. I remembered Lev's care when I swam with him – it would stay with me forever.

Suddenly breakfast wasn't sitting well as I tried to bat away images of the whales being stripped of their blubber at Fredelighavn.

'Something wrong with the pancakes?' Nancy hovered close.

'No, they're delicious.' We chatted over coffee and then I went up to my room to put in a call. I was eager to start trawling through Erling's papers but I wanted to set up a meeting with Snow. If I didn't find anything about the tunnels today, I could leave the women searching while I went to re-establish a connection with the one person who might be able to tell me what was going on at Fredelighavn. I looked up his department at Harvard online, found the number, and dialled. After a while a woman picked up the phone.

'I was wondering if I could speak to Professor Andrew Flynt please? It's Doctor Alvarado calling.'

'I'm sorry, Doctor Alvarado, but Professor Flynt isn't with us.'

'He's not come in yet since Antarctica?' I asked confidently.

She paused. 'Professor Flynt is no longer on staff.'

I went silent with shock, and tried to gather my thoughts. 'When did that happen? I mean, when did he leave?'

'A few months ago. Back in July.'

I felt the blood drain from my face. 'Do you have a contact where I can reach him?'

'I'm sorry, I can't give out that information. Is there someone else who can help you?'

'Thanks anyway.' I hung up and sat on the bed, realising now the folly of my plan. Why had Snow lied? I thought of how he'd ignored me on the trip back to America, and how evasive he'd been when we'd arrived. Was Georgia right about him?

I hauled myself up and stared out the window at the boats in the harbour. The *Sankaty* was coming in again, slowly approaching the dock.

How would I find Snow now? And he certainly wouldn't be pleased to see me. I looked at the time. Georgia would be asleep, so I sent her an email.

Nancy called up from the bottom of the stairs. 'Ready to head to Helen's?'

'Could I just have a few more minutes, please?' I called back.

'Take as long as you need, Laura. Come down when you're ready.'

I went back online, searching for Sam Wiltshire, a colleague I knew at Harvard in marine biology, who I'd worked with in Melbourne. I found his email address and sent a message, saying I was in the States briefly and would love to catch up. Could he contact me as soon as he could?

I stared out at the harbour again, trying to make sense of what I'd just heard about Snow. I longed to speak to Georgia, but Nancy was waiting in the kitchen.

The day was mild, with a fresh sea breeze as we walked around to Helen's house. Birdsong filled the air. Most of the trees were bare, their skeletal branches overhanging the street. High up, I caught sight of a bright red bird. The reddest bird I'd ever seen, flitting between a few vibrant orange leaves that still clung on.

'Whatever's that?' I stopped to gaze at the bird.

Nancy peered up. In a red flash, the bird flew to another tree. As it perched, I saw it had a top-notch sticking from its head. It was cheeky and sublime. And perfect. A fiery, audacious bird.

'That's a cardinal. There's a couple live out back in my hydrangeas,' said Nancy. 'In fall they seem to move about the streets. One of the prettiest birds you're likely to see.'

The cardinal seemed full of hope as it flitted from tree to tree, its striking red burning against the pale sky.

Helen opened the door seconds after we knocked. 'Come in, come in, I have a pot brewing. No doubt you've had breakfast but I've baked some blueberry muffins.'

All hint of yesterday's tension had disappeared. She took my arm and led me down the passage, smelling of spicy cranberries, like me.

I loved the homeliness of the kitchen, its warmth and sweet aromas. Helen had set three mugs on the table again, which she filled with dark, rich coffee. She took the blueberry muffins from the oven and arranged them on another creamware plate. Although I was full, I couldn't resist eating one – and then another. I had to force myself to stop or I would've eaten the whole batch. They were sweet without being cloying, and the blueberries, plump and juicy, were even tastier than the cranberries in Nancy's jam.

'So, I've been going through the boxes in the attic,' said Helen, 'but I stuck to my promise and have waited for you to bring them down.'

'Let's go,' I said. 'I can finish my coffee as we look through.'

Both Helen and Nancy scowled. 'Those papers are precious, my dear,' said Helen. 'There'll be no drinking or eating while they're out. I have cotton gloves for us to wear.'

'All the originals are here,' said Nancy. 'The archives only have copies.'

'Isn't that the opposite of what you'd normally do?' I asked, surprised, and they both laughed.

'We do as must needs,' said Helen. 'I could never part with Daddy's papers, and he didn't want me to either. He left strict instructions.'

'You're very lucky that you're going to see these,' said Nancy.

We quickly finished our coffee and climbed a broad staircase. At the top of a second flight of stairs was a small door. Helen went ahead and opened it.

Old timber shelves lined the walls, filled with boxes of paper-work, neatly filed.

'What you want is over here,' said Helen, leading the way.

I carried down a total of twenty-four boxes. We placed them in chronological order on the kitchen table, and on sofas in the adjoining lounge room. Helen passed us each a pair of cotton gloves and once they were on, she opened the first box and brought out a stack of papers browning at the edges. They were hand-written, in English.

'Let's see what we have here,' she said. 'I've never been through these.' Her hands trembled as she began to look.

'Well, we each need a heap,' said Nancy, 'or we'll be here all year.'

I took my batch and found myself staring at research notes. They seemed to be for Erling's book. For the first hour I scanned ghastly descriptions of how, by the time Erling and his family arrived at South Safety Island, some of the ships had been adapted to process the whales on-board rather than have to take them all to shore. Pelagic whaling allowed the whalers to slaughter and process thousands more whales, stripping off the blubber either on factory ships, or towing the whales to a safe harbour and flensing them beside the boat. They were killing so many whales, there wasn't room for them all at Fredelighavn. But the shore station used the whole of the whale with no wastage, and Erling's father Lars, and later Erling and his brother Olaf, enjoyed processing guano as well as oil. Erling gave vivid descriptions of the various cookeries involved along the way. I started to scan quickly, whipping through page after page, not wanting to fill my head with the horrible images.

'You're a fast reader,' said Helen. She'd only got through a few pages, savouring every description of her father's – which meant she probably didn't have accounts of whale slaughter.

'May I?' I said, and reached out to her pile.

'You don't like yours?'

'It's about life on board the ships and what they did to the whales.'

'Then here you go.' Helen gave me the rest of her stack. 'This stuff's interesting.' She opened a fresh box while I started to read through my new papers. She was right – it was a daily description of life on shore: the operation of the bakery, fights between the pigs, which ships were being fixed in the repair yard and problems with the conveyor belts around the station. There was, however, no mention of tunnels. I moved to another box and pulled out its yellowed papers.

These were about the entertainment at Fredelighavn: a list of films that were screened in the late 1940s and early 1950s. Mainly old horror movies, a lot from Val Lewton: *Cat People*, *Curse of the Cat People*, *The Body Snatcher*, *I Walked with A Zombie*. I smiled to think of the whalers and their families enjoying being spooked at the end of the earth.

They'd also put on plays, organised by Ingerline. There was plentiful description of the productions – surprisingly, Shakespeare, and a few Rodgers and Hammerstein musicals. Ingerline seemed to have become anglicised. It occurred to me I hadn't yet asked an obvious question.

'Did Ingerline come to Nantucket?'

'Granny Inga? Of course. Winter, she was always in Antarctica, because that's summer down there. But each Northern summer when it was winter in Fredelighavn she lived right here with us. Every second year, that is. In between she lived with Uncle Olaf or Uncle Julius in Larvik in Norway. Uncle Julius ran the company from there. The Larvik Fishing Company. It was a real family affair. Granny Inga had raised her sons well. And she hoped we'd all go into the company one day, me included.'

'What was she like?'

Helen's face relaxed and her eyes twinkled. 'Fun loving. Adored the theatre and movies. But she could be strict and stern too. After my granddad died she really was the force behind the company. A true matriarch. And of course it was Granny who expanded Fredelighavn and made it into a real village, and that was early up, in the twenties. Daddy didn't put that in his book, I told him he should have. But I think he thought it might make his father look weak.

'Granny wanted men to be with their families down there so they wouldn't go rough. She organised those homes to be built. Before it was just barracks, with two separate bathhouses. A few years back I took a cruise down to Antarctica, when they started opening things up to tourists. Of course we couldn't go to Fredelighavn but the ship stopped in at Grytviken on

South Georgia. That was another whaling station run by Norwegians. Although the operations were actually owned by an Argentinian company, as Granny Inga liked to point out – so it wasn't through and through Norwegian like ours.'

'I know it,' I said. 'I've been there.' I smiled to myself. I'd always thought of Grytviken as Norwegian because both the station and the South American company had been set up by a Norwegian captain. Granny Inga would have chided me.

'Then you'd see it's a very different place. Just one big house for the Station Head, and the barracks. It had the bakeries like us, and all the blubber-boiling sheds and guano sheds and all. But it doesn't have the houses, does it? Not the civilised village. Although it does have a church. Granny Inga wanted hers to be more beautiful. That's why she put that gold orb on top of the steeple.' Helen sat back and grinned.

'Did Ingerline run Fredelighavn for a long time?' I asked, growing increasingly amazed by the woman, a pioneer who had been largely written out of Erling's official history.

'Granddad Lars passed away in 1948. I was only six, so I don't remember him much. It was Granny I knew, the way she organised everything through the toughest years. The whale numbers were declining and there was growing hostility about the entire whaling enterprise. But Granny stuck to her guns. I loved being with her. Down at Fredelighavn and here on Nantucket. We all treasured her. The whole island – she was like a piece of living history.'

'I adored Inga,' said Nancy. 'She was a formidable dame.' The two friends laughed.

'She died in 1982 at ninety years of age,' said Helen. 'She was determined to meet that milestone, and she did. Of course by then the company had been wound up years before. But Granny still alternated her time between Nantucket and Norway.'

It was remarkable to hear Ingerline spoken of with such familiarity. I was beginning to know her. The portrait I'd seen in Fredelighavn hadn't captured her at all. If the whaling station were ever opened up to tourists, I would recommend historians record an oral history from Helen. If there were to be a museum, Ingerline would be given her rightful place in history. Apart from the sickening fact it was wholesale slaughter she was leading, her feats in designing the village were noteworthy.

Fredelighavn stood for so much. The vision and bravery of those who'd formed it was extraordinary, given they were building in the most inhospitable place on earth. That they were so bright and yet so wrong in what they were doing at the Larvik Fishing Company was a tension that might create a fascinating quandary for tourists to ponder. The ignorance about whales could be compared to the ignorance about global warming; how people could be caught up in something they didn't, and couldn't, comprehend.

'A penny for your thoughts?' said Helen. 'You look a million miles away. Perhaps you need more coffee. If you go into the lounge room, I'll bring some. But don't go near the boxes.'

Nancy and I hurried in, eager for refreshment and more blueberry muffins.

'I do hope you open up Fredelighavn,' said Nancy. 'I'd so love to go there.'

*

By the end of a very long day I knew a lot about the village but there was still no reference to tunnels. I'd scoured everything to do with the cinema and new bakery, the area where poor Peter had supposedly fallen through the ice, but there was nothing to indicate any underground structures. Of course they might not have told Helen the truth about where the boy had met his fate. If he had fallen through into a tunnel they might have wanted to keep her well away for safety. And if the family company owned everything, how much better did it seem that it was an accident of nature and not one of human negligence.

Helen declined Nancy's invitation to dinner and so it was just the two of us who walked through the icy night back to Annie Coffin's Inn. Nancy had left a chicken-and-tomato stew cooking slowly all day, and now its aroma filled the air, the homeliness bringing a prick of tears to my eyes. We ate rapidly, starving after our long hours of reading.

'We'll find those tunnels,' said Nancy, as we turned in for an early night, 'don't you worry.' Neither she nor Helen had asked further details about why a boy might have been in an ice cave. That was their way, it seemed. Helpful but not nosy. The opposite of my mother.

I quickly put my mother out of my mind as I hopped into bed. She'd emailed twice asking me to phone, and I was avoiding it. I couldn't deal with listening to her endless string of woes at the moment. No doubt her university was still pressuring her to retire and I didn't want to be the one to tell her they were right. Although that would give her more time to interfere in my life. On second thoughts, I hoped she'd keep her job.

Just as I was falling asleep my phone pinged. I thought it would be Georgia, who hadn't yet returned my email – but it was Sam Wiltshire, from Harvard. He could meet tomorrow.

I emailed back and set a time for lunch.

The next morning, I wolfed down pancakes perfect with fresh lemon and sugar while Nancy promised that she and Helen would keep searching Erling's papers in my absence. She didn't pry about my dash to Boston.

The buildings of Main Street twinkled in the early light as Nancy walked me down the hill. We passed an old pharmacy with the original counter and chairs for soda pops, a true traditional drugstore; there was an inviting bookstore, and shops with enticing displays of sofas, snug woven rugs and island artwork featuring bobbing sailboats in the colours of the rainbow. It all spoke of cosy rooms waiting to be filled with beauty and ideas, just like the ones I was leaving for the day. I looked forward to coming home to dinner and hearing how Helen and Nancy had fared.

We walked past sturdy brick buildings centuries old and up onto Straight Wharf. A few tourists were queuing in a snaking line, waiting for the ferry. There was a small shop, already open, selling exquisite drink coasters of colourful yachts, painted by a famous local artist. They were just the type of thing my mother loved, and I made a mental note to buy a set on my way back. In spite of everything, I did like bringing Mum souvenirs, especially nautical ones that made her too-big house feel more homely.

'I'd better love you and leave you,' said Nancy as I took my place in the ferry queue. She pressed a shiny penny into my hand. 'Throw this when you go past the lighthouse at Brant Point. It means you'll be back. It's good luck.'

I thanked her. 'And happy hunting,' I said.

Nancy grew serious. 'I know it would take a weight off Helen's shoulders if she felt she knew the truth about her brother after all these years. And if you're right that there's a boy down there now ... Well, I'd better hurry, hadn't I?' She kissed me and hugged tightly. 'It's just the way we do things here,' she said warmly.

Her hair bobbed in the breeze as she strode back towards town.

I boarded the ferry and went up to the top deck, through the cabin and outside to the stern. We drew away through calm water the colour of forget-me-nots, grey and white houses peeking through bare branches sweeping up the hill, and little cottages crowded around tiny wharves at the edge of the harbour echoing the soft silvery hues. The *Sankaty* was docked, loading up cars and goods to take to the mainland. Higher up, a white church with a golden steeple caught the morning sun.

As we passed the lighthouse I hurled my penny into the churning sea. I looked back at the sandy spit, yachts bobbing in the Sound behind, receding as we picked up speed. Nantucket had already taken a place in my heart.

At Hyannis I hired a car, and two hours later in Boston Sam and I were sitting near the harbour in Little Italy, hunched over bowls of pasta full of sweet seafood in a spicy sauce. After catching up on news of mutual friends, I came to the point.

'I met a fascinating scientist on South Safety Island at the Alliance Base. Professor Andrew Snowden Flynt. People call him Snow. I was wondering if you knew him?'

Sam's curly brown hair and thick eyebrows set off his bright, animated face. 'Can't say I do. Is he at Harvard?'

'Well, that's the thing. He was but he's just left. I was curious to know why.'

Sam frowned. 'That's an odd question.'

'I was quite taken by him.'

'So you're keen on him?'

'You could say that.'

'Still single, then?'

'Yeah, tell me about it.'

'I'll see what I can find out. I'm guessing you want to contact him?' Sam grinned.

I nodded, smiling. Amused, Sam picked up his phone and tapped a contact. After a while a man's voice came on the end of the line. 'It's me, Sam. Just wondering if you had a number or an address for Snow Flynt?'

I listened but couldn't hear what the other person was saying.

'An old friend wants to pay him a visit.' Sam winked. 'Wants to take him some flowers to thank him for something he did for her.' Sam pulled out a pen and wrote the address on a paper napkin, along with a phone number I knew I wouldn't use. Some things must be done in person.

As he went to end the call, I signalled for Sam to ask why Snow had left Harvard. Luckily Sam was quick on the uptake and did my bidding. After he'd hung up he leaned forward eagerly. 'He got a position down there in Antarctica. Chose to give up his professorship. It must have been a big promotion. Although, my mate hinted he may have left under a cloud. There was no farewell, just an announcement and a sudden departure. Not the usual fanfare and emeritus and all that. So I guess he's not really even a professor any more. It's not like he went to another university.'

I tried to take in what I was hearing but it was making my head spin. Sam passed across the paper napkin with the contact details.

'You sure you want to follow him up?' Sam's dark eyes caught mine. 'Harvard's not the sort of place people leave like that.'

An hour later I was back on the road, heading to Cape Cod where Snow lived in the small community of Chatham.

I looked at the map on my GPS – Chatham was quite close to Hyannis, and lay 90 miles south-east of Boston. It stuck out on the right elbow of the Cape, just before the land hooked up to the stretch that led to Provincetown.

As I drove into Chatham I was struck by how pretty it was. Houses were traditional grey-shingled cedar with white windows; gardens were lush and neat as a pin, with towering trees, many bare-branched at this time of year. Their leaves had all been picked up, as if an army of elves were keeping everything in order, letting nothing fall out of place. It was designer heaven, and it had a surprisingly calming effect on me. If only life could be like this in reality. There was no litter, no tackiness. It was a truly genteel, pleasant place. And when

I wound down my window, there was the tangy, revitalising smell of salt.

Snow's house was past the commercial harbour, and through the town. In Main Street the stores were alluring: little jewellery shops, bookstores, cafes. Many were open, their lights ablaze in the darkening afternoon. From the map I could see that Snow's place was perched on the water, overlooking the wild Atlantic Ocean.

Huge gulls flapped in the wind like white and grey mop-rags. I passed an extensive lighthouse complex that hosted the US Coast Guard; the lighthouse itself was a tall white beauty with a black top striking up into the grey sky.

The navigation misled me and I ended up in a dead-end, at a private marina. Boats were moored along a canal, and on the other side, vessels sat hoisted and housed on a dry dock. There were a couple of men in a shed, working on an engine.

I parked and braved an icy wind to ask for Ocean Street. A man in oil-stained overalls, eyebrows crusted with salt that was whipping off the sea, directed me. In two minutes I was driving slowly by the house of Andrew Snowden Flynt, past but not present Harvard professor. I couldn't see much because it was hidden behind a green hedge and tall, established evergreen trees. The grey-tiled roof looked impressive and high. I reached the end of the street and turned around, cruising slowly past again. I still couldn't get a proper view.

I pondered whether to drive up to the solid timber gates and press the intercom. But I needed to collect my thoughts, so I drove back to town, parked in Main Street and went into the lone cafe that was now the only one open. The town had shut quickly. It was already five o'clock and the last ferry from Hyannis to Nantucket was at six-thirty. It would take me at least half an hour driving down the Cape to get there. I couldn't linger, but neither did I want to leave.

'Can I help you?' A waitress with dirty-blonde hair bunched into a ponytail took my order. I asked for a coffee, figuring I'd have plenty to eat when I got back to Annie Coffin's Inn.

When she brought a steaming mug of dark liquid I asked for a recommendation for a place to stay, as I was planning to return tomorrow.

'There's a very good inn just off Main Street.' She scrawled the name and directions on a coaster. 'Highly recommended. What brings you to us?'

I thanked her and pocketed the coaster, wondering how much to give away; in a place like this everyone was sure to know everyone. 'I'm just passing through, but while I'm here I thought I'd look up a friend. I don't suppose you know him – Snow Flynt?'

Her face changed just a fraction, and her body tensed, but she covered with a broad smile. 'Can't say I do. He live here?'

'Just down the road. I'm going to pay him a surprise visit.'

This time her face clouded over. 'Uh-huh.' She made herself busy and disappeared out the back. I checked my watch. I couldn't miss the ferry, so I called goodbye and hurried through the freezing air to my car. From her sudden vanishing act, I suspected the waitress did know Snow – and didn't like him.

17

Nancy and Helen were waiting as I clanged down the gangplank into the misty night.

'How was your day, dear?' asked Helen, brimming with excitement.

'You look like you've found something,' I said, my own excitement growing.

They beamed.

'A reference to tunnels,' said Helen.

'Two references, in fact. A few years apart,' chimed Nancy.

I caught my breath. 'Where?'

'Well, we don't know yet,' Helen said. 'Daddy didn't exactly say where. But both times he said the tunnels were holding up well. That was in 1949 and 1952 – the last was just three years before my brother . . .' Her voice trailed away. I linked my arm through hers as we headed up Straight Wharf.

'Now we know the tunnels exist,' I said, a thrill zipping through me. 'That's a huge step forward.' *But not enough – we urgently needed to know where the tunnels were.*

'Isn't it just?' said Nancy proudly.

'It's been strange going through Daddy's things,' said Helen as the old-fashioned streetlamps of Main Street came into view, golden haloes in the fog. 'It brings him right back, you know. He had such a way with words. And to think of Fredelighavn after all these years. I was wondering, Laura, do you have photographs? I'd so love to see how it looks now.'

'Of course.' Although my report was confidential, the photos might jog Helen's memory to reveal something useful. 'I'll bring them over.'

'Tonight? We have dinner ready at my place.' Her voice was light with anticipation.

'You *have* been busy.'

'We girls are good multi-taskers,' said Nancy. 'You go freshen up and then join us.'

Back in my room, I took out my camera and computer and assembled a slideshow of Fredelighavn. My fingers flew over the keyboard as I reconstructed the village.

After Nancy cleared the dishes we moved into the lounge and sat in front of the television. I plugged in my laptop and started the slideshow. The first image was of the flensing platform and the cookery sheds, because these were what Helen would have seen as she sailed in. She sat upright, absorbing everything. The next images were taken as I walked up a street of houses.

'Could you tell me when we get to Ingerline's place?' I asked.

'Not in this street,' said Helen. 'We're going away from the harbour, so it's further over to the left.' My skin felt like it was being pricked with tiny needles. We were heading, house by house, towards the large pink and blue home with the gramophone where I'd seen the ghost of Ingerline in the mirror. 'Stop!' Helen cried as I reached it. She hunched forward and breathed in quietly. 'That's Daddy's house.'

So Ingerline's ghost – not that I believed in ghosts – had been in Erling's home.

'Where did Ingerline live?' I asked.

'Well, Uncle Olaf lived right next door to my father in the beautiful rose-coloured house, and after Granddad passed away Granny sometimes stayed there; when we were down she stayed in Daddy's house with us. Other times she went back to her own place.'

'Was that the orange house?' I asked, my body tingling as I remembered Ingerline's portrait.

'The house opposite? Yes, that one's hers. It was the grandest place in the village. Granddad Lars made sure of that.' Helen chuckled. 'With those fierce portraits. That artist didn't capture them at all. Missed their spirit, everyone said. Gave us a good old time teasing Granny Inga. She'd wanted another but Granddad wouldn't spend the money.'

I went through the photos of Erling's house, the convex Regency mirror on the wall, the furniture sitting snugly, the gramophone and records, and Helen's eyes welled. 'Nothing's changed,' she said in a hushed voice. 'Nothing at all. It's as though we could all be there still, listening to that beautiful music.' Tears streamed down her face. I remembered how the notes had filled the house when Kate played the gramophone.

'Oh my word. Daddy just loved classical. And so do I. What I would give to have those records,' said Helen.

It was an interesting thought. Who did own the records now? Perhaps I could repatriate them to her when my report was done. I could certainly raise the issue with the Council.

'I might be able to do something about that,' I said.

'I would be most grateful. The records and the gramophone. I wouldn't be able to play them otherwise.' Helen smiled gently.

'Wouldn't that be swell?' cried Nancy, clapping her hands together.

I continued to screen the photos, moving through the kitchen and upstairs to the bedrooms. 'This one's mine,' said Helen and her face dropped. 'It's been stripped. How odd. Why would Daddy have done that?'

I looked at the photo anew. Perhaps Erling hadn't done it. Had the intruders at Fredelighavn shifted things around? It was entirely possible.

'Your Dad didn't bring things back here?'

'No, he brought nothing. When Fredelighavn closed, it was a very fraught time. Everyone thought the whaling would continue. But one year – 1957 – it just stopped. The politics and the finances and the lack of whales – what they'd call now a perfect storm. When November came round, no one went back. The place was abandoned. But some workers had seen the writing on the wall and already left. They were the ones who moved their stuff. But Daddy and Granny and Uncle Olaf – they were believers. It hit them hard. And if it hadn't been for the Antarctic Treaty, I think they would have tried to go back. I'm sure they left everything there. Daddy was very clear, and so was Granny. I remember because I was upset. I threw a tantrum – I wanted my things. So I don't understand what happened to my room at all.'

Her brow was creased, anger brewing. 'You say no one's been in?'

'Not officially.'

'Well, clearly someone has. My daddy did not dismantle my room. It was a beautiful room. A wonderful hand-made quilt, all my pictures around the walls. No, something's off here. Who did this?'

'I don't know,' I said. 'I wish I did.'

'You saw a boy – goodness knows who he was, or who he was with. Someone's tampered with my property. In a zone where no one's meant to be, in a place where I'm not allowed. Things are amiss down there, aren't they, Laura?'

Her pale eyes pierced mine.

'I think so,' I said.

'Then you must do something about it.' Helen sat frowning – she looked spent. Nancy said nothing, but she radiated anger on behalf of her friend. I decided it was not the moment to show photos of the area where they'd said Helen's brother had died. But before I left I was determined to see the references to the tunnels they'd found in Erling's notes.

Helen pulled out the pages, her earlier enthusiasm drained. It was just as they'd said: two notes, three years apart, commenting on the state of the tunnels. Frustratingly, there were no details as to where they were.

Helen was white and frail. I felt guilty I'd kept her up.

'I'm heading to Cape Cod for a night or two, tomorrow,' I said. 'If you have time, could you keep looking for more references to the tunnels? But I'd understand if you've had enough.'

'We'll keep looking, all right,' said Helen, clear-voiced, and relief surged through me. 'But now I do need to get to bed. Seeing those photos is like being back there. It's a lot for me to think about.' Her pale eyes didn't tear up this time but Nancy still gave her a tight hug.

As we headed off into the night Helen called, 'Take care, Laura. Come back safe.'

I went up to my room and emailed Georgia, telling her about the existence of the tunnels, and the story of Helen's brother Peter falling into the ice near the cinema. I urged her and Kate to check under the stage when they could.

Then I packed. I decided to take everything, even though I was expecting to return. Given a couple of days, I was sure that Helen and Nancy would find more details.

The next morning the shops were hidden in a thick fog as I made my way down Main Street to Straight Wharf. Nancy had given me breakfast but had been keen to get to Helen's, which I'd encouraged, so today I was alone. I felt a melancholy tug in the silky half-light. I wished I could stay and delve through Erling's papers and find more about the tunnels. And I was indecisive about the best way to make contact with Snow.

I had plenty of time, so before I reached the end of Main Street I turned left to detour past the whaling museum. It was in a huge old red-brick building, with a white-pillared portico and a sunburst over its double doors. I could just make out on top, shrouded in fog, a viewing deck with a small white-windowed room. A whale was spinning slowly on a weather vane; I could see from its square nose that it was a sperm whale. It was Wednesday morning. Alice from the museum would be back for Saturday, and so should I.

Nantucket Sound was glass-calm as the ferry headed off. I went out onto the top deck and threw a penny back towards the lighthouse as we rounded the point. I didn't want to risk not returning.

My hire car was waiting where I'd parked it. I fired it up and drove the half-hour route through the Cape to Chatham, which was as pretty today as yesterday. The serenity and uniform beauty of the houses soothed me. I followed the waitress's instructions to the inn off the main street, turning right by a stately old Methodist church, its steeple shrouded in mist.

The inn was actually a motel – but not a typical string of small rooms lined up like ducks in a row. These were pictur-esque two-storey cottages arranged around lush gardens and a swimming pool that had been drained in readiness for winter. I parked and went into reception, where I was greeted by a woman with a blonde beehive hairdo, who looked almost identical to the waitress in the cafe except for the hair. As I went through the process of checking in I peered closely – the woman was wearing a wig.

'Have we met before?' I finally asked.

'Yes darling, in the cafe.' She smiled, swiping a red fingernail over the key to my room. 'Two-one-two, top floor. You have a gorgeous view to the sea.'

'You work two jobs?' I said.

'Many more than that at this time of year, honey. I'm here and at the cafe, and I clean the houses of the rich people who won't be back till summer. I'm trying to set up my own company selling kitchenware online, and in my spare time I paint church steeples.'

I laughed, but she was serious.

'In this economy, off-season, you do everything you can. By training I'm a musician. I'm Wendy Slattery.' She leaned across and shook my hand. 'I do a few shows here and there.'

'I'm Laura,' I said, but she already knew that from the check-in paperwork. She smiled back graciously.

I found my cottage and carried my bags up the stairs to the top floor, all the time wondering what to make of Wendy; I was certain that she knew things about Snow. I just had to work out how to get her to open up.

Wendy's description of my room proved accurate: it had a spectacular view out to sea. The water was grey and mist swirled above the surface. I stood gazing at the waves, trying to think how I could contact Snow. Part of me wanted to ring the intercom at his gate and announce myself. I'd take flowers, say I was in the area. But how would I claim to have found his address? It wasn't in the phone directory – I'd checked.

I sat down on the bed and pulled up my email. There was still nothing from Georgia, so I sent an email to Kate, asking if they'd had a chance to look under the stage for a tunnel entrance, and if she could get Georgia to contact me. Perhaps they were both camping again at Fredelighavn, and were out of range.

My mother had sent more emails, but I wasn't in the mood to reply, so I didn't open them.

I went for a drive to Snow's house, as though it might help me work out the best way to approach him. As I passed, the hedge and evergreen trees hid everything but the roof. I kept driving, and again ended up at the private marina. Fog hung low over the sea. Boats were perched high on the hydraulic double-storey dry dock – they were substantial pleasure craft. Other boats were tied in a canal, slapping gently against their moorings. A man working in a shed saw me. I drove off.

As I went back to town I stopped at the lighthouse with the Coast Guard sign that warned only *authorised personnel* could enter. Opposite down below was a wide, sandy beach, and sea that stretched for miles, limpid grey, peeking through a white shroud. Pale strips of sand bars cut the water. The lighthouse foghorn boomed, startling me. A long beam of light swept through the fog in a yellow arc. Atlantic gulls cried, lonely and forlorn.

I drove on past immaculate mansions with thick green lawns and well-tended gardens. Squirrels played beneath trees, grey feathered tails curled high as they scampered about. On one lawn a large hare wandered, grazing casually.

I parked outside the cafe. I was in luck: Wendy was behind the counter and I was the only customer. I bought a stack of fresh sandwiches and water to take away and ordered a coffee to have there.

'You visit your friend yet?' she asked, bringing over my drink. She'd taken off her wig and her hair was thin and lank, tied again in a ponytail. It was unnerving how she ping-ponged between glamorous and plain.

'He doesn't exactly know I'm coming.'

Wendy stopped and hovered.

I shrugged. 'I've only met him a few times but I really liked him.'

Wendy pulled up a chair and sat facing me from the next table. 'Honey, I think you're barking up the wrong tree there.'

'So you do know Snow?'

'The professor? Uh-huh.'

She seemed not remotely worried that she'd lied to me yesterday, or maybe she didn't remember.

'I do some cleaning, on account of there's no lady of the house.' Wendy pulled her chair closer, scraping it along the timber floor. She lowered her voice and glanced around, even though we were alone. 'I can see you're heading for trouble. You've got love written all over your face.'

Thank goodness Wendy had an imagination. I thought all I was showing was curiosity.

'Honey, I don't think there's *ever* going to be a lady of the house, if you know what I mean. The professor only lets me clean certain areas, other rooms are closed up tight. He's very particular. The other day I arrived early and he wasn't happy about that. I could have sworn I heard teenage boys laughing in the basement. He moved me upstairs quick as you please. You seem like a nice girl. Don't go getting yourself hurt now.'

A flush burned my neck right up to the tip of my head. Teenage boys laughing in the basement. My flesh crawled. And Snow was in residence, here in Chatham.

'Sisters need to look out for each other,' said Wendy, tapping my arm. 'Am I right?'

Before I could speak, an elderly couple bustled in and Wendy stood up. 'Just watch yourself, honey,' she whispered as she ducked back behind the counter to greet the new arrivals.

I left a fifty-dollar tip, hoping I wasn't stepping outside the bounds of the friendship we seemed to be establishing. As I headed towards the door, feeling shaken by Wendy's news, she swept the greenbacks off the table.

'Come again,' she called.

Back in my car I drove to Snow's place, parking a little way up the tree-lined street. My mind was racing with the idea of teenage boys in his basement. But Wendy had said they were laughing. Could they have just been students from Harvard visiting? Wendy hadn't seen them – how could she tell their age? Except Snow wasn't at Harvard any more, I reminded myself.

My neck was stiff with tension. I checked my emails. There was nothing from Georgia, but Kate had replied. Georgia was letting her go every day to Fredelighavn to observe the gentoo penguins along the shore from the whaling station. She was happy. She wished she could return to her own Adélies, but

Georgia hadn't wanted to trouble the base by requesting a plane. Rutger and Georgia were still going through the village documenting everything, but for now, Kate was busy with the gentoos and also recording chinstrap penguins and a couple of macaroni penguins. I emailed back asking if I could use the data and if she could also record any whale movement in the harbour.

It made me feel slightly better. Kate's work would help my report. At least I was moving forward on one front. I opened a sandwich and bit into it – roast beef with a hot mustard kick. It was kind of Georgia to let Kate back in the field but also strange: I would have thought she'd want everyone possible looking for the tunnels.

I kept staring at Snow's huge white gates, hoping to see him come in or out. I waited until dusk, when I could just glimpse lights coming on.

Once it was dark, I ventured out of the car and walked quickly up the street, grateful that neighbouring houses seemed empty, their owners tucked away in Boston and New York at this chilly time of year. I stopped by the hedge of Snow's house and peered through the trees.

Someone was definitely home. Lights were glowing on both floors. But if anyone was in the basement, I wouldn't be able to see. The air was so cold it felt like icicles were forming in my nose. I went back to my car and huddled inside where it was only slightly less Arctic but I didn't want to start the engine to put the heating on.

By midnight I was debating whether to go back to my

motel when the gates swung open. I sank down into my seat, my pulse quickening. Here at last was a sign of Snow – or was it?

A black SUV crawled slowly onto the street and turned left, away from town. The gates swung firmly shut. I waited until the SUV was a distance down the road, and followed. I could see from the receding red lights of my quarry that we were heading for the private marina.

By the sea, the fog was rolling in again, hiding activity. I parked down the street and walked, the damp air chilling my bones.

The SUV had stopped by a boat that was moored in the canal. I arrived just in time to see six small bodies slip out of the car and move towards the boat. Boys. Teenagers. Dark-haired, in warm coats, scarves and gloves. The last one out of the SUV was Snow. He walked casually as he ushered the boys onto the mid-sized fishing vessel, which roared its engines to life and blasted a beam into the night. Snow stood on the dock and held one hand into the air, waving, as the boat cruised out through the fog into the breakers, finally disappearing into a grey–white soup.

My breathing was strained; I had nowhere to hide as Snow turned back to his SUV. Fearing I'd be caught in his headlights I sprinted to the nearest greenery on the other side of the car park. Had he seen me? It was impossible to tell as I crouched behind a prickle-filled bush. His car rolled smoothly out of the car park and went back up the street towards his house.

I waited for ages before I dared to get up. My knees were

stiff and my shoulders ached from stress and the heavy, cold air. My stomach wrenched. The boys were similar in age to the boy I'd seen in the ice. Should I call the police? But what would I say? What I'd seen didn't prove anything. I felt I should have intervened, but the scientist in me knew I didn't have anything of substance to back up my concerns.

The US Coast Guard stationed at the lighthouse would be aware the boat had sailed. There was no doubt they'd have the most sophisticated equipment, but what I didn't know was whether they would be tracking the children: it wasn't against the law to take kids on a motor around the harbour at night.

I phoned Georgia but she didn't pick up – it went straight through to messages. 'Georgia, Snow's just sent a boatload of boys out to sea. Please call me.'

I hung up, my head pounding as my frustration built. *Why* wasn't Georgia getting back to me?

I phoned Kate, trying to work out what time it was on South Safety, but I was too frazzled. Would she still be at Alliance, or already down at Fredelighavn for the day? Her voice came on the line.

'Leave a message and I'll get back to you. Too busy with my penguins. Seeya.'

'Kate, call me. It's about Snow. It's urgent!'

I waited.

And waited.

A rosy sunrise crept into the sky.

I was dizzy but realised I needed to get out of the marina. The boat hadn't come back and workers would be arriving soon.

As I drove slowly past Snow's place I couldn't see anything. There were no lights on.

At the motel, I looked up the US Coast Guard online. I desperately wanted to put through a call. Doing nothing was making me shivery, like I was coming down with the flu. I forced myself to be calm. Georgia must get back to me soon, and I'd be able to discuss everything with her.

I slept briefly, and then went down to a small dining area and rushed through a late breakfast, gazing at my phone, willing it to ring. I couldn't stop thinking that there was a boatload of boys. The boy in the ice, boys put to sea under darkness . . . it was all too strange and I couldn't stand by and do nothing. I could wait no longer – I hurried back to my room and called the Coast Guard. A man with a deep, stern voice picked up. I gave my name and explained my fears that a group of young boys had been put on a boat in the middle of the night. With some reluctance, I mentioned Snow's name – and was met with stony silence.

'Thank you, ma'am, we'll look into it.'

'Can I come down and make a statement?'

'All maritime activity is monitored, ma'am, so there's no need. Thank you for your call, Doctor Alvarado, we appreciate your vigilance. Please phone back if there's anything else you'd like to report.' He hung up.

I had no idea whether he'd taken me seriously. He'd given nothing away. It was a small place, and people knew each other. In my worst-case scenario, the man I'd spoken to could be in on whatever was happening. What if he told Snow that I was here, reporting on him? It would be easy to track me down at my motel. Growing increasingly paranoid and anxious, I couldn't stop myself from phoning again. The same man picked up.

'I was just wondering what you were going to do?' I said.

'Ma'am.' This time his voice had an angry edge. 'As I've said, thank you for passing on the information. We will be investigating. And may I ask you what you were doing at a private marina? Do you have a boat there?'

'I couldn't sleep, so I went for a walk.'

'That's private property. I don't think you should go there again unless you have business. Thank you again for your vigilance, have a good day.' He hung up and the skin on the back of my neck prickled.

Where was Georgia? I needed to speak to her, badly. Without any evidence of wrongdoing, I was stuck. I only had my instincts, which I knew weren't always right. It seemed I'd been wrong about Snow.

Exhausted, I lay on the bed to think, but quickly fell into a troubled sleep with feverish dreams of the boy in the ice. And now he wasn't alone: Snow's group of teenagers had joined him. In the ice cave sat a circle of men, and the boys stood naked in the middle. It was a witchcraft ceremony. There was a guitar-strum rhythm – incongruous, intrusive – as the men rose and walked slowly towards the boys—

I sat up covered in sweat and realised my phone was ringing. I snatched it up.

'Laura it's me, Georgia,' said the familiar voice on the other end. My body slumped with relief. She sounded rushed, like she was running.

'Thank God you rang,' I said. 'Did you get my messages?'

'I certainly did. I can't speak for long, I'm in Madrid, about to catch a connecting flight. I think the boy you saw in the ice is going to be arriving in Venice by boat. Laura, I've been working with David White and British detectives and now we're getting the Italian police involved. We believe there's a paedophile ring operating on South Safety Island. What you've just seen in Chatham is quite likely part of it. I need you to come to Venice and identify the boy you saw in the ice. Can you do that? You're the only one who's seen him, and that's going to be crucial.'

Horror pulsed through me. The boy flashed in front of me, his dark hair, pale face, mouth wide open screaming for help. *What were they doing to him?*

'I'll catch the first flight out,' I said, my heart thumping in my chest. I heard a loudspeaker crackle in the background.

'That's my final call,' barked Georgia. 'Meet me at my hotel – I'll text the details.' She hung up.

I tried to take in what I'd just heard. My head was splitting from stress and lack of sleep. *A paedophile ring*, Georgia had said. My poor boy. And the other boys – were they heading to South Safety Island? I should have stopped them. I should have pulled them off the boat. Whatever happened to them now was my responsibility. Fighting a wave of dizziness, I trawled through airlines to find flights to Venice.

I didn't have time to check out of the motel. I left the key on the bed and hurried down the stairs with my luggage.

I hoped there weren't traffic police about as I sped past every car on the road.

*

At Boston's Logan Airport, I just made the plane. I was heading to New York, from where I would fly to Venice.

As we waited on the tarmac before take-off, I texted the motel to check they had my credit card number and to thank Wendy for my stay. Then I texted Nancy and explained that I couldn't be back on Nantucket for a while but to be in touch if they found anything. I knew I should contact my mother, but I was too tired and preoccupied.

My hands were shaking, and as the plane taxied down the runway I braced myself. What had the boy in the ice been through? And what was happening to him now; why was he heading to Venice?

18

The Italian countryside spread below like a patchwork quilt in shades of lush green; the limpid grey sea came ever closer as we touched down at Venice Marco Polo airport.

It was 11am and there were crowds of tourists. I turned on my phone and saw that Georgia had texted her address: Hotel Leone Alato, her favourite place, nestled between St Mark's Square and the Accademia Bridge.

A water taxi whisked me over the lagoon, the crumbling buildings of Venice looming into sight, thrusting up from the water like a magical fairytale. The last time I was in Venice I'd been on my own, trying to reconcile myself to losing Hamish, and hoping to forget Cameron. Attempting to feel all right about being single, rather than surrounded by a happy young family.

Slowly the city had calmed me, washing around, soothing; the soft, muted colours of the palazzos and dark winding alleys were a perfect environment in which to grieve. The locals had been friendly. Some of the men too friendly. I ended up spending time with an American woman. We toured galleries and islands, and even went on an exorbitantly expensive gondola ride, serenaded under a star-filled sky. I had felt lonelier that night than ever before. The next day I'd left for Naples and had never been back.

The water taxi stopped at the tiny wharf of Hotel Leone Alato. I paid the driver and he grabbed my hand and hoisted me up onto the deck, then passed my luggage.

Two glass doors slid open and I walked into a gloomy lobby.

'*Buon giorno*,' called a throaty woman's voice. 'Can I help you, signora?'

'I'm Laura Alvarado. I'm meeting Georgia Spiros.'

'Ah, welcome, welcome.' As my eyes adjusted to the light, I saw the woman behind the counter was in her late fifties, with flowing brown hair and silver jewellery draped artistically around her throat and chest. Huge rings adorned every finger. She jangled towards me and shook my hand.

'I'm Silvia. I have a beautiful room for you with a view of the canal.'

'I might just go straight up and see Georgia.'

'Georgia? No.' Silvia looked concerned. 'She is not in.'

'Did she say when she'd be back?'

Silvia shook her head and quickly, efficiently, checked me in, then took my case and led me to a tiny lift. We just fitted, squashed together like sardines. It was slow and creaky but we finally made it up to the second floor.

My room was decorated with sumptuous Venetian fabrics and through double glass doors twelve feet high was a tiny stone balcony.

'We are in an old palazzo, so please, you tell me if you need heating or air, and I switch on from downstairs. We keep the temperature adjusted for the murals.' Silvia pointed to the ceiling, where a beautiful colourful fresco showed angels leaping in all four corners. 'Sixteenth century,' she said.

As soon as Silvia left I phoned Georgia but was diverted to voicemail. 'I've arrived,' I said. 'Can't wait to see you.' It hadn't occurred to me that Georgia wouldn't be here. Perhaps events had moved faster than expected but I was surprised she hadn't left a note.

I stepped out onto the balcony. Sleek black gondolas full of tourists floated beneath, the gondoliers serenading in their blue and white striped tops and wide-brimmed hats. Two middle-aged women waved up at me, sending memories flooding back. I blocked them and retreated inside, firmly closing the doors.

In the silence, the piercing shrill of the hotel phone startled me. I picked up.

'Laura, *prego*. There is a man to see you.'

'I'll come straight down,' I replied, wondering who it could be.

In the dark lobby a tall, thin man in his sixties, with silky white hair, intense amber eyes and tanned skin, stood waiting. He spoke with a rolling accent and a soft, deep voice.

'Doctore Alvarado?' He shook my hand. 'I'm Professor Fabio Natuzzi from Venice University. I'm very pleased to meet you. Georgia's told me everything. But I was expecting her to be here, no?'

'So was I. She'll be back soon, I'm sure.'

Professor Natuzzi frowned, deep lines etching his brow. He took me gently by the elbow and led me away from the reception desk. 'But Silvia says that Georgia didn't come home last night. Is this like her?'

I stopped and stared at him. 'Absolutely not.'

'She not play with the men?'

'She has a husband and two beautiful kids. Never.' I grabbed my phone and looked at when Georgia had texted me the address. It would have been early evening here, last night.

'Silvia,' I called. 'When did you last see Georgia?'

'Before dinner yesterday. She went out.'

'When did she come back?'

Silvia shrugged awkwardly. 'I don't think she did. Her bed's not been slept in.'

My blood turned to ice. 'Can I see her room?'

'Normally no, but . . .' Flustered, Silvia grabbed a key from its pigeonhole and led me to the lift. We squashed in.

'I'll follow. Which room?' said Fabio.

'Room three-eleven,' said Silvia as the doors closed.

The lift clunked up. 'Did she ever do this before when she stayed?' I asked.

'No, never. Georgia's my friend. I'm very worried.'

I followed Silvia down an ornate passage on the top floor. Georgia's room was grander than mine with a view over rooftops to St Mark's Square.

Silvia handed me the key, which felt cold and heavy against my skin. 'Lock up and come down when you're ready.'

The bed was still made up. Georgia's clothes lay strewn across a thickly embroidered gold bedspread that hung in neat lines.

In the bathroom, Georgia's make-up cluttered a tiny marble shelf. Everything said she'd gone out into the night to meet someone – most likely, a man. A faint trace of perfume hung in the air, sweet and familiar.

Georgia would never be unfaithful. But what had she been doing, and why wasn't she here?

'Anything?' Fabio called from the doorway.

'It looks like Georgia went out to meet someone,' I replied, coming back to the main room.

'And didn't come back.' Fabio frowned as he walked in, picking up a few clothes and putting them down again.

'Should we call the police?' I asked, thinking I would have to make another call – to my ex-husband David White, who was working with Georgia. I assumed he was still back in Australia and not over here, but I hoped he could shed light on what was going on.

Fabio went to the old black phone sitting beside the bed and dialled. He spoke urgently in rapid Italian, as I moved a few steps away and found David's number in my phone's contact list. I sucked in my breath. I hadn't spoken to him since our divorce two years ago. His voice came on the line, authoritative and calm, ordering me to leave a message. 'David, it's Laura. I've just arrived in Venice and Georgia's not at the hotel, or answering her phone. They say she hasn't been here since last night. Can you call me urgently? Thanks.' I hung up, rattled.

Fabio crashed down his phone.

'The police will look. They are worried to hear this news. They have been working with Georgia – a team met with her yesterday. The meeting ended in the early afternoon. I'll call the hospital.' He dialled, spoke intensely, waited, thanked the person on the other end and hung up. 'She's not there, so that's good news.' He moved to a chair, indicating for me to sit opposite. 'So tell me, Georgia said you saw a boy in an ice cave? Could you please tell me everything? It's all right, we can stay here. I think this is the best place to stay.'

Georgia hadn't said anything about Professor Fabio Natuzzi and I didn't have any idea who he was.

'I'm sorry, but could you let me know a bit about yourself?' I asked.

'Of course,' he replied assuredly. 'I am a human rights lawyer. Georgia and I have been corresponding, and we met here yesterday. She wanted me to come back this morning. Georgia first phoned from Antarctica, and I knew immediately what she meant when she asked about pale-skinned boys, boys who looked like they hadn't seen sun in a long time. I am what you would call an expert in the movements – illegal – of children.'

He pulled out a packet of cigarettes. 'Do you mind?'

I shook my head, shuddering at Georgia's description – *pale-skinned boys.*

'Would you like one?' Fabio proffered the packet. As I declined I was reminded of the cigarettes at Fredelighavn. Fabio took a long drag of nicotine as I opened the balcony doors, aware the smoke might damage the ancient mural of angels and devils overhead.

'So,' he said, unfurling a line of smoke, 'there is quite a trade here in illegal child migrants. A flood of humanity that arrives on our shores at night and disappears through Italy, making their way to whatever countries will hire cheap, hidden labour. You might be surprised to know that England hides many illegal children.'

'Where do they work?' I asked, alarmed.

'There's manufacturing still in Britain.' He took another long draw of his cigarette. The smoke was starting to make me nauseous. 'Here in Europe they do whatever they can. A lot of these children are economic refugees. They have no real need to leave their home country, which often has a good education system. But the children have parents and relatives, whole villages even, who pay for their travel with people smugglers. They put up, say, ten thousand American dollars, and the children arrive here in Venice. Then they go and work, and send money home. Everyone who paid for their journey gets their share accordingly. The children become like a stock, and send home dividends. They are boys. About twelve. Maybe fourteen. They view it as an adventure, as a rite of passage. They are from very poor families and are helping out.'

He took a tiny silver box from his pocket and butted his cigarette into it emphatically, then lit another cigarette.

'So, I do not like this. There are *true* refugees, as I'm sure you are aware, children included, whose lives are at stake for religious and political reasons. People who *must* flee their country. We have more and more of these asylum seekers, an overwhelming number. More than at any time since the Second World War.'

I thought of my mother, and the boatloads of refugees desperately crossing the Mediterranean to Italy in leaking vessels. The photo of the two small girls, drowned, face down in the shallows . . .

'The economic refugees clog the already overloaded system,' continued Fabio. 'They should not come. But when children are sent by their parents and villages it is wrong and I try to help. Some we repatriate here. Italy is kind to children. And although every child should be reunited with their family, maybe sometimes this is not so good, if their parents have let their young ones go in this way to be exploited as child labour.' He tapped cigarette ash into his silver box with a staccato movement.

'Your boy in the ice. He may have been picked up from here and taken to Antarctica, or they may have picked him up elsewhere. But we think they drop the boys back in Venice. If they've been doing unspeakable things, where better to lose the children when they grow too old?'

I flushed with fury and concern.

'Here in Venice,' continued Fabio, 'they can join the throng of refugees disappearing into the shadows. They have the chance of work, exploitative as that will be. You'd be surprised how many of these refugee children make good. They become engineers, doctors even. Some would say the end justifies the means. But not me. And if children have been abused, we must do whatever we can for them.' He leaned forward, his amber eyes bright.

'Georgia and I together filled in the jigsaw of the pale boys. And this morning, I have word. A shipload of boys, unearthly white, has set off from Turkey, earlier than we first thought.

We'd been told it would be tomorrow, but now we think it will be tonight that your boy will arrive. I've left a message for Georgia about this.'

A surge of maternal instinct rose through me.

'Will you come with me to the dock?' he asked.

I nodded, overwhelmed, trying to imagine how I would feel seeing the boy again.

'The most important thing is that you identify him, otherwise it will be just another boatload of refugees among the flood of asylum seekers. We will have detectives and immigration officials with us, and we will stop this paedophile ring that takes children to South Safety Island. With your help, we can prosecute. This is a human rights violation. This is my specialty and the reason I get up in the morning. Often it is hard to have any impact at all. But tonight, it is perhaps possible.'

Fabio finished his cigarette, squashed it into the silver box, and stood stiffly.

'I will come for you at eleven o'clock. I trust Georgia will be back by then. Now, I must go, I have an appointment at the university.'

After he left, I looked around the room for any notes, or a phone, or computer. I couldn't find anything. Surely Georgia would have brought her computer? Although maybe not. She could have just had her phone, and she would be carrying that on her.

I tried again to call her but was sent straight to messagebank.

I caught the lift down to my room and took a shower to wash off the cloying smoke. Anticipation built that I would be meeting the boy tonight, but I was feeling increasingly uneasy

about Georgia. I phoned the Italian police and was transferred from person to person. One woman acknowledged that
Georgia had been reported missing; no one could find anyone
who was working with her.

I looked up Professor Fabio Natuzzi online, and there he was,
smiling out – a law professor at Venice University, a specialist in
human rights, just like he'd said. He'd written many papers on
child refugees, including reports for the United Nations.

I phoned Kate but she didn't answer. I cursed – I really needed
to talk things through. I asked her to call, and then I left further
messages for Georgia and David.

In the lobby, I gave Silvia my phone number and she promised
to let me know as soon as Georgia came in. I needed air, and
so I went out into the grey afternoon and walked, joining the
throng of tourists heading for St Mark's Square. As I moved
under a high stone arch, the square stretched before me. At
the far end, the golden cupolas of St Mark's Cathedral glowed
dimly in the light and the Doge's Palace loomed white and
mysterious – but in between stretched a vast sea of blue–green
water. St Mark's Square was a giant swimming pool. It was
acqua alta, high tide. Snakes of raised duckboards had been laid
across the square and people were trotting along on top, as if
promenading on trestle tables. An orchestra still played, on its
stage, outside the sumptuous Caffè Florian and, remarkably, the
shops spread around the square on three sides under the grand
stone arches were open, plying their glittering wares of gold
and gems and luxurious fabrics. A group of men, tall, ebony-
skinned, possibly illegal refugees, had set up a table selling cheap
plastic overboots that looked like luminous green garbage bags.

I bought a pair and put them on over my shoes, tying them above my knees.

I couldn't keep still, thinking about Georgia. It was unlike her not to come back to the hotel last night. Perhaps she was staked out somewhere, gathering information on the boy's arrival, and didn't have time to call? She was a detective. If anyone could look after themselves it was her, but no matter how many times I told myself that, I still felt sick.

As I clambered up makeshift steps to the duckboards I held my phone, waiting for someone to return my calls. The sea slopped beneath me, a dull, dirty colour up close, brown through the green. There was a hush over the square.

Perhaps David was here with Georgia, and they were staked out together?

I kept walking, not really thinking about where I was going. I reached the other side and waded through water that splashed up my legs, then I went down an alley of shops winding towards Rialto. The tourists thinned out: I'd chosen an alley that wasn't a main one. Sound hollowed, and I was suddenly alone.

The shops evaporated, replaced by blank-faced houses as the walkway became impossibly narrow, flooded by a canal that had spilled over in the high tide. The alley stopped in a dead-end, where water lapped, making a quiet hissing noise. I retraced my steps, but soon I became even more lost as I waded through polluted seawater looking for something familiar, or a sign back to St Mark's Square or on to Rialto. But every intersection was just more houses with crumbling, blank walls. I tried to pull up a map on my phone, but it wouldn't load.

I looked at the time – 4pm. It was growing darker by the minute on this dull day. Panic rose, my hands were clammy. I felt like I'd never find my way, trapped in a maze. I was in a run-down area. There was nobody on the street.

Just as I was about to phone Silvia at the hotel to ask for help, I saw a roughly-sketched arrow scrawled on a wall, announcing Rialto. I followed it, only to get to an intersection where there was no arrow, and three alleys shot off in different directions. I took a stab at the middle one. After five minutes I heard voices echoing and the sound of feet sloshing through water. Turning into another alley, I met up with a crowd of tourists. I tried to calm down as I followed them to the Rialto Bridge. Arching over the Grand Canal, the pale stone steps of the bridge rose up, tiny shops on both sides twinkling with lights. I went across, looking everywhere for Georgia, peering into jewellery stores packed with luminous silver and gold rings and necklaces, specialty shops selling handmade note-paper, other shops full of Murano glass decorated in gold leaf. Georgia was not inside them. But of course she wouldn't be. She wouldn't be shopping if she hadn't come home last night. I turned back.

My feet were aching as I trailed more tourists up an alley with a sign pointing to St Mark's Square. There was an unreality to the twilight as it clung to the old stone walls, turning colours sickly. A dead rat floated past.

The tourists were laughing, voices booming; I didn't let them out of my sight. We went under an arch and St Mark's Square, still submerged, stretched in front. I wanted to hug my unknowing guides. The snaking duckboards were far away from this entry, but I was happy to wade through the water to the exit I knew. I found the broad walkway that led towards my hotel. Bustling shops were lit up brightly. Beside a window filled with sleek leather gloves, I turned right into a tight alley, then right again. The hotel was at the end, a beacon of hope.

I hurried in, not stopping to take off my overboots. 'Silvia, have you heard from Georgia?'

Silvia looked confused. 'No, but I would have called you, of course.'

'I was just hoping,' I said, deflating.

'This is very bad. The professor told me he reported it to the police. I'll call them again.'

She spoke intensely down the phone, listened, and hung up. 'Nothing. No sign of her.'

I tried Georgia's phone, and when it went straight to messages I gave another plea to call, joining the ones I'd already left. My head throbbed. I texted David, sick of hearing his voice when I asked him to ring me.

'Have you eaten?' said Silvia. She clunked down a multilingual sign – *Back in 5 minutes*. 'Prego, come.' Upstairs in her tiny apartment, she put a hearty pasta in a microwave, zapped it and handed over the steaming bowl aromatic with basil and tomato. She picked up a stick of bread and pulled an open bottle of white wine from the fridge. 'Here, take these to your room.' I declined the wine, which was difficult because it might have helped to settle my nerves, but I needed to be alert for the boy's arrival. Tonight I could save him.

*

At 10.30pm I sat waiting for Fabio in the empty lobby. Reception was closed, Silvia tucked away in her apartment. I was rugged up in a coat, scarf and gloves. I'd put my plastic overboots back over my shoes. As soon as the sun had set the temperature had plummeted and the night was icy – a dank, close cold, unlike the clear chill of Antarctica.

There was still no sign of Georgia, nor any word from David. I prayed that I would meet up with Georgia at the docks where the children were due to arrive. The more I thought of it, the more convinced I became. I was uneasy about going without hearing from her, but my overwhelming emotion was for the boy.

I jumped as my phone pinged with an email. For a moment I didn't recognise the name – and then I remembered that Astrid Bredesen was the translator at Harvard.

I flipped up her message. She had found a reference in Ingerline's diary to the tunnels. Strangely, her attention had been drawn to it by a small handwritten annotation in Spanish, scrawled in the margin: *Read this. The entrance.* My eyes flew over the translated extract, where Ingerline outlined the importance of the tunnels for storing alcohol and cigarettes. It appeared that in the later years of the whaling station, the Halvorsens had branched out to make money another way as the whaling stocks declined. They had traded in hard liquor and tobacco, and I suspected none of it was legal. The ships picked up the contraband on their way over, proving useful for ballast. Then, when the oil and other whale by-products were low because of a poor season, the ships had taken the alcohol and tobacco back to Norway, or sold it en route.

The tunnels were a tightly kept secret. At the bottom of the page, Ingerline mentioned an entrance: through a false door at the rear of the kitchen pantry in her house. The house where her portrait still kept watch. A shiver tore through me. I'd looked in all those cupboards. And Ingerline's house was where I'd seen the man – and where the boy's T-shirt had been found. Now I knew how they'd got there, and where they'd gone. From underground, they'd come up into the kitchen, and then retreated back down under the ice by the time we'd returned. Hope rose: if the boys from Chatham were destined for South Safety Island, replacing the boys who were coming to Venice, *we would be able to find them.*

'You're here. Good.' Fabio walked in briskly. He saw my overboots. 'You won't need those.' He looked around. 'Where's Georgia?'

'She's still not back. Do you think she might already be at the docks?'

'Yes,' said Fabio, which gave me some comfort. 'She knows the time and location from my message. There must be a reason she's not here.' He frowned. 'Our police in Venice give very little away. Georgia could be acting under orders.'

'Do you think it's all right that I'm coming?' I knew Georgia probably hadn't meant me to actually be on the docks, but rather to identify the boy at the police station.

'Of course. You must.' Fabio was definite. And I wanted desperately to make sure the boy was safe when he arrived.

I took off my overboots and left them under the chair. Fabio crooked his arm through mine and we went out into the night, where heavy clouds scudded across a full moon, and a mist hung low, swirling over cobblestones. The tide had gone down; the footpaths were dry.

I tried to digest the news about the tunnels, dying to tell Georgia about the entrance. We finally had what we needed to crack open the ring. I wanted to phone and leave messages for both her and David, but Fabio was leading me through dark alleys and there was an urgency to the task at hand. As we went down a space between buildings so tight we had to walk in single file, I ran into Fabio's heels when he stopped at a dead-end. A canal splashed in front, its water black and opaque beneath a thin veil of mist. My heart thundered, and for a terrible moment I wondered who this man was. He was a human rights lawyer, but I only had his word that he had been in contact with Georgia. What if he wasn't? I'd been so preoccupied I wasn't thinking straight. I'd just walked into a blind alley with a total stranger, in the middle of the night, in the middle of nowhere. My legs turned to jelly.

But a sleek boat came swishing along and Fabio helped me down into it. 'We go to Porto Marghera,' he said. 'On the other side of the lagoon, on the mainland. To the container depot.'

As we motored away, the elderly driver, silver-haired with a sailor's weatherworn face, said nothing. Inside the small cabin, Fabio lit a cigarette. I pulled out my phone and texted Georgia and David, saying I was on my way to the docks.

The mist thickened to fog as we sped up and headed out across the lagoon. The water was choppy, the boat slapped over waves. The temperature plummeted further.

The mainland came into sight like an impressionist painting through the fog, and we slipped up the coast past several huge container ports, their lights blazing, seeping into the ghostly air.

Finally, we stopped at a wharf piled high with towering multi-coloured steel containers, and three men ran down to meet us. We climbed a steep ladder up to the dock and the boat took off. I tensed as I realised I was even more isolated here in this vast industrial wasteland. Anything could happen. I prayed I was right to trust Fabio. What if there wasn't a shipload of boys coming at all?

We hurried along through the swirling mist. One of the men, an overweight giant, grabbed my arm and propelled me faster, pinching my flesh. Who were they? They didn't look like detectives or immigration officials. They looked like thugs. Where were the police? And where was Georgia?

The giant pulled me past containers stacked high. Ahead, there were loud mechanical clanks. In the fog I could just make out a monster crane lifting containers onto a ship.

We moved quickly, heading to a dark area at the end of the dock. There was nothing there. Panic set in. I wanted to run. I'd been an idiot coming on my own. I must still be toasty from Antarctica, not thinking straight. Should I flee onto the ship that was being loaded? The giant held me tight. I tried to calm down, but couldn't. Had Georgia been lured here by Fabio last night, before she vanished?

The moon appeared, full and bright through the clouds, as a blustery gust momentarily parted the fog. A boat was puttering slowly towards the dock.

Fabio reached out and pulled me into black shadows. The giant flanked my other side. If there weren't boys on the boat, it could be me heading out to sea. I tried to keep my fear under control, preparing to sprint for my life if the boat was empty.

A man called quietly, and the giant and another man ran down and caught thick ropes that were tossed up. They tied them tightly to the dock as the boat bobbed in the water.

And then they came, one by one, through the fog. Young teenage boys, dark-haired, their faces as pale as ghosts. One, two, three. And then two more. I ran over with Fabio as they clambered up a ladder. '*Hola*, *hola*,' they mumbled. '*A dónde vamos?*' Where are we going, they were asking. In Spanish.

I replied rapidly in Spanish, and the boys blinked. I told them they were in Venice and we were going to look after them; all the time I was looking over their shoulders, for the boy who looked like Hamish. But he didn't come.

'Is there another?' I asked in Spanish. 'Another dark-haired boy, thin-faced, brown-eyed?' They each shook their head. They all fitted that description, but my Hamish wasn't there. Claws of pain slashed through my stomach.

We spoke in Spanish. Fabio watched us, and I noticed he was discreetly filming everything on his phone. 'Where are you from?' I asked the boys.

'Mexico,' one replied.

'Guatemala,' said another, 'but I came through Mexico.'

'Me too,' croaked a tiny boy who looked about ten.

'After that?' I said.

'They took us somewhere. A big house. Down below, in a basement. And then we went to sea. Then we flew. Far away. Vamoose. To the ice.' The boy worked his hands this way and that, illustrating the length of his journey.

'Under the ice?' I said, trying to keep my voice calm, and they nodded.

'Are there boys still there?' I demanded. 'A boy about twelve, thin and dark?'

They nodded. My chest tightened.

'How many?'

They shrugged and said nothing.

I paused, praying my boy was still at Fredelighavn and nothing had happened to him on the journey. 'Did everyone who set off get here?'

'Yes,' said the tallest boy.

My knees went weak with relief. At least my boy hadn't drowned. 'What happened to you down there?' I asked.

They shut their mouths tightly. Fabio repeated the question, gently, speaking Spanish. He'd understood everything we'd said.

The boys stayed silent.

'We get paid,' the tallest boy said finally. 'We go now.' He took a boy's hand on either side and headed off.

'Where are you going?' I asked, following.

'We meet someone. We thought you, but not.'

The boys hurried away in a pack. I raced after them, with Fabio. 'Don't be frightened!' he called. 'Please don't be afraid!'

But the boys were running fast now, galloping down the dock like startled animals. Fabio grabbed one and the boy kicked him in the shin. The other men who'd come with us stood staring, by the boat. As I glanced back I saw money changing hands with the man who'd brought the boat in.

Fabio was lunging at the boys, trying to grab them, but they kept slipping away. Again I wondered who he was. He could be a paedophile himself, snatching the new arrivals. But that made no sense – why would he have wanted me along if that were the case? To lull the boys into a sense of security before spiriting them away? And then dealing with me. My blood drained.

The boys were getting away. They were nimble, darting through the shadows, swallowed into the fog. Fabio was losing ground. I sprinted faster, but now we were among the containers and the boys split up and went down different aisles through the dark metal boxes. I chased the smallest boy. He took corners faster than I could, leading me in a circle, and then he disappeared. I stopped, a stitch burning my side, my breathing raw in the freezing air. I was alone. I stood stock still, listening. But all I could hear was the wind and the roar of the crane and machines loading ships.

The moon came out again and the fog cleared momentarily. I was surrounded by empty shadows.

I tried to decide what to do. Could I trust Fabio to get me back to Venice? Or should I go off into the night and find another way back? I was tired; my bones ached. I was bitterly disappointed that Hamish wasn't here.

There could be any number of dangers in the shipyards, and in a wave of anger, I headed off away from the dock. And then it hit me. Fabio was a *professor*. Snow, too, had been a professor. I started to run. I could hear Fabio calling me, and when I turned I saw him following. I sped up, increasing the distance between us, weaving through containers until I lost him.

I ran into a deserted street leading out of the port. Breathless, checking no one was behind me, I staggered to hide in bushes at the side of the road and phoned Silvia at the hotel. There was no answer. I checked my email – still no reply from anyone.

Georgia hadn't been at the docks. I felt desperate about her, and helpless.

I stayed in the undergrowth until the fog lifted and pink clouds filled the dawn sky, then I tried again to reach Silvia. No answer. Trucks roared past. I sat back into the bushes and kept calling until finally the phone clicked at the other end.

'*Pronto?*' Silvia's voice was thick with sleep. I gabbled what had happened. At first she couldn't understand who I was or what I was saying. Then finally she did.

'Stay there,' she said. 'I'll send someone. They'll phone as they come up. It's early and who knows what men are on the docks at this hour. Please don't come onto the road until you get the call.'

Twenty minutes later my phone rang. A girl announced herself as Chiara, and moments later a stylish woman in her early twenties drove up in a red sports car. I clambered in. 'I'm Silvia's daughter,' she said, shaking my hand. 'We go to the airport and I arrange a *motoscafi*. I get you back to the hotel. You are safe now.'

19

Silvia rushed onto the tiny landing as my water taxi pulled in. 'Why were you at Porto Marghera?' she said as she hauled me up and ushered me through into the lobby. 'It's a terrible place to be at night. No place for a woman.'

'I went with the professor. I hoped Georgia might be there,' I replied, deliberately vague on detail. 'We were separated and I got lost. And then I called you.' I hugged her. 'Thank you so much.'

Silvia hugged me back, her arms strong and reassuring. 'And still no sign of Georgia?' Her face was lined with worry.

'No,' I said desolately. 'Can we call the police again?'

Silvia picked up the telephone, spoke rapidly, and waited. When she put down the receiver, she was grim. 'No news.'

Despondent, I went into the lift and clunked up to my room,

where I checked my phone yet again. *Why* wasn't David replying?

I lay on the bed. What were they doing to my boy who looked like Hamish? And where was Georgia? A sick, leaden feeling weighed me down. Georgia had been gone too long.

I woke to strange, musical sirens wafting through the air. Two angelic tones, repeated over and over. They sounded eerie but not urgent, like humpback whales singing to each other. I rubbed my dry eyes and checked the time: 11.30am. I sat up as last night's events came flooding back. Was I right to have run or was Professor Fabio Natuzzi genuine? Even in the light of day I couldn't tell. Why had one of his men given the boat captain money? Fabio had led me to believe there would be police there – and it hadn't looked to me like there were. Certainly the thuggish men hadn't identified themselves as police.

I still had my clothes on from last night, but I didn't want to waste time showering or changing, so I went straight downstairs.

'Anything from Georgia?' I asked Silvia, hoping against hope.

'No, *bella*. I call the police again. They are searching – but nothing. And the professor's phoned, asking if you got in safely. I said you were sleeping.'

'Thanks.' An involuntary shiver ran through me. Fabio knew where to find me, and that wasn't a good thing. Even if he was legitimate, I didn't want to see him again. The boys had disappeared into the ether and my Hamish wasn't with them. I needed to get back to Antarctica, urgently.

'Laura?' said a deep male voice.

I turned. Silhouetted in the glass doors that led from the canal, suitcase in hand, stood David White. I blinked and stared as my ex-husband came at me like a bear. His aftershave, so familiar, almost knocked me off my feet as he shook my hand with a firm grasp.

'Georgia said you'd be here,' he said confidently.

'Did you get my messages?' I asked.

'My SIM card's not working properly. I've been held up in Dubai for hours. I was meant to get here last night, but Georgia probably told you that.'

'David, Georgia's missing.'

David looked confused.

'No one's seen her for over twenty-four hours.'

David watched my face for a few moments, then spoke briskly. 'Can I borrow your phone?' I passed it over and he called the police. He knew who to ask for. After a brief and difficult conversation in English, he hung up, furious.

'They have no idea where Georgia is, and they were too busy with a flood of asylum seekers who arrived last night to send anyone to the docks. They're not coping with all the refugees. And Professor Natuzzi asks them to go to boats all the time. Without Georgia's involvement, they weren't going to send police a day earlier than had been arranged for the operation.'

'I went with Natuzzi,' I said. David glared at me, surprised. 'The boy I saw in the ice didn't turn up,' I continued. 'Others did, though. And they'd definitely been in Antarctica. The men with Natuzzi paid cash to the boat captain.'

'And no one was arrested because there were no police there,' said David darkly.

So the men with Natuzzi weren't police – I was right about that, but who were they?

'You shouldn't have gone to the docks,' said David sternly. 'You were meant to ID the boy at the police station.'

'What was I supposed to do?' I replied, tired and defensive. Within seconds of seeing each other we were getting into a fight. I wasn't in the mood. 'I couldn't contact anyone. *You* weren't returning my calls. And I thought Georgia might be at the docks.'

David, concerned, turned to Silvia who was listening worriedly. 'Can I see Georgia's room, please?'

I took David up in the lift, filling him in on the details of last night.

It was chilling to enter Georgia's room and see it exactly the same as yesterday, with her clothes strewn on the bed. David looked methodically through everything. He took my phone and called the police again; the detective on the other end put him on hold. David cursed, his body pumped with rage – something I remembered from seeing him work difficult cases.

David stabbed the phone on to speaker, and as we waited I told him about the tunnel entrance in Fredelighavn; he listened intently. 'Georgia told me about the Chatham boys,' he said. 'We've been in contact with American and British colleagues. Snow's record's clean, but these sort of men are smart, so that's not surprising. Connaught's shady – up until his early twenties he was known as Harold Westley, a primary-school science teacher in North London. When a father accused him of inter-fering with his son, Westley physically attacked him. He was charged with assault, but nothing else was proved. It was enough to make Westley change his name, though. And the boy's family moved to Australia. You've met the boy – now grown up.'

I looked at him mutely, confused.

'Simon Huxtable,' said David. 'The pilot at Alliance. So we think the Base Commander and Chief Pilot are in on this. And your original boy's still down on South Safety Island?'

I nodded, reeling at the news that Simon was involved. He'd always seemed like one of the good guys.

'Another pilot, Reg, tipped Georgia off that he thought Simon might have been doing irregular flights for quite some time. Simon's fudged his records, but we managed, with help, to trace where we suspect he's been. A line of Middle Eastern countries, where people smugglers then take the boys a short distance overland to boats. A British detective put Georgia in touch with Natuzzi, and with Natuzzi's information we formed a pattern. Natuzzi heard that another group of pale boys was on its way. The people smugglers notice these boys because they're as white as ghosts.' David turned red, bottling up his emotions.

'We have no idea yet how many men on South Safety are involved. Recently, an electrician at Rothera Base was convicted for sending indecent images of children over the internet. We haven't found a connection between him and Alliance, but we know scientists aren't exempt from being paedophiles, and Antarctica can be a magnet for people who don't fit in anywhere else.'

I grimaced.

David softened. 'But now with the details you've provided, we can mount an operation. Good work, Laura.'

I felt sick to my core. My boy was still there, with Connaught and Simon, being violated by them and who knew who else. Possibly even Travis. Vomit rose in my throat.

'We have to get back to South Safety,' I demanded. 'And who *is* Natuzzi? Do you know him?'

'Not personally. Georgia was dealing with him. You look like you don't trust him?'

'I don't.'

David looked surprised. 'Well, when someone bothers to speak to me I'll find out more about him—' David stopped as a male voice came down the line. 'David? Hello?'

David took the phone off speaker and lifted it to his ear, but before he could say a word, the other man spoke rapidly. David grew as still as a statue. 'We'll be there,' he said, hanging up. He looked at me. 'They may have found Georgia.'

'Is she all right?'

He didn't answer as he tugged me out of the room, his face a rigid mask of anger.

'David?'

'Near La Fenice opera house, do you know the way?'

'David, tell me she's okay?'

'Just get me to La Fenice; I'll find it from there.'

I'd seen the signs to La Fenice – it was near the hotel. I led us, running faster than I ever had. We flew up to the main thorough-fare and after a few moments we turned at the sign. As the grand stone façade of the opera house came into view, David detoured down an alley, and then another, twisting towards a canal. The tide was rising, lapping across the narrow footpath. A distance away, uniformed police and plainclothes detectives huddled. It was a quiet, desolate area, devoid of tourists, at the back of buildings; there were no entrances onto the footpath.

As we ran into the clump of police I looked for Georgia –

she wasn't among them. They were all staring at something slumped against the wall. Lying with its face turned away was a bloated body. The jeans and white shirt, slimed with green, could have belonged to anyone. The hair was dark, blood-stained, covered with seaweed. But there was something about the hands that made me stop.

In death there was still a strength to the hands, a vitality. And then I saw Georgia's rings – her sapphire engagement ring bit into her grey flesh, the gold wedding band on top. I heard a sharp cry and knew it had come from me. I was moaning, rocking back and forth. David bent over her body. I went to follow, numb.

'Get her away!' yelled David, lunging up and grabbing my arm. 'Laura, get back.' I pulled away and again moved towards Georgia, but two policemen forced me back. Filthy canal water rushed over my feet. Georgia must have washed up here yesterday at *acqua alta*. If she hadn't been found, she would have floated away on today's tide. I thought of the bruised, murdered woman being hauled, feet-first, out of a dank canal in Georgia's favourite film, *Don't Look Now*. Georgia's body in front of me, and the one in the film, started to jumble together. Had Georgia fled down dark alleys before she was killed? Had she been terrified? I stared at her body wedged against the wall and couldn't believe what I was seeing, the horrible, unreal finality of death.

As I sat in a small, poorly lit room at the police station while David went in to make a formal identification of Georgia, the scene played over and over in my mind. Georgia's broken body, blood oozing from her head, dark and gelatinous.

Georgia had always been so animated when she spoke of Venice; she'd been looking forward so much to bringing her family next year when Stacey graduated. Georgia was such a loving mother – how would her children cope? And Jeff, her husband? They were each other's world, a tight-knit family. My loyal, caring friend had been murdered. *And she would never have been involved if it wasn't for me.* Tears seeped out; my head felt like it had been cracked by an axe.

Who had done this? Had Connaught and Simon arranged it? Or was it Snow? And was Professor Natuzzi involved?

Which one had sent her to a watery grave in the city she loved?

I was full of fear for my boy. If they had killed Georgia, what terrible things were they doing to him?

I had to find him, and the other boys, before it was too late. If whoever was behind this had even a hint that we were onto them, they could close things down. My heart started to race. If Natuzzi was in on it, they might have already taken the boys away when they couldn't dispatch me into the freezing sea with Georgia.

David burst into the room, eyes ablaze with rage and adrenalin. 'Come on,' he said. 'There's no more we can do here.'

'Natuzzi. Are they speaking to him?'

'Right now. He's legitimate. He wasn't in on it. He's a big name in Venice, internationally renowned. He pays the boat captains so they bring the kids to him. Natuzzi and his bodyguards are devoted to helping them.'

So the thugs were bodyguards, and it seemed I owed Fabio an apology for running away. But I still wasn't sure about him.

'So we have no idea who did this,' David said, lowering his voice so no one but me could hear. 'I suspect that Connaught and Simon are behind it, and probably Snow Flynt. But I feel there's someone involved this end as well. Two detectives, one from our squad, and one from the Australian Federal Police, are flying over with Georgia's family tomorrow. And the AFP Commissioner has spoken to her Italian counterpart, so they'll be pulling out all stops in the investigation.' He was now whispering in a low rumble. 'As far as the Venetian police know, I'm staying here. But we need to get down to South Safety – and no one here is being told that, for operational reasons.'

I nodded, grateful for David's plan.

'Can I see Georgia now?' I asked.

'No.'

David stood with his legs apart like he was about to have a fight.

'Please, David, I need to say goodbye.'

'I think you don't.' He sat beside me and held my hand. 'Remember her like she was. She wouldn't want you to see her like this.' My body tensed and then crumbled – I started to sob uncontrollably. David held me tight.

Five hours later we were on a plane, on our way to Buenos Aires. Venice drifted below, lights twinkling in the dusk, soft and deceptive. I could barely see through swollen eyes. Tears kept seeping out.

David was hunched over my computer the entire flight looking at the photos of Fredelighavn. I explained everything I knew, but he kept asking questions, trying to ascertain all angles, tapping notes into his own laptop.

I wanted desperately to contact Kate but David wouldn't let me. We needed to arrive unannounced, he said tersely. Our friend, and one of his own, had been killed. We were set to avenge her death. Fury rose in me, unstoppable, at what they'd done to Georgia.

At Buenos Aires we were met by an Argentinian pilot, who flew us to Ushuaia. There we transferred to a smaller plane and flew to Base Martinez, an Argentine station on the Antarctic Peninsula. The irony didn't escape me that my Spanish compatriots were going to play a key role in the mission. Argentina and Britain were usually at loggerheads over their disputed territories down here, but children at risk had united them – along with a firm directive from the Antarctic Council. If the boys on South Safety were like the others, they could be Mexican, Guatemalan, and other Spanish speakers who'd been sent across the border from Mexico into the United States, hoping for a better life, only to end up with Snow.

As we touched down at Base Martinez, waiting for us were two British detectives, Ben and Heather, mid-thirties, untalkative, and an Argentinian detective, Carlos, who was whippet thin with warm, animated eyes and a grin as broad as Georgia's. I took one look at him and burst into tears again, remembering my vivacious friend. David squeezed my hand impatiently. 'Keep a lid on, Laura,' he whispered. 'We need you to concentrate.' A white heat of anger blazed through me. Here was the patronising

David I'd left behind. Rather than explode, I walked away, gazing at the sea to try to calm down. *Focus*, I told myself, just as two sleek, black humpback whales came cruising through the water, a mother and her calf. A sign.

When I walked back to the group I was strong. And full of rage.

We just fitted into the small propeller plane that had skis beneath its wheels. As soon as we were strapped in, the plane took off. David and the detectives leaned towards each other and spoke soft and fast. I didn't know why I was being left out but I didn't care. I thought only of my boy.

South Safety Island came into view and my heart skipped a beat. It was a sparkling afternoon and I could make out pods of whales – humpbacks, orcas, southern right and the small minke – gliding through the pristine water. On the giant blue icebergs, Adélie penguins huddled, staring at the water until one brave bird went first and the others followed in a mass of black and white.

Small bits of icebergs, growlers, floated in the deep blue ocean, and smaller bergy bits bobbed about. Summer had arrived.

As we banked over Alliance Bay and flew above the red rooftops of Fredelighavn, the giant, bleached whale bones stood out starkly on the beach. At Alliance Point, the Adélie rookery was packed with hundreds of thousands of birds stretching up the hill as far as the eye could see. Leopard seals roamed the water beneath the cliff. Elephant seals lolled on the beach and Weddell seals swam between the rusted hulks of the abandoned ships.

As we circled and came in again I saw the gentoo penguin colony and, a short distance away, off to one side, a tent.

Kate must be staying with her penguins. I couldn't see her but I hoped it was the reason she hadn't returned my earlier messages – that she'd been out of phone range.

The plane landed on its skis in the vast white ice behind the village. As I stepped out I sucked in the crisp air and put on my gloves. David handed us torches, strong police ones. The pilot stayed guarding the plane with Ben, one of the British detectives, as the rest of us headed off.

I led the way, not missing a turn as we hurried through the streets, a tight commando unit. When we arrived at Ingerline's orange house we rushed up the stairs and into the hallway. I glimpsed Ingerline's portrait staring at me as I ran up the passage and felt a sudden chill, like an icy hand on my back pushing me forwards. But I didn't believe in ghosts.

As I pulled open the pantry door I understood why the shelves were empty – to allow greater ease for opening and closing the route underground.

'Step aside,' David ordered, pushing past, grabbing the middle shelf and pulling with all his strength. He staggered back as the shelves swung out easily, revealing a stairway down into the ice. I peered in, amazed – I was staring at a tunnel. Its walls were reinforced with timber and tar. The air had a strange smell, one I couldn't immediately place. Not musty, but not fresh either. Clinical, like a hospital. And mixed in was the distinct odour of sweaty socks.

We turned on our torches and David went first, followed by Heather and then me. Carlos came last. All three had guns, standard-issue police revolvers. I was the only one unarmed. There was an unreality to being surrounded by cops. It should have made me feel protected but it didn't. The fact their bullets could kill a person filled me with dread. Whatever Snow and Connaught had done, I didn't want them to end up like Georgia. I wanted them in prison. For life.

Our torchlight beamed off the walls. It was warm underground, the ice insulating. Before our tunnel went down, there was another that branched off at a ninety-degree angle to the right. Did it connect to Erling's house? It would be in the right direction – and would explain the sudden disappearance of Ingerline's ghost that day.

We went deeper into the ice. The tunnel plunged at a steep decline and then levelled out suddenly, where it widened and went off in three directions. We stopped, shining our torches down each tunnel. 'Laura, come with me,' said David in a hushed voice, and indicated for Heather to take the left tunnel and Carlos the right.

David and I went straight on, and after a few minutes we came to a fork. David stopped and whispered urgently, 'Which way?'

I tried to get my bearings. Were we beneath the cinema by now? But maybe we hadn't come that far. My attention was taken by shelves along the left-hand tunnel, full of bottles of liquor. David followed my gaze. The shelves stretched into the distance. We followed them. And then we heard shouts from behind – men's voices; one sounded like Connaught, another was definitely Snow. A gunshot echoed through the tunnel.

David and I looked at each other. A surge of care ran between us like an electrical current. 'Stay here,' he said. 'Turn off your torch and don't move.' I obeyed, and he ran off towards the sound of another gunshot. I waited until he was swallowed into the gloom, praying he'd be all right, and then I flicked on my torch and quickly moved in the direction we'd been heading. I knew the tunnels must lead to rooms somewhere, and I couldn't wait, I had to find my boy.

My ears were ringing from the gunshots as I started to run flat out, my torch beam bouncing in front. The light was announcing me, so I shone it down close to my feet and kept going.

Another fork. I stopped. The harbour would be on my right. Or was it? Would the rooms be close to it or further away? I may as well have just tossed a coin. I went left. I could be anywhere.

Up ahead, light spilled around a corner – it seemed more stable than torchlight. I stopped, breathing hard. I needed to quieten my breath. After a few moments I went on, placing each foot carefully in front of the other to make no noise.

I turned left into a blazing corridor, lit from above by electric lights, and saw a room behind a glass door. A bright, white laboratory. There was no one in it, but at the back of the room was another solid door leading to a further room.

I opened the glass door and went inside, struck by an overwhelming smell of disinfectant. I looked at the vials of samples along one wall and tried to understand what was marked on them. They were long formulas, and that was only part of the sequence of numbers; fuller mathematical equations were taped on the bench below each sample. If I had to guess, I'd say they were genetic sequences.

Several microscopes stood on a bench on the opposite wall. I looked closely at each, but they were empty, no slides in the glass. A tap dripped suddenly into a sink and I nearly screamed.

It kept dripping, running through my body like a freight train. I walked up to the door at the back and opened it a crack.

I couldn't believe my eyes: a man in a white coat turned, as surprised to see me as I was to see him.

I knew his face. The brown hair greying at the temples, the smooth skin, pale and unwrinkled. The black eyes, as dark as my own.

'Hello Dad,' I said.

20

Professor Michael Green was so shocked he couldn't speak. He looked right through me, as though he couldn't understand that I was standing there. I was having a hard time believing it myself. I'd longed to see him for so many years, and here he was. In completely the wrong place, and nothing like my fantasies of how it would be to meet up with him.

'Laura?' His deep voice finally came, now not in a phone message, but in real life. Goosebumps crowded my arms. I didn't know what to say. My mind was scrambled. We stood staring at each other. From the next room I could hear the tap dripping.

I glanced at test tubes sitting in holders on benches around the room. Mike Green was a microbiologist. His specialty was influenza. The last article I'd read of his came flaring back: he was researching a cure for a flu pandemic.

'What are you doing to the boys?' I said, but I feared I already knew. It wasn't a paedophile ring at all. They were testing human guinea pigs.

'If I told you that I'd have to kill you,' he deadpanned. 'And then I'd have to face your mother.' He smiled, cool under pressure. I obviously took after the emotional Spanish side: I wanted to lunge and punch him. I'd seen my boy's face. Terrified. Screaming. Desperate for help.

'Where are they?'

'Who?' He was surveying me, taking me in. It was over a decade since we'd met in the flesh – he was appraising how much I'd changed. Part of me couldn't help but feel flattered that he was taking an interest. I caught myself. *Don't be absurd.*

'I have people with me, Dad. Detectives from Australia, England and Argentina. It's over. There've already been gunshots. If I can say you helped me, maybe they'll go more lightly on you. So please take me to the boys.'

'Why do you think what we're doing is illegal?' he said, full of confidence.

'Because I saw the boys when they were let off in Venice.'

Now he was taken aback.

'Nothing about them seemed legal, Dad.' A wave of nausea swept through me. The world suddenly stood still. My adrenalin drained. Here was the man I'd admired my whole life. An immoral criminal, experimenting on children, out of the world's gaze. Abusing his scientific knowledge, or, no doubt

325

in his mind, using his phenomenal skills for the greater good. My head spun.

He seemed calm but a bead of sweat trickled from his temple towards his eye.

'We pay them, Laura. They're employees. They send money back to their families and we do safe experimentation with the drugs. It's a win–win. No one gets hurt. I would never test anything if I thought it was dangerous.'

'Then why not do it back in Australia or America?' I couldn't believe I was having this conversation. With my brilliant scientific father, who'd been my god. If he was capable of this . . . who was I? Professionally, I'd styled myself in his image. I felt my world crashing in.

'The climate down here. It's a perfect environment for what I need. Laura, you're a scientist, you should understand.' His dark eyes pierced mine. 'Are there really police with guns?'

'Yes.' I walked over to a test tube. I wanted to start smashing them one by one until he told me where the boys were, but I knew that wouldn't be safe. I thought I could scare him at least. I picked up the one that had the most paperwork beneath it, hoping it meant it was the most important. He rushed at me.

'Put that down *right now*, Laura!' I was suddenly eleven years old and he was back to being my father. I turned with the test tube stuck out like a sword. 'Tell me where they are or I'll drop this. What is it, anyway? It's something genetic, isn't it?'

'It's a superstar,' he said, his voice a mix of pride and anger. *Superstar.* The same word I'd seen when I'd looked up Snow's research online.

'This is important to you, I can see, but what's a rock star doing here?' I taunted.

'A *superstar*, Laura. A random gene, one in a trillion that behaves like no other. With this gene, we can stop a pandemic that could kill half the world's population.'

His eyes were blazing.

'And it works. My vaccine *works*. Those boys you saw, all healthy, right?' He was starting to puff up with self-importance.

'If I drop this, will we get infected?'

'You wouldn't be so stupid.'

I couldn't see what else I could threaten him with. I tossed the vial at him and he caught it, horrified. And then I ran. I fled down the corridor, passing scientists in white coats running in the other direction, not stopping to wonder who I was. They were flushed with fear.

I looked for another room. There was a fork ahead. I listened for my father, but he wasn't following.

I tried to think where I might be but I couldn't focus. I turned left. Then I changed my mind, retraced my steps and turned right. Halfway along the passage, there was a glass door. It was a class-room, with a whiteboard out the front, colourful posters on the walls and a dozen desks with computers.

I went in and looked around. They were teaching the children down here. Boyish handwriting was scribbled on a pad. Notes of some kind. I blinked – it was in Spanish. *We're in room two doors down, on right.* I ripped off the page and ran.

Which way did he mean? It must be further on. I'd never had so much trouble thinking in my life.

The door was solid, I couldn't see in. I pushed it open. At the front of the room stood the ghost of Ingerline, wearing the 1950s dress, blue with white bands. But she wasn't a ghost, she was flesh and blood: the tall, blonde woman I'd seen in the mirror. She was a teacher. In front of her sat a group of teenage boys. Half were dressed in 1950s checked shirts and trousers, and half in modern T-shirts, jeans and tracksuits, no doubt a part of my father's experiments. All were staring at me – but I was looking straight at the boy in the ice. And this time he was grinning, dark eyes shining, his black hair, longer, hanging shaggily around his imp's face. He was wearing a blue T-shirt and jeans, and seemed just like I imagined Hamish would have been at that age. A sweet, handsome boy.

He leaped up and ran into my arms. '*Que hayas venido!*' he cried. 'You've come.'

21

I was hugging my boy so tightly I was worried I'd crush him, but he was clinging to me just as fiercely, his thin pale arms as strong as a lion. I could smell his skin, soft and fresh, and a soapy shampoo in his hair. His warmth infused me.

'Quickly, we must go,' I said in Spanish. The other boys sat frozen. The teacher hadn't moved.

'They're too scared,' he said.

We spoke in Spanish. 'What's your name?' I asked gently.

'Santo.' He looked into my eyes and hugged me again, sighing. 'I left T-shirts. And I moved the diaries to the church. You found them. I knew you'd come and get me.'

I covered his hand in mine. 'We must leave.' Santo nodded emphatically but the other boys wouldn't budge. The teacher watched us mutely, terrified. I was desperate to get Santo safely away, and he started to tug, trying to lead me out of the room. 'I'll come back,' I promised the boys, as Santo yanked me into the corridor. 'Which way out?' I cried as we broke into a run.

'To Ingerline's house?'

'No, not there.'

'To Erling's place? Or Olaf's?' *So there were entrances in all three houses.* But I didn't want to go in that direction.

'No.'

'The church?'

An entrance there too. But if Santo knew it, his captors would too.

'The ice cave, where you saw me?' he offered. 'But the door will be locked.'

I tingled at the memory of Santo screaming in the cave and my eyes clouded with tears. I'd found him.

'Have you ever been to the cinema?' I asked.

'We watch films there. We get to chase the seals away. And after the movie they let us play with the penguins on the hill.'

My temper flared. Not only were they doing human experiments, they were letting children out among the wildlife. I could only imagine what teenagers in an angry mood might have done to the Adélies.

'Is there a tunnel up to the cinema?'

'No, we walk there from Ingerline's.'

'If there *was* a tunnel, could you tell where it might run off down here?' I kept flashing to Helen's description of where her brother had fallen through the ice. And if Santo didn't know of the tunnel entrance in the cinema, maybe nobody else did either. If it existed.

Santo gripped my hand tighter and stopped. He thought for a moment. My heart was pumping so fast I hoped it didn't give up on me.

'This way,' he said and we retraced our steps before he pulled me down another corridor. We wove around in the labyrinth of corridors until we started to rise on an incline.

'Is there *really* an entrance into the cinema?' he asked, amazed.

'I don't know. I hope so.' It was only the slightest thread of a hunch. It seemed unlikely to me that Helen's brother had fallen directly through the ice into a tunnel; more likely he'd gone underground, where something awful had happened.

Santo stopped suddenly. 'I think here,' he murmured, and turned into a tight passage that was so dark I hadn't noticed it. 'I've always wondered where this one went,' he said.

I flicked on my torch and the beam lit the way like a beacon. There was a flight of narrow stairs, rising steeply. We clambered up about thirty steps, having to take great care not to slip. The steps were poorly made, and dangerous. At the top, there was a landing, and a small steel door, crawl-height, blocked the way. I tried to open it but it was locked from outside. There was nothing I could unlatch from this direction. Santo swore under his breath.

'Stand back,' I said, and started to kick as hard as I could. Santo wanted to help, and when I was completely out of breath he took over. He was making a loud clanging, and when he tired, there was silence for a moment. And then there was clanging from the other side, the sharp twang of metal on metal. Someone was trying to hammer the lock open. I froze.

Santo grabbed my hand and pulled me back as the door swung inwards, nearly knocking us off our feet.

Torchlight slashed my eyes. I couldn't see who was there.

But I knew the voice.

'She's here,' said Kate. 'With a boy.'

'I'll help you out.' The torchlight swung away and Travis grinned down. Relief surged through me as he reached in and took my hands.

'Santo first.' I stepped back. 'This is Travis,' I said to Santo. 'A good friend.'

Santo sprang into Travis's arms and Travis barked with laughter.

Then as Travis pulled me out I felt a wave of fear. 'Where are the seals?'

'Gone. In the harbour. There were just a few and sorry, we did have to scare them out when we heard you banging.'

'How did you know I'd come here?' I looked around the dark cinema, wanting to check for myself we weren't in danger from the bull seal. The room stunk of seal but there were none in residence.

'You kept thinking there was an opening here,' said Kate.

'Well, here and everywhere else.'

'We should go,' said Travis urgently, pulling out a satellite radio. 'Okay, Reggie, you're on!'

Kate and Travis led us to the bay. As we ran, Santo gripped my hand so tightly I lost blood flow. I could hear an approaching plane, and a Twin Otter with floats flew low overhead. It landed in the sea, close to shore, and cut its engine.

'We'll have to swim,' called Travis.

'Can you swim?' I asked Santo. He shook his head, terrified.

'Just go limp in my arms. I'll tow you.'

We rushed towards the icy water. It was so cold we would last only minutes – but I knew from Polar Plunges that we'd be okay, if we were quick. In the distance, men came running. One was tall and lanky – Jasper. Another was unmistakably Simon. He raised his right arm towards us and there was a glint of metal just before an almighty crack rang out.

We lunged, as one, into the sea. The chill hit me so hard that I almost stopped breathing. Santo's eyes filled with panic and then he flung back and went limp in my arms, and I towed him the few metres to the plane. Reg – the pilot I'd been told never to fly with, who'd helped uncover everything – hauled Santo on board, and then me, as Kate and Travis were hauled in by Moose. There were towels and blankets waiting. Reg slipped into the cockpit, and the engine spluttered to life. I shielded Santo with my body, willing the plane to take off as shots whirled past. Simon – seemingly the only one with a gun – thankfully had a poor aim.

After long moments we were airborne, heading out over the sea.

'We're going to Base Martinez,' said Travis. 'They're waiting for us.'

'How do you know?' I asked, confused.

'David White's been in contact.'

'Do you know where he is now?'

'No. But all hell broke loose when you arrived.' Travis grinned, and I noticed how blue his eyes were, the same colour as the cobalt water below us. Kate reached across and held Santo's hand. 'We've been looking everywhere for you, mate.'

Santo nodded awkwardly and nestled into me, his teeth chattering from cold. I dried his hair and wrapped him in three blankets. He opened up the woolly mass and snuggled me under with him. Then he leaned his head on my shoulder and closed his eyes.

22

Barbara Preston, a British detective who specialised in child protection, and Doctor Mariano Ramos, an Argentinian child psychiatrist, met us at Base Martinez. They ushered us into a warm room and gave us dry clothes. Santo wouldn't leave my side. Over the next hour they quietly, gently interrogated him in a recorded interview.

Santo spoke in fluent English, which he'd learned from his teacher – the ghost in Ingerline's blue and white dress – and he'd also taught himself Norwegian. He was shy with the other adults, his voice a whisper.

'We'd do things together, like carry chairs from house to house, sit around and eat in one kitchen and then another. They dressed half of us in old-fashioned clothes, and the rest of us in normal stuff.

I don't know why; something to do with how we'd cope with the cold. One week, we carried cigarettes from the tunnels and put them in a house, because they'd found us smoking them, and that wasn't allowed. Sometimes we'd do repairs on the houses. Sometimes we'd just stay and sleep. Every week Doctor Mike would inject us.'

He shuddered violently and my chest tightened. Doctor Mike. My father.

'Did that make you ill?' Doctor Ramos asked in a deep, resonant voice.

'Sometimes. Some boys got rashes. Half the time I felt I was going to be sick. Other days I was okay. The injections hurt as they went in. I wanted to leave but I couldn't.'

Tears seeped into his eyes. I wished I could storm out and confront my father, but he wasn't here. Neither was David, which worried me.

'Did anyone touch you – inappropriately?' asked Barbara Preston gently.

Santo clammed up.

'Somewhere you didn't want to be touched?'

'No.' Santo answered simply.

Silence hung in the air. We couldn't know if Santo had understood, or was hiding something, or simply telling the truth.

'How did you feel about Professor Connaught and Simon?' Barbara continued.

Santo tensed every muscle in his body.

'Did they come down?'

Tears flooded Santo's cheeks. He shuffled his chair closer to mine and leaned in, his bony shoulder sticking into me. I wrapped my arm around him.

'Harold and Simon would choose one boy from each group. There were three groups who came while I was there.'

'That is Harold *Connaught* and Simon *Huxtable*,' Barbara said into the tape recorder. My skin crawled at the thought of Simon: a victim himself, having been abused by Connaught as a child, who went on to perpetuate the cycle.

'They took the boys to a shed they kept locked.'

'Did you go in the shed?' I asked, not knowing if I could bear the answer, thinking of the one locked shed we'd come across and its pile of mattresses.

'No. But the chosen boy would come back and tell one of us. The rest would warn each other. When I didn't leave with my group last week, I knew it was my turn.' Santo put his warm hand, sweaty and trembling, in mine. I gripped it tightly.

'My *whole group* left except me,' he said, his face crumpling. 'I'd been down there for ten months. I wanted to go so badly.' I hugged him to me, rocking us back and forth.

Doctor Ramos passed Santo a tissue and he blew his nose.

'Did they come down again then? Simon and Harold?' asked Barbara.

Santo shook his head. 'No. Everything changed. New boys arrived with Snow, but people were nervous. Doctor Mike kept giving us injections, but Simon and Harold didn't come. And you'd gone, Laura.' He pronounced my name the Spanish way. I felt a surge of love, even as my head reeled. Doctor Mike, the medical scientist, giving injections to innocent boys kept trapped in the ice; boys who were being abused at the whim of monsters. Was my father part of that too? Bile rose in my throat, burning sharply.

'I couldn't see you in the cameras any more,' said Santo, looking up at me. 'I thought you'd left me.'

So there *were* cameras. Well-hidden, like everything else.

'I'd never do that,' I said.

'So no one touched you?' asked Doctor Ramos again gently. Barbara watched closely.

'No.' Santo sat up straight. 'But Harold and Simon would have if Laura hadn't found me.'

I thought of Georgia: her actions had saved Santo from abuse from which he would never have recovered.

'Did Snow touch the boys?' asked Doctor Ramos.

'No,' said Santo.

'And Doctor Mike?'

I held my breath, fighting another wave of nausea.

'No.' Santo leaned back into me.

But surely my father must have known what was going on?

'Santo, I'll be back.' I raced out, just made it to the bathroom, and vomited. I couldn't stop thinking about my father, the person I'd admired above everyone. What kind of man was he?

I walked slowly outside, gulping the cold, clear air, and phoned my mother, needing to tell her about my father, hoping somehow she could make me feel better about myself. I was his bloodline; he was a part of me. Had she suspected all along what he was really like? Had she been protecting me all these years?

'Hello?' The voice was deep and slurred. I checked the number – it was Mum's.

'It's Laura. Can I speak to my mother, please?'

'Laura, it's me.'

I froze. 'Mum, what's wrong? You sound dreadful.'

'I've just come out of surgery.'

'What for?'

'If you'd called, you would have known. I was diagnosed with breast cancer.'

My legs felt hollow. I needed to sit, but I was standing on ice. 'So they operated?'

'Yes.'

'Did they get it all?'

'Well, I hope so. I'll have to have chemo for a few weeks, and then tablets for the next two years. But the prognosis is positive. They're very good. Cancer treatment's moved in leaps and bounds, you know.'

Because of research done by clever people like my father and Snow. No doubt they were convinced they were advancing medical science. And they probably were. Unethically. Trapping children and holding them like prisoners; using them as human guinea pigs. And turning a blind eye to the despicable actions of the two men they needed onside: the Base Commander and the Chief Pilot.

'Are you sure you'll be okay?' I asked, tears rolling, fat and wet, down my face.

'Laura, when will you be home?'

'I'm so sorry. I'll come as soon as I can.' I couldn't stop crying, my body shaking, as she hung up.

23

I tucked Santo into a soft bed in a bright blue room at Base Martinez. 'Buenas noches,' I said, as a surge of tenderness shot through me. He looked up with wide, tired eyes. 'Laura – thank you,' he replied, his voice hoarse with exhaustion. He squeezed my hand, and I felt the hot prickle of my tears. Within seconds Santo's breathing fell into the gentle rhythm of deep sleep. My phone beeped with a text from David.

'All safe. Will be in touch.'

My shoulders relaxed a little, but I wished he'd given more details. I was very relieved to hear from him.

I found the mess hall, a huge room abuzz with scientists and tradespeople speaking Spanish, loudly. Travis and Kate were eating dinner, a bottle of whisky glowing amber on the table in front of them. Kate's eyes were swollen from crying; Travis was sombre. After phoning my mother, and with Santo out of earshot because he was still with Doctor Ramos and the detective, I had relayed the awful news about Georgia.

I distractedly chose a plate of paella, and sat down to quiz Travis about what he did and didn't know. Kate listened, swaying slightly, a little drunk.

'I got wind of a tunnel,' said Travis. 'It was rumoured to start to the east of base, about twenty minutes out, and people were saying vehicles were going down there. Moose and I thought it might lead to Fredelighavn, and we searched for an entrance, but we couldn't find anything. That's what I was trying to hint at before you left for Nantucket.'

Travis's tan had deepened while I'd been away, and the shadow of stubble on his face brought out the strength in his jaw. 'But what I *did* discover was fuel-oil in the tanks at Fredelighavn, and that convinced me there was something underground. A mirror-world with its own electricity.'

'That was a brilliant idea of yours to check in the tanks,' I said, and he glanced at me with such proud intensity my stomach fluttered.

'You know Rutger high-tailed it back to Berlin as soon as Georgia left,' said Kate, sniffling.

Tears started to flow down my cheeks at the thought of Georgia. Travis's eyes misted up.

'Anyway,' Kate said, blowing her nose, 'I headed down to camp with the penguins. And Travis came every night to check that I was safe. We'd go into Fredelighavn and keep searching for entrances.' She grinned slightly, focusing on me.

341

'Travis drove me to distraction because he wouldn't stop talking about you.'

Travis blushed scarlet and my whole body tingled in a way that wasn't at all suitable for a sister towards a brother. A sob erupted out of me, and Travis rubbed my back soothingly with his warm, strong hand.

'I did some more sleuthing at base, too,' he said. 'Eventually I found a couple of guys who reckoned that Jasper has a liking for date-drugging girls. He's never been caught, but last summer there were evidently two incidents, and Jasper was close by when they happened. He didn't follow through with anything, it seems he just likes scaring women, so the whole thing was swept under the carpet.'

I shuddered, remembering my lost day – and how Jasper had volunteered to be with us in the lab. What sort of kick had he been getting out of it?

'Seems I was right about him being the one who slipped something into your whisky,' said Kate, her green eyes bloodshot.

'Then I'll be reporting him for that,' I said firmly. 'Travis, do you think the men will talk to the detectives?'

'I'll try to persuade them.' Travis didn't look hopeful. 'And if they won't, I'll give David their names,' he offered, and I loved that he'd be brave enough to take a stand in the world of men at Alliance.

I didn't want to ask the next question, but I had to. 'Travis, did you ever suspect Simon?'

Travis paled and sat back in his chair, his body seeming to shrink. He looked at me directly as I held my breath and waited for his answer. Kate watched, her brow creased with worry.

'No,' he said, 'and that makes me feel terrible. That he was a friend, doing that under my nose, and I never had a clue. He was so clever, pretended he didn't like Connaught. I never even saw them together socially.'

I exhaled and breathed more easily, relieved to hear Travis confirm his innocence.

'I've been thinking about that Adélie,' said Kate into the silence. 'The one we found in the cupboard. It might actually have wandered in there and died of natural causes. I couldn't find any evidence of viruses in the penguin colonies, so thankfully that's at least one bit of good news.'

I'd been wrong about everything with that Adélie – but now happiness flashed through me to hear the penguins were virus-free. 'That is truly great news,' I said. Kate poured another whisky, and refilled our glasses. 'To Georgia,' she said suddenly. 'She might have kept me from my Adélies, but she was a bloody good woman.' I saw the glasses blurrily as we clinked them, and I sculled the liquor down, hot and fiery, which seemed fitting for Georgia. 'Although we really should drink beer for her,' I commented sadly.

Travis rose. 'Let me.' He went over to the bar.

I turned to Kate. 'Remember that man we saw at Fredelighavn the night we stayed? I'm now *certain* that it was Snow. I still can't quite believe that he's behind all this. I wonder what Harvard found out about him?'

'It must have been really bad, because we've seen how universities can close ranks around professors,' said Kate forcefully.

She was right. Universities kept those matters confidential. We would never know. 'My father will lose his position at

Sydney University,' I said and stopped as memories came flooding in. Dad's dark eyes, so familiar, his smooth skin, the antiseptic smell around him. I had wondered if I'd unwittingly met up with him in the blubber cookery the first day I went to Fredelighavn – but I'd decided that man was shorter and fatter. Another scientist.

Kate squeezed my arm supportively. 'You're thinking about your dad, aren't you?'

I nodded. 'But I don't want to. Not now.' *Not ever, if I could help it, but that was unlikely to be possible.*

Travis came back with three beers.

'To Georgia,' we toasted again. As the cold beer slid down my throat, a shiver convulsed me. I could feel Travis watching. I glanced across, and as my gaze locked into his blue eyes that were full of concern, I realised the more time I spent with him, the more I thought of him in a very different way. A man who was loyal, who liked to say yes, and who grew more handsome every time I looked at him.

'Hello, Helen?'

'Laura! We've been so worried about you.' Helen's voice, clear and strong, came down the line. I pictured her standing at her kitchen table in Nantucket, and wasn't sure how to break the news. I was sitting in the empty mess hall and could barely stay awake, but felt I had to speak to her.

'We found the tunnels,' I said. I could hear Helen breathing but she said nothing, waiting for me to continue.

'There were steps, very steep, narrow steps, leading down from under the stage. In the dark, your brother wouldn't have seen them.'

I didn't know how to say that he probably broke his neck, without it coming out too shockingly.

I didn't need to.

'I understand,' said Helen. 'Thank you, Laura. It helps me very much to know that—' She gasped.

'Helen? Are you okay?'

'My dear, yes. You wouldn't read about it, but a cardinal has just flown right up to the sill. The brightest red I've ever seen. It was little Peter's favourite bird.'

The next day, David Skyped me from Alliance. He had the strained, slightly wild eyes of someone who hadn't slept. I sat in a small, dark computer room. No one else was around.

'We've arrested your father and Snow, as well as Connaught, Simon, the teacher and four other scientists,' he said and paused, shifting in his seat. 'I'm sorry about your dad, Laura.'

'It's okay, I don't really know him,' I replied, feeling the truth of my comment. *He was like a complete stranger.* 'Any news from Venice?' I asked dismally.

'The Italian investigation's going at full speed.' David tensed up. 'We suspect that Connaught and Simon arranged Georgia's murder through mafia, and someone in the Venetian police force – most likely part of Connaught and Simon's paedophile network – tipped them off that she was there.' He stopped, looking like he might break down, then collected himself. 'A detective is being interrogated as we speak,' he continued angrily. 'He could be the man who Georgia was planning to meet the night she disappeared. Someone she trusted, who'd been working the case with us. And this bloke's senior enough to have made sure no police went to the docks the night the boys arrived.'

A vein throbbed in David's neck, his face deepening red as he fought to keep his grief and rage under control. 'Of course Connaught and Simon are swearing they had nothing to do with Georgia's death. But they've given up the names of other paedophiles – including your mate Rutger Koch, whose visit down here wasn't his first, and the artist-in-residence who'd painted the Hägglunds. They're desperate to cut a deal.' David smiled grimly. 'Which they won't get.'

So Rutger *did* know Connaught well. Horribly well. My stomach tightened into a thick knot. 'What about my father and Snow?' I braced for the answer.

'They're trying to persuade us they knew nothing about what Connaught and Simon were up to, and they're adamant they were only doing safe experiments on the boys. And Stan, Simon's co-pilot, is saying that he knew nothing either. He managed to fly with Simon on all the flights except the ones with the boys.'

People who chose not to see, I thought, my temples throbbing. Like people close to atrocities throughout history, who convinced themselves that doing nothing meant that they weren't complicit. My father and the others had made choices. Choices, without conscience. Thinking that no one was watching, or would ever find out. *And that no one would ever judge them for their decisions.*

'Snow's still trying to be a leader,' David was saying as I tuned back in. 'Refused to name the multinational pharmaceutical company that's clearly involved in the drug trial. Won't admit government involvement either, but he can't substantiate how he could have funded the whole operation himself. Everything was financed through accounts in Snow's name in the Cayman Islands. The boys were paid. Every fortnight, money was wired to their families.'

My father had been telling the truth about that after all. They were kids who had been sent out to make money, and they had succeeded, I noted miserably.

'Their families didn't know where they were. Snow kept that vague. He was pretending they were working somewhere in Europe.'

I listened tiredly, my limbs heavy, my blood feeling thick and slow, as David outlined how my father and Snow were facing prosecution for unlawful drug testing on humans, for which they had pleaded guilty, and charges relating to the trafficking of children, which they were fighting. They were also to go before an international court for having placed protected wildlife in grave danger with their experiments, letting children out among the penguins and seals. If the flu had spread to the penguins as avian flu, the whole ecosystem could have been at risk. They were claiming everything was carefully controlled, and the children never had active flu. As for their pragmatism in keeping Connaught and Simon compliant, by looking the other way to the sexual abuse of the boys, the law seemed not to have caught up to charging them with that. Yet. But laws were changing, and inquiries could be retrospective, so one day they might be brought to account for that too. In my mind, my father was as guilty for allowing the abuse to happen, as he was for everything else. I was disgusted, depressed and haunted to be his daughter.

'I *won't* go back there! I told you yesterday, and I'll tell you tomorrow, I won't!' Santo's pale face was flushed with fear and anger, his voice raised, as he spoke to Doctor Ramos.

My heart wrenched as I sat with them in a room that looked out across a field of ice to the sea, grey and choppy under thick clouds, matching the mood inside. Santo's parents had been killed in the Guatemalan drug wars, and Santo had been sent across the border from Mexico to the United States by an uncle who had eagerly received the money wired to him by Snow's Cayman Islands company. Santo was adamant he didn't want to go back to the relative who had exploited him, and he had no other close family.

The ten boys who were found at Fredelighavn had now all been brought to Base Martinez for psychological and medical assessment. After two emotional days it had been established that five wanted to go back to their families in Guatemala, and the rest, like Santo, were begging not to return to their homes. Professor Fabio Natuzzi had graciously accepted my apology for doubting him, and was already working to settle boys in schools and families in Italy, but Santo didn't want to go there either.

And so I'd asked Professor Natuzzi for help, and was desperately waiting for his answer.

My phone rang and I trembled as I saw it was him. His voice came down the line, full of calm authority. 'I've pulled a few strings, Laura,' he said, 'and I've managed to organise for Santo to be placed temporarily in your care.'

It took me a few moments to register what I'd just heard, and then I looked across to Santo, my body humming, a broad smile stretching across my face.

24

It was early afternoon in April when I finished the final draft of my report to the Antarctic Council. I had almost met the deadline, which would have pleased Georgia. I sighed deeply. Georgia appeared most nights in my sleep, usually her vivacious self, but on a few occasions her bloated body swam slowly through dark water towards me. The Italian police had arrested a man from Naples, linked to the mafia, who had given up the name of the detective in the Venetian police force. The detective then implicated Simon and Connaught. The trial would take place later this year, and David and I would be there, ensuring our dear friend, who we missed so greatly, at least received this justice.

I looked back at my report, thinking Georgia would have hated my recommendations.

In summary, taking all aspects into consideration, this remarkable wilderness has a chance of not only keeping its vast number of species, (refer appendix 1), but also increasing the population of each species.

The industrial architecture and streets of detached domestic dwellings at Fredelighavn Whaling Station are unique and would attract large numbers of tourists. However, given the importance of the wildlife, it is my strong opinion that this piece of Antarctica should remain an Exclusion Zone in perpetuity.

Regarding the buildings, due to their special nature, I suggest a photographic display of them be housed at Grytviken Museum on South Georgia Island; deposited in the archives of the Nantucket Historical Association in Massachusetts; and approaches made to Commander Chr. Christensen's Whaling Museum in Sandefjord, Norway, situated in the Vestfold region where the Larvik Fishing Company was based, to include a set of photographs in their archives.

Ingerline Halvorsen was instrumental in creating a domestic summer village on an island south of the Antarctic convergence and for this, I believe, she deserves a place in Antarctic history alongside the explorers we already commemorate. An oral history could be sought from her granddaughter Helen Halvorsen, a Nantucketer who spent four summers at Fredelighavn, between 1950 and 1955. I would ask the Council to consider repatriating a gramophone player, records and family portraits back to Helen Halvorsen. The other contents of the houses could be placed with museums.

The buildings themselves could be left to decay with the weather and the years, or, if funds were supplied by participating treaty nations, all structures could be removed by a specialist company. I have spoken to several leaders in the field who estimate it would take five Austral summers to complete the dismantling. They would be happy to quote if the Council feels this is the appropriate path.

Given the difficulties of monitoring the activities of the nearby Alliance Base, and in light of recent violations of the Exclusion Zone at Placid Bay, I would recommend the base be relocated elsewhere in Antarctica and that South Safety Island, in its entirety, be closed to all human visitors.

I pressed send, dispatching it to my Australian superiors. My email pinged – it was Kate, who, writing up her Adélie research, was sending daily photographs of the penguins and their chicks, who had hatched, grown and headed out to sea. Today's image was of penguins Isabel and Charles with their two fluffy chicks, standing happily between the tripod legs of the fixed camera. Smiling, I emailed Kate back, reminded that human presence didn't have to hurt wildlife in Antarctica. As scientists we couldn't leave everything alone, or we would miss learning important facts.

Was I then a hypocrite to want to close South Safety Island? Nancy on Nantucket swept into my mind; her justification of the whalers. I didn't agree with her – but I knew that she was also right. The whalers, including Erling and Ingerline and their families, hadn't thought what they were doing was wrong.

Incredibly, I didn't think my own father did either. Or Snow.

My head started to ache and I closed my computer. Sunlight played through the gauze curtains, which billowed in the breeze. I looked out to a dusty patch of ground and saw Santo kick a soccer ball high into the blue sky, and Travis race to it and bounce it off his head. My mother, tall, brown-eyed, tufts of grey-brown hair sticking out like a penguin chick after her bout of chemotherapy, ran to the ball and kicked it. I was surprised by how far it went.

I stood up stiffly and walked outside, where the sweet scent of cherry blossom filled the air. It was my first time in Spain, and we had rented a house in Valle del Jerte in Extremadura, where Granny Maria and Papa Luis had spent their idyllic childhood, before Franco. The cherry trees were in full bloom, as white as driven snow, stretching far into the distance. Bees buzzed contentedly, gathering nectar for honey. Behind, mountains rose in a purple haze.

Santo ran and hugged me. 'Kick the ball, kick the ball!' He squeezed tightly.

Professor Natuzzi was helping us with the legalities required to allow Santo to continue to stay away from Guatemala. In time, after passing through a maze of bureaucracy, we hoped to adopt him.

In the meantime, Santo was going nowhere without me. He'd made his choice; and he was as stubborn as I was. I bent and quickly kissed the top of his head, and he tickled me, laughing merrily as I squealed.

My mother came towards us, the awkward run she'd always had, lopsided, hands splaying out to the sides. She was happy with life after her breast-cancer scare – a scare for which I'd given no support because I hadn't answered her calls. I realised, now, how much I loved her, and how unfair I'd been to her over the years. She'd been looking out for me all this time, saving me from the darkness she knew was in my father. She'd seen his lack of ethics early on, had argued with him – and then asked him to leave when his sense of right and wrong was crushed beneath his overwhelming ambition. My mother had given me a moral compass. I'd misunderstood her – and now, like a lens flipped, I saw her for the brave, caring woman she was, and was sorry I hadn't noticed before. With her reprieve from cancer, I was grateful I'd get a second chance to be as good to her as she'd been to me.

I smiled at Mum and she caught my eye; a moment passed between us, solid and strong, and then I kicked the ball and she cursed playfully as it went flying. Santo ran like the wind, glancing it off his boot and darting it to Travis.

Crickets chorused gently in the still air and an owl hooted somewhere far in the distance. The night was crisp. Santo and Mum were asleep in the adjacent rooms, and I stretched my body into the bend of Travis's arms, luxuriating in his warmth. Next week, he planned to take us all for the promised lobster dinner in Kennebunkport, Maine. On our way, we would stop in Nantucket. Helen and Nancy were excited to meet Santo, and he was keen to try their famed chocolate-chip cookies and blueberry muffins.

I'd finally learned Travis's age – twenty-seven. As he shifted and held me tight, his breathing light and steady, it didn't escape me that he was the same age as Cameron had been when I was pregnant with Hamish.

Just as the Spanish Civil War had sent my grandparents to England for a new beginning, the Guatemalan drug wars had sent Santo in search of a new life in America. Now I was having a new beginning with Santo, a boy the age that Hamish would have been if he'd lived, and with Travis.

Migration. A shifting world. The sea of humanity seeking new homes.

We were lucky to be here.

'Look!' Santo pointed excitedly, binoculars glued to his eyes. 'Here they come!' The wind buffeted us as we stood with Travis and Mum on the cliffs at Aireys Inlet on a cloudy, late autumn afternoon, where we'd been scouring the water for hours.

A spout of mist shot up above the grey waves, and Santo yelped as a humpback leaped into the air, breaching. Near it, huge flukes rose, black and white, and slapped the sea. The whales were on their annual migration from Antarctica to the warm waters of far north Queensland.

'Is it Lev? Is it Lev?' Santo cried. Through my binoculars I studied the giant flukes as the humpback lobtailed again.

'Different pattern. It's one I don't know.' I ruffled Santo's hair as his face dropped in disappointment. 'It's a new one, just for you. You must name it,' I encouraged, and my boy's face lit up. 'I'll call it . . . Travis 2.'

'Travis 2 can be my *little brother*,' joked Travis, and I pulled my binoculars down just in time to catch his twinkling blue eyes meet mine. 'You dag,' I said, inwardly pinching myself that this beautiful man was here with me.

'Don't worry Gran, I'll call the next one Cristina,' promised Santo. Mum grunted and put her arms around him. 'I might call it Santo instead,' she replied. 'I already feel like too much of a whale.'

I was so relieved that Mum had gained weight steadily in our travels, a reassuring sign of her recovery.

'Ooh! There she is! Cristina 2!' called Santo happily as another whale shot its flukes out of the water like a black and white butterfly in the dwindling light. I held my binoculars closer. Was I imagining it, or could I just make out the markings I knew so well, with a diagonal scar running through?

'*That one* already has a name,' I went to say, but my voice caught in my throat. Was it possible? *Could it be Lev?* But before I could utter a word, he slapped his flukes one more time and disappeared down into the darkening sea.

As night gathered around us, and a lighthouse swept its yellow arc across the water, we made our way back to Melbourne, where we were living with Mum in the too-big house in the leafy street, and I had a family of my own.

25

Sometimes I wake in the middle of the night to whale song. I imagine the humpbacks swimming in the harbour, Fredelighavn creaking in the wind. Penguins and seals overrun the buildings, as they slowly decay.

On a sparkling day, the Adélies dance on the ice, heads to the sun, tiny wings flapping, leaping from foot to foot.

And the white–blue ice cave sits, pure and still.

ACKNOWLEDGEMENTS

I am very grateful to the teams at Simon & Schuster UK and Australia for their hard work and support. In the UK, I would particularly like to thank Jo Dickinson, Publishing Director, Fiction, for her wisdom and guidance, which I truly appreciate. My thanks also to Suzanne Baboneau, Managing Director, Adult Publishing Division, Gill Richardson, Sales Director, and publicist Jess Barratt. Sian Wilson and Nick Castle have created a wonderful cover, and I thank them both.

In Australia I owe an enormous debt of gratitude and thanks to Roberta Ivers, Managing Editor, and to Head of Publishing, Larissa Edwards. Roberta has an extraordinary ability to see exactly what I am trying to write, and make it so much better. Her keen eye for themes and storytelling, and her astonishing flair has helped this book in a myriad of ways. Larissa Edwards is astute and generous, and gave pivotal suggestions that enabled the story to take flight. I am very lucky indeed to be guided by such talented women.

Thanks also to Dan Ruffino, Managing Director, for the great care he takes of authors and our books. A special thanks to Carol Warwick, Senior Marketing and Publicity Manager, who comes up with fantastic ideas and is a dream to work with; to Marketing and Publicity Director Anabel Pandiella for her clever thoughts; Anna O'Grady for her work with festivals; and Ellin Williams for her diligence.

ANN TURNER

Sales Director Elissa Baillie does an exceptional job, and I thank her. I owe a particularly large debt of gratitude to Nicki Lambert, Account Manager, for her excellent suggestions on the manuscript and her inspiring support, and for the magnificent work that she does handselling into the beautiful bookstores in Melbourne, Adelaide and Tasmania. I thank, too, Melinda Beaumont, Key Account Manager, for her wonderful feedback on an early draft and her great encouragement, and for her tireless work handselling my books into the equally beautiful bookstores in Sydney. Liz Bray, Vicki Mayer and Georgina Rhodes undertake incredible work, which makes such a difference to the life of my books. Jo Munroe does a spectacular job with the ebooks, and also deserves my deep gratitude.

Claire de Medici I thank for her copyedit and her insightful advice, which made such a difference to the manuscript.

A special thank you to Christa Moffitt at Christabella Designs for creating beautiful covers for my books.

I am indebted to my patient readers: Jenny Sweeney, Katie Edwards, Julie Wells, Carmel Reilly and Rivka Hartman, who gave brilliant suggestions. I thank Mary Damousi, and Kathy and Myles Vinecombe for their helpful feedback and Evangelina Vinecombe for her energetic encouragement. Sue Maslin gave razor-sharp advice, David Cramond shared my enthusiasm for Antarctica and provided insightful comments, and Ruby Kerrison read a late draft and gave me a valuable perspective – I thank them.

I am very grateful to Kerry Landman for her support through the writing of this book. Kerry was so generous in allowing me to co-opt the use of *Superstar* for the purposes of my story, and for helping me gain insight into the workings of a scientific mind. Her suggestions were always inspiring. Annette Blonski has taken a very long journey with me: the idea of writing about Antarctica took hold over twenty-five years ago, and Annette has shared my passion for this landscape through all these years. With this manuscript, she has patiently read drafts and given invaluable comments, and I thank her very much.

For their professional help along the way I would like to thank Mike Middleton for sharing his pilot's knowledge of planes, and the ins and outs of skis and floats on Twin Otters (all mistakes are my own); Warwick Anderson for his medical guidance (any mistakes are definitely mine); and Leigh Dale for her expert advice regarding a key moment in the book. Thanks to Mary Tomsic for her help that allowed me to travel overseas for research, and my sister Judy Turner for introducing me to the beauty of Nantucket and Cape Cod.

I would also like to thank the booksellers, reviewers and readers in the UK and Australia who were so supportive of my debut novel *The Lost Swimmer*. I am indebted to you, and delighted by you.

And finally, my love and thanks go to Joy Damousi, for her encouragement, patience, support, wisdom, endless enthusiasm, and inspiration, for which I am truly grateful.

Ann Turner
2017

ABOUT THE AUTHOR

Ann Turner is an award-winning screenwriter and director, avid reader and history lover. She is drawn to salt-sprayed coasts, luminous landscapes, and the people who inhabit them all over the world. Her films include the historical feature *Celia*, starring Rebecca Smart – which *Time Out* listed as one of the fifty greatest directorial debuts of all time; *Hammers Over The Anvil*, starring Russell Crowe and Charlotte Rampling; and the psychological thriller *Irresistible* starring Susan Sarandon, Sam Neill and Emily Blunt. Ann has lectured in film at the Victorian College of the Arts.

Her bestselling debut novel *The Lost Swimmer* investigates the consequences of love and trust. In her second novel, *Out of the Ice*, a mystery thriller set in Antarctica, Ann explores the dark side of human progress and a past and present of tragedy, deception and survival. Ann was born in Adelaide and lives in Victoria.

Visit Ann's website at AnnTurnerAuthor.com

BOOK CLUB NOTES

1. Antarctica is a unique setting for the novel. How does the location add to the suspense, and how crucial is this setting to the story? What place does Antarctica hold in our collective imagination?

2. Laura Alvarado has a troubled past. Do you think that this has played a part in her strong feelings towards Antarctica and its wildlife? How has it affected her view of the world? Is Laura an unreliable narrator?

3. How would you interpret the title *Out of the Ice*? Does it have more than one meaning?

4. Migration, of both wildlife and humans, is a theme in *Out of the Ice*. How is the long history of migration depicted?

5. The destruction, but also the survival of family is a continuing theme in the story. Does the book explore more than one type of family? Ultimately, does it raise questions regarding the notion of family and what it – and home – can mean?

6. The story looks at how the whalers' actions in the past are judged in the present. It links this with global warming and how the potential destruction of the environment is perhaps not understood by some in the same way that the whalers didn't comprehend the level of emotion that whales feel, and their evolved communication skills. Do you agree, or disagree, with these ideas? How do you view the past through the prism of the present?

7. Scientists conducting experiments are depicted in *Out of the Ice*. Can science ever be justified as being above ethics and morality if it is for the greater good of humanity?

8. Discuss how the book looks at human progress – from the whalers, to the scientists, to the migrants and refugees in search of a better life. How vulnerable are children in this?

9. Friendship between women is a fundamental aspect of this story. How is the friendship depicted between Laura, Kate and Georgia? And between Helen and Nancy? How does friendship help these women? And how do women fare in isolated, male-oriented environments?

10. Fredelighavn Whaling Station is a haunted place, and Laura feels a presence there, although she believes in ghosts of memory, not the supernatural. But in sites of bloody violence, can ghosts visit?

Praise for *The Lost Swimmer*

'A vivid, suspenseful thriller.' *Sydney Morning Herald*

'Reminiscent of Patricia Highsmith's *The Talented Mr Ripley* . . . In the best thriller traditions, this exciting novel's end-game contains an unexpected twist.' *The Age*

'An expertly scripted psychological thriller . . . A tense, evocative and absorbing tale of trust and betrayal.' *Australian Book Review*

'The definition of a page-turner.' *Marie Claire*

'A smartly constructed, tense thriller that will leave you guessing until the very end. It's a remarkable debut from former filmmaker Ann Turner, who's destined to become a prominent name in Australian writing.' *Better Reading*

'I knew *The Lost Swimmer* had won me over when I was standing in line at the supermarket and all I could think about was what was going to happen next in Ann Turner's impressive debut novel. A suspenseful and dramatic thriller.' *Readings*

'We had pins and needles trying to unravel the truth throughout Turner's crisply written, cleverly plotted tale of deceit.' *iBooks Editor*

'Everything flows and nothing abides,
everything gives way and nothing stays fixed.'

Heraclitus c. 535–475 BC

1

The sand was washed clean today, stretching wide at low tide. I ran along the glistening shore thinking of something I'd read last night: that you could travel a thousand miles and never notice anything. I suspected that this was as false now as when it was written by a Greek philosopher in the fifth century BC. Surely powers of observation would eventually take hold?

Two parrots were swinging upside down, a blaze of red and blue, sliding beaks and claws along a tree root that erupted from the stark ochre cliff. They swirled upright and bobbed about in a crazy dance, then one suddenly bit the other and flew off screeching in an ear-shattering blast as Big Boy, my border collie retriever, torpedoed from the shallows in a black and white streak and snapped at my heels. Years ago we'd rescued this shaggy giant from an animal shelter; now that the kids, James and Erin, were away at university in Melbourne, Big Boy was my reason for fitness, my daily coach.

The low rays of the sun tingled my skin as I scanned the ocean, a burning sapphire glowing with the promise of a long, hot summer on the Surf Coast. Hugging around the base of Victoria, this stretch of bush and beach lay exposed to dangerous storms off Bass Strait. But today there was no fierce swell; the waves rolled in gently, crystal clear. And yet for all the pleasure this morning gave, a hard fist gnawed deep inside my gut, clenched and pushing and out of control.

Heart pumping, I pounded up the cliffs through the moonah trees, resistance in my muscles making me aware of every one of my forty-seven years. Slamming through the pain, minutes later I rounded the bend to where our weatherboard home perched atop a steep drive, one massive glass door peering out like a Cyclops to the bleached timber deck. The house floated in a pale eucalypt haze, as if it might untether at any moment and drift away.

On the kitchen table a note lay bathed in sunshine. *Sorry, couldn't wait, see you tonight xxx*. Carelessly scrawled, unlike my husband Stephen's usual meticulous handwriting. He must have been in an extraordinary hurry. My stomach kicked again as I strode to the bathroom, stripping off my sweat-stained clothes and dropping them on the floor. I caught myself in the mirror, shoulder-length dark blonde hair plastered to my face, blue eyes clouded with frustration. What was so important that meant he couldn't wait? As water pounded my skin I cursed. Although I'd been an archaeologist for twenty years and a professor for five, this was my first stint heading the School of Classics and History at Coastal University, whereas Stephen, an economics professor, had led his department twice. I was used to sifting through dirt for fragments of the past, writing about the daily life of lost cultures and supervising my students, but dealing with the problems of colleagues, often urgent, was challenging. We were under pressure from budget cuts and I desperately needed Stephen's advice on several issues.

Suddenly I heard a volley of barks rising to a crescendo of growls. I stilled beneath the water, listening for Big Boy to stop, wondering what had set him off. When he escalated into frantic yelps I leaped from the shower.

The dog's claws were scratching like razors, raw against the glass. I wrapped my towel tight and peered out.

A kangaroo and her tiny joey lingered in the shadows at the edge of our lawn.

'Shh, it's okay.' Relief flooded through me but Big Boy's yelps grew more hysterical. Slipping my fingers beneath his collar I banished him into the depths of the house, and then I crept back and watched as the mother began nibbling tender shoots and the joey, tentative at first, bit down on the sweet blades. The kangaroos moved slowly through the dewy grass as they grazed. The mother had a fluorescent tag in her ear and a red band around her neck, on which BONNIE was written in large black letters – she was part of the local mob being tracked by a university study. The joey looked up shyly. Bonnie tensed and rose to her full towering height. Strong and proud, she stretched almost two metres from the ground. Our eyes locked and she became instantly still.

Bonnie had never been this far down the hill before. Her gaze was calm, alert, full of trust.

In a flurry of upside-down crumpling the joey fled into his mother's pouch, a wisp of tail the only clue to his existence until he righted himself and his perfect little head popped out, peeping back, emboldened. Bonnie turned abruptly, her powerful legs propelling her and her son silently up the hill in seconds.

Amid the tranquility I realised I was late for work.